In Situ

THE ROADS TO SANTIAGO DE COMPOSTELA

Texts written with the collaboration of Julie Roux
This book was written with the help and advice
of the Centro Estudios Camino Santiago – Sahagún
and of Humbert Jacomet, Conservateur
Translated by Barbara Da...

D1374263

MSM

S U M

1

Santiago, cathedral cloister

Ladies Towers of the Alhambra

James and John, Cámara Santa, Oviedo

M A R Y

Saint Luke, San Isidoro in Leon

Chevet of Saint Sernin, Toulouse

Detail of Angoulême Cathedral

1

HISTORY

1

FROM THE SEA OF GALILEE TO GALICIA

Called by Jesus while he was fishing in the waters of the
Sea of Galilee, James was called *the Greater* because he
was the first among the twelve apostles to bear the
name. To this *Son of Thunder* who became a fisher of men,
was assigned the evangelization of Spain, which, in the
first centuries of our era, had a rich and tumultuous
history. The Romans had to cede to the Visigoths, who
were themselves threatened by Byzantine power. But the
founders of the Hispano-Gothic nation, weakened by their
divisions, were carried away by the surge of the Muslim
wave. Al-Andalus had hardly been created when, in the
north of the peninsula, the idea of *Reconquista* was born,
and the apostle James the Greater's tomb was discovered.

Trial and condemnation of Saint James the Greater, St James altar in Pistoia

Martyrdom and glorification of St James the Greater, St James altar in Pistoia

APOSTLE AND MARTYR

The son of Salome and Zebedee, brother of John the Evangelist and, like him, a fisherman in the Sea of Galilee, James was one of the first of Christ's apostles. According to the *Acts of the Apostles* (12.2), the man known as James the Greater was beheaded in Jerusalem on the orders of King Herod Agrippa, in about 44 AD. The reasons for the condemnation of the son of Zebedee, the first apostle to become a martyr, remain obscure. By persecuting the new Church, Herod Agrippa, who also had Peter imprisoned, was trying to satisfy his influential subjects, followers of traditional Judaism. Perhaps too, James, this *Son of Thunder*, had been guilty of seditious words or acts, and at the time beheading was the usual punishment for all political crimes. In his *Ecclesiastical History*, Eusebius of Caesarea (265-340) tells how James, on the way to his death, allegedly miraculously healed a paralyzed man under the eyes of his denouncer, Josiah. Convinced by the miracle, the latter was converted and became a martyr alongside the apostle. The *Acts of the Apostles* and the *Epistles*, so instructive about Peter's missions and Paul's travels, the two "pillars" of the Roman Church, say nothing about James's evangelism. And it was not until the beginning of the 5th century that Jerome, in his *Commentary on Isaiah*, attributed the evangelization of Illyria and the Spanish lands to the fishermen of the Sea of Galilee.

James healing the paralyzed man

SON OF THUNDER

On his way to Jerusalem with his disciples, Jesus wanted to spend the night in a small village in Samaria. But nobody was willing to offer them hospitality, so James and John, sons of Zebedee, wanted to call on lightning to strike such uncharitable inhabitants. Their Master chastised them severely, but the incident certainly provided the two brothers the fiery nickname "*Boanerges*", "Son of Thunder" in Greek.

ABOUT JAMES

The adjective "the Greater" describing James, son of Zebedee, distinguishes him from the other James, son of Alphaeus, called "the Less", because he came into Jesus' following afterwards. James the Less is often confused with a third James, the brother of Jesus, who did not belong to the group of twelve disciples. Was this James another son of Mary and Joseph, as Protestants tend to believe because of their reticence about the Marian cult? Or, as Catholic doctrine has it, was he a cousin of Jesus', and the term "brother" in Aramaic having a wide meaning. This brother of Jesus, the head of the first Church in Jerusalem, allegedly supported a Judaic tendency, in opposition to Peter and Paul. The Nag Hammâdi manuscripts however, present him as the privileged dispenser of Jesus' teachings, and James was to play an essential role in the constitution of the Church. After the first Christian Council, the Jerusalem Assembly, he also decreed that circumcision was not necessary for pagans to be converted. From being a reformist movement within Judaism, Christianity was affirmed as an autonomous religion. The brother of Jesus was condemned to death by the Great Priest Anan in 62 for breaking the Law. Tradition attributes to him the Epistle of James, admitted into the canon of the New Testament. But in fact, it is probably a pseudo-epigraph, composed in his honour by one of his disciples.

James and John, Chartres

THE SON OF MAN

"… he saw two other brethren, James the son of Zebedee, and John his brother, in a ship with Zebedee their father, mending their nets; and he called them."
(Matthew 1, 16-20)

Herod the Great was ruling Palestine by rights from the Roman Senate and the Emperor Octavius Augustus governing Rome when, between the years 6 and 4 BC, was born the son of the carpenter, Joseph, his legal father, issued from the line of David, a descendant of Abraham, and the Virgin Mary. In the Gospel according to Luke, the event took place in Judea, in Bethlehem, the town of David, where Joseph and his pregnant wife, who lived in Nazareth in Galilee, had had to travel for a census. As soon as the child was born, in a state of complete destitution, shepherds, to whom the coming of the Messiah had been revealed, came to the manger where Christ, in other words the anointed of Yahve, the King who was to save the people of God and definitively establish His kingdom, had seen the light

The manger

of day. According to custom, the newborn child was circumcised eight days after his birth and Joseph gave him the predestined name, Jesus. Then, after the prescribed forty days for his mother's ritual purification, as the first born son of

his parents, Jesus was presented at the Temple to be consecrated to Yahve. There, the devout Simon and the prophetess Anne recognized him in their turn as the long-awaited Christ. According to Matthew, the Magi or Wise Men, coming from the East and having seen the Star, came to Bethlehem to pay homage to the mysterious child, the "King of the Jews" who had just been born. But their action soon awakened the anger of Herod, whose bloodthirsty despotism was equalled only by his submission to the Empire, and who ordered the massacre of the children of Bethlehem. Joseph fled with his family to Egypt, before returning to Galilee and Nazareth at the death of Herod, in 4 AD. Rome had by then decided the succession of the king of the Jews by dividing Palestine among his sons: the eldest, Archelaos, received the title of ethnarc of Judea, Idumea and Samaria; while his brother, Herod Antipas, as tetrarch, became governor of Galilee. However, in 6 AD, Archelaos was deposed by Augustus, who had decided to administer Judea, Idumea and Samaria directly through a prefect, and then through a procurator. Raised in a family that faithfully respected the precepts of Mosaic Law and its practices, Jesus received an education based on traditional Judaism. He learned to read the Bible and came to know it remarkably well. Since he accompanied his parents on their annual pilgrimage to Jerusalem to celebrate Passover, according to Luke, at the age of twelve, his wisdom and pertinent answers astounded the doctors of Law with whom he stayed to talk in the house of His Father, unknown to Joseph and Mary. He nevertheless returned to Nazareth with them, remaining their submissive son. At Joseph's side, he became a humble carpenter. During the fifteenth year of the

government of Tiberias (14-37), in about the year 28, Jesus's public life began. Aged just over thirty, he was baptized in the waters of the Jordan River by John the Baptist, who was preaching in the deserts of Judea about the coming of Christ and his kingdom,

The baptism of Christ

calling upon people to convert. After his baptism, during which a celestial voice proclaimed him the Son of God, guided by the Spirit, Jesus retired to the desert for forty days where he confronted the Devil, before beginning his ministry, which was to last a little more than two years. First of all, he preached in Nazareth and Capharnaum; and not far away, on the western shore of the Sea of Galilee, he called his first disciples to him: Simon-Peter and his brother Andrew, both fishermen. Soon James and John left their nets and fishing boat, where they worked with their father Zebedee, to follow the man calling upon them to become "fishers of men". With Peter and Andrew, James and John, these sons of Zebedee that Jesus nicknamed *Boanerges*, that is, Sons of Thunder, probably because of their fiery character, were to be among his closest disciples. From the shores of the Sea of Galilee, Jesus pursued his life as an itinerant preacher across Galilee, multiplying miracles on his way. His travels took him to Judea, to Jerusalem where he went several times, to Samaria, to Perea and as far as the borders of the Jewish world, in Syrio-Phoenicia and the West Bank of the Jordan River. Without renouncing Mosaic Law, he addressed man a message of love, exchanging the image of a vindictive and terrible Yahve for a benevolent and merciful *Abba* or Father. His concern for the poor and the cures he carried out aroused enthusiasm among crowds, edified by his teaching and parables. His *Beatitudes*, pronounced during the Sermon on the Mount renewed a profitable alliance. During his life on Earth, he reserved for Peter and the Sons of Thunder, James and John, the revelation of his divine power over life. All three had the privilege of attending the resurrection of the daughter of Jaire and the Transfiguration. But Jesus' preaching was rapidly contested in Pharisaic and Sadducean circles, the principal representatives of religious authority and Sanhedrin policy, alarmed by his growing popularity. Members of a Jewish sect, often assimilated into Scribes or doctors of the Temple, the Pharisees saw themselves as scrupulous observers of the Law. They also followed some non-biblical traditions, later described as Oral Law. The Pharisees reproached Jesus and his disciples for their negligence of ritual purification, dietary prohibitions and Sabbath observance. In turn, Jesus denounced their formalistic attitude, their sticking to the letter rather than the spirit of the Law, badly concealing their hypocrisy. The Sadducees held with rigorous observance of the *Torah*, challenged Pharisaic oral law as well as certain other Jewish beliefs inherited from the prophets, in particular those concerning the resurrection of the dead and the immortality of the soul, that appear in Jesus' teachings. But above all, these teachings threatened the political-religious system in place under Roman occupation, of which they were the main supporters. By incarnating the hope of the Messiah-King, establisher of the universal kingdom of God prophetized in the Old Alliance, whose imminent coming he announced, Jesus fulfilled a twofold desire of the Jewish people: a "new David", to free Israel, occupied by Roman armies since 63 BC, allowing its people to recover national independence; furthermore, by predicting the destruction of the Temple, giving the Torah a new interpretation, many saw in him the beginning of a period of religious freedom that was until then paralyzed by the grip of the priestly class. However, the kingdom announced by the man from Nazareth was spiritual above all, and people were to be disappointed by it. When Salome, the mother of the Sons of Thunder, James and John, requested that her sons sit on his right and left in his kingdom, he promised his disciples, first of all, the cup of suffering from which he himself would drink, without being able to decide celestial rewards. At his entrance into Jerusalem, eight days before Passover in the year 30, the jubilant crowd acclaimed the "Son of David" and threw palm leaves on the road to celebrate his coming. The religious authorities decided to finish with the preacher from Galilee. They managed to corrupt one of the twelve disciples, Judas Iscariot, who led them to the Garden of Gethsemani, at the foot of the Mount of Olives, where Jesus and his apostles used to spend the night. A few hours before his arrest, the Son of Man confided to Peter and Zebedee's two sons, James and John, his anguish at the approach of death. Arrested, Jesus appeared before the members of the Sanhedrin, presided by the Great Priest Caiaphas, then before the Roman procurator Pontius Pilate, who agreed to the Sanhedrin's request and condemned Jesus to be crucified, a method of torture reserved for slaves and rebels against the Empire. Jesus died at the beginning of the afternoon, in a festive Jerusalem, shortly before the beginning of the Sabbath and the celebration of Passover. A short time later, he appeared to his eleven disciples, giving them the mission of converting "all the nations", and of being his "witnesses in Jerusalem, in all of Judea and Samaria, and as far as the ends of the earth".

The Crucifixion, Treasure of Aachen Cathedral

The forum of Ampurias, city in Tarraconensis

The Visigothic Kingdom of Toledo

The Iberian peninsula was colonized by the Romans during the second century BC. During the Roman empire it was divided into six provinces: Baetica, Lusitania, Galicia, Tarraconensis, Carthaginensis and the Balearic Islands. The administrative diocese of Hispania was composed of these provinces, along with Mauretania Tingitana, and was joined to the Gaul prefecture. During the 3rd century, barbarians invaded the Empire. Having crossed the Pyrenees in 409, the Western Germanic peoples, Vandals, Suevi and Alans shared out the Iberian provinces among themselves several years later: the Siling Vandals took over Baetica, the Alans seized Lusitania and western Carthaginensis. Galicia north of the Meseta was annexed by Asding Vandals, while the Suevi took over its western section. Tarraconensis passed into the hands of noble Romans who had rebelled against imperial authority. Simultaneously, the Visigoths invaded Italy and sacked Rome in 410. Settling in Gaul by 412, their king Wallia ultimately signed a treaty with the emperor in 416. As soldiers of the federation, the Visigoths' task henceforth was to eliminate the other barbarians from the Iberian peninsula, and they soon crushed the Alans and the Siling Vandals, who had occupied the richest and most Romanized provinces. In 418, the future emperor Constantius established the Visigoths and their king, Theodoric 1st (418-451) in the province of Aquitaine II, which would become the first Western

Barbarian invasion of the Iberian peninsula	409
Foundation of the Toulouse Visigothic kingdom	418
Victory of Clovis over the Visigoths at Vouillé, end of the Toulouse Visigothic kingdom	507
Byzantines occupy Baetica and Cartaginensis	552
Recared converts to Catholicism	587
The Council of Toledo proclaims Catholicism as the official religion of the Visigothic kingdom	588
Byzantines chased out of the Iberian peninsula	625
Muslims invade the Iberian peninsula, fall of the Toledo Visigothic kingdom	711

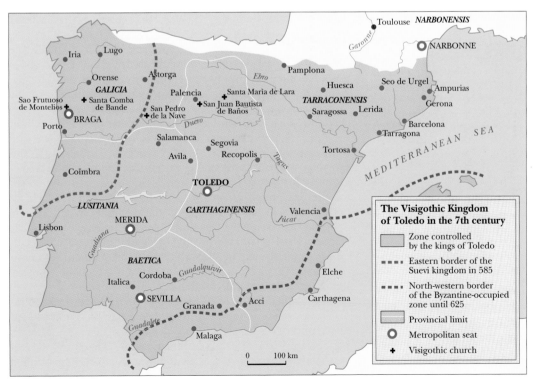

The Visigothic kingdom of Toledo in the 7th century

The ramparts of Tarragona

JUSTINIAN'S CONQUESTS

T he Western Roman Empire
had already been weakened
and dismembered by the great
barbarian invasions when, in 476,
the barbarian chief Odoacer took
power in Rome. From then on, the
West belonged to Germanic tribes:
the Ostrogoths possessed Italy, the
Vandals controlled North Africa,
and the Visigoths had the Iberian
peninsula and southern Gaul. The
Eastern emperor governed what
remained of the great Roman
Empire, which consisted of the
Balkan peninsula, Asia Minor,
Syria, Palestine, Egypt and
Cyrenaica. But in the 6th century,
Emperor Justinian (527-565)
reconquered most of the provinces
of the western Mediterranean
basin, where he attempted to
restore the former Roman
administration. In 534, his troops,
commanded by Belisarius,
recovered North Africa from the
Vandals. Soon, Illyria, Dalmatia,
Italy and Sicily, Sardinia, Corsica,
the Balearic Islands, and last of all,
Baetica and Carthaginensis in the
south-east of the Iberian peninsula
came under Byzantine control. But
Justinian's restoration did not last
longer than he did and his empire
collapsed under assault by
Lombards in Italy, Bulgars in the
Balkans, Persians in Asia and Arabs
in Syria, Egypt and North Africa.

barbarian kingdom, with Toulouse as its capital. In the peninsula, the Asding Vandals, pushed southwards by the imperial armies, crossed the Straits of Gibraltar in 429. Still masters of Galicia, the Suevi settled around Porto, Lugo and their capital, Braga, tried to extend their domain by carrying out multiple raids of Lusitania, Baetica and Carthaginensis, and starting in 450, even in Tarraconensis. In 446, they routed the Roman army that had come to restore imperial authority. But ten years later, the Visigoth king Theodoric II (453-466), alarmed by the incursions of King Rechiaire (448-456) into Tarraconensis, crushed the Suevi army before Astorga in the name of Rome, took Braga and killed the monarch. After the departure of Theodoric II, the Suevi remained in the north-west of the peninsula in scattered groups whose chiefs fought for power. One of them, Remismond, gained the support of the king of Toulouse by adopting his religion, Arianism, and by marrying a Visigothic princess. He thus restored a Suevi kingdom, of which Lisbon, Merida, Palencia – strongholds controlled by the Visigoths – marked the limits. With the decline of the Western empire, the Visigoths gradually became the main representatives of authority in the peninsula. In 472, their king Euric (466-484) occupied Tarraconensis. For his Visigothic subjects, he had a code of laws written in Latin by Bishop Leon of Narbonne – the Code of Euric. By 476, the kingdom of Toulouse had become completely autonomous and consisted not only of most of the peninsula, but also half of Gaul located south of the Loire River. Euric's successor, Alaric II (484-507), had a Breviary containing texts of later Roman law compiled for his Roman subjects, while the Visigoths remained under Euric's code and mixed marriages were forbidden. In 507, with the victory of the Frankish armies under Clovis at Vouillé, the kingdom of Toulouse collapsed. Alaric was killed and the Visigoths, whose kingdom had just lost its entire area north of the Pyrenees, pulled back into the Iberian peninsula. With the help of the Ostrogothic king of Italy, Theodoric the Great (455-526), they managed to rebuild an Arian Gothic kingdom that included, north of the Pyrenees, Provence and Narbonensis, reconquered in 508, and in the south, Tarraconensis as well as parts of Carthaginensis and Lusitania. Theodoric divided the peninsula's administration among Ostrogothic magnates and Hispano-Romans and until 549, except for the brief reign of Amalric (526-531), the son of Alaric II, Ostrogoths held power throughout the peninsula. When Amalric was assassinated in 531, Theodoric's former military commander, Theudis, was elected king by the Ostrogothic aristocracy. Theudis (531-548) tried to extend his authority into the southern regions of the peninsula, which were in the hands of the Catholic Hispano-Roman aristocracy hostile to Arianism. He also undertook the conquest of Ceuta, but clashed with Emperor Justinian's (527-565) troops, who were in the midst of reconquering the former North African provinces from the Vandals. Assassinated in 548, Theudis was replaced by one of his former generals, Theudisel, the last Ostrogothic king who, during his eighteen-month reign, continued the work of his predecessor by reinforcing Gothic power in Baetica. When Theudisel was himself assassinated in 549, Agila, elected king

GOTHIC ARIANISM

Towards 320, Arius, (280-332) a priest in Alexandria, began to preach a doctrine founded on strict monotheism, questioning the divine nature of Jesus Christ. Postulating that God was not only uncreated, but also unengendered, Arius argued that the Son, created *ex nihilo* and engendered through the will of the Father, could not be God's equal. According to him, there was a time when God was not the Father, and when the Son, in fact inferior and posterior to God, did not exist. The conclusion of Arian doctrine was hence the affirmation of three substances (from the Greek, *ousiai*, essences) that were separate and dissimilar, of the Father, the Son and the Holy Spirit. Arianism was condemned by the first ecumenical council held in Nicaea by Emperor Constantine in 325. Declaring that the essence of God was not identifiable with the concept of unengendering, the council composed a declaration of faith claiming that the Son, "a true God born of a true God, engendered and not created [was] consubstantial (*homoousios* in Greek)with the Father", then excommunicated Arius and his disciples. Arius was condemned to exile by Constantine, but his ideas had started a debate that was to last over half a century, opposing the "Nicaeans" led by the Alexandrian bishop Athanasis and the "Arians", an assorted coalition gathering Arius's supporters and theologians opposed to the symbol of Nicaea. In an attempt at a union that was more political than religious, Emperor Constantius II (337-361) called two councils, one in 359 in Rimini for the western bishops, and one in 360 at Seleucia for those from the east. Subsequently, a mitigated Arianism –recognizing an undefined similarity between the Father, the Son and the Holy Spirit, but affirming their inequal-

ity– was ratified as an article of faith in the entire Empire. This was the doctrine embraced by Ulfila of Cappadocia (311-383), who was to become the apostle of the Goths. Born in Gothia on the shores of the Black Sea, near the mouths of the Danube River, Ulfila was at first a prisoner of the Gothic people. His parents had been brought from Cappadocia as captives by the Visigoths, after raids carried out during the second half of the third century. Intelligent and able to speak Greek, Ulfila was sent to the Roman Empire on a mission by his adopted people and there he came into contact with Arianism. Towards 341, he was consecrated as a bishop in Constantinople by the Arian bishop Eusebius of Nicomedia, and then undertook to convert the Gothic people. He invented a literary Gothic language for his preaching, with an alphabet and writing derived from the Greek and translated a large part of the Bible and the New Testament. In 360 Ulfila took part in the council of Seleucia called by Constantius II. However, the symbol of Nicaea triumphed and Arianism was widely rejected under Theodosius the

Constantine and his mother, Helen

Great (379-395). The second ecumenical council called in Constantinople in 381 concluded with the definite wording of trinitarian dogma, completing the Nicaean credo with the affirmation of the divinity of the Holy Spirit. Jesus, the only Son of God "true God of a true God, engendered and not created [is] of the same substance as the Father" and the Spirit "that proceeds from the Father [is] adored together with the Father and the Son". Theodosius imposed the symbol of Nicaea-Constantinople as the official credo of the entire empire and, starting in 383, Christian heresies like Arianism were harshly repressed. Because he died at about this time, Ulfila, who had drawn up an Arian credo, escaped persecution. But his missionary action was to have considerable results. When the Goths began their mass conversions to Christianity at the end of the 4th century, they adopted the symbol of Ulfila, meanwhile considered a heretic, even as they encouraged the conversion of the majority of other Germanic peoples. Furthermore, the emergence of Gothic literature, strongly linked to their religion and for a long time considered as a sign of ethnic particularity, provided the Goths with a certain prestige and put an end to a feeling of cultural inferiority with respect to the Romans. Arianism became one of the major obstacles to the fusion of the Visigoths and the Hispano-Romans, attached to the Nicaea-Constantinople symbol, into a single people. The obstacle would be overcome by Recared, the first Catholic Visigothic king of Toledo, in 587. The city of Uppsala in Sweden has some important fragments of a biblical manuscript, the *Codex argenteus*, the last pieces of the Gothic literature that was systematically destroyed during the 6th century because of its heresy.

by the Visigothic aristocracy, immediately began to raid Baetica's main cities, like Cordoba, that were in the hands of the powerful Hispano-Roman aristocracy. But in Sevilla, a Visigothic magnate, Atanagild, supported by local authorities, proclaimed himself king. Civil war broke out. In 551, Atanagild asked for help from the Byzantine emperor, who called on some of his forces stationed in Sicily. The imperial army landed in 552 and occupied a large part of Baetica and Carthaginensis. Rapidly routed, Agila was assassinated in Merida in 555 by his own soldiers, who had joined forces with his enemy. With unanimous recognition of his kingship, Atanagild then tried in vain to push back his former Byzantine allies. He finally gave up to Justinian the lands occupied by the imperial army, including Cadiz, Cordoba, Malaga, Carthagena and perhaps, Sevilla. Until 624, these were to constitute the imperial province of Spain and were annexed to the African prefecture. Pressed northwards, Atanagild made Toledo the capital of his kingdom. The Byzantine occupation strengthened trade, as well as cultural and religious exchanges, between the peninsula and Constantinople, Italy and Africa. Furthermore, taking advantage of the troubles caused by the civil war, the Suevi kingdom underwent a new period of expansion while, in the northern mountainous regions, Asturians, Cantabrians and Vascons became practically independent. Atanagild was assassinated in 567, leaving no heir. The throne remained empty for five months before being filled by the duke of Narbonensis, Liuva, who rapidly brought his brother, Leovigild, into power with him. This pre-empted any possible civil war, since his brother was a favourite of the Toledo aristocracy. Quickly, Liuva retained the government of Narbonensis for himself, and his brother, who had in the meantime married Atanagild's widow, governed the kingdom of Toledo. Leovigild considerably extended Visigothic domination over the peninsula and unified it politically, thus founding Visigothic *Hispania*. From 570 to 573, he attacked the south occupied by the Byzantines, devastated Baeza and Malaga, then took back Cordoba and Medina Sidonia. From 573 to 577, he fought the northern

Antique theatre in Merida

MERIDA

T he administrative capital of Lusitania during the Roman period, Merida, *Emerita Augusta*, was also, starting in 297, the residence of the *vicarius Hispaniarum*, the delegate of the prefect of the Gallic praetorium, whose role was to administer the entire Hispanic diocese. The formerly prosperous city has retained numerous antique relics, such as its theatre, its amphitheatre and its aqueduct.

Aqueduct of Los Milagros de Merida

The horreum in Narbonne

Visigothic tower in Narbonne

Gardens in Sevilla

THE TRINITY

T he oldest depiction of the
Trinity appeared in the 4th
century, in the shape of an
equilateral triangle. Starting in
the 5th century, it was symbolized
by three similar persons, like on
this Flemish tapestry from the 16th
century.

mountainous regions, subjecting Cantabria after taking its capital, Amaya. He also pacified the area of Orense, the border with the Suevi kingdom into which he led armed incursions. To celebrate his victory and glorify the monarchy, Leovigild created a city that he named Recopolis in the honour of his second son, Recared, and had a vast palace, with a Palatine chapel and basilica, built in Toledo. He had Euric's code revised and brought in the *Codex revisus*, later known under the name *Leges antiquae*, that removed ethnic and judicial obstacles to the fusion of the Goths and the Hispano-Romans, hence creating a national law code, applicable to all its subjects. In 579, the king entrusted the government of Sevilla and Baetica to his eldest son, Hermenegild, who was married to a Merovingian and Catholic princess, Ingunde. But Hermenegild immediately tried to create a provincial uprising against his father by converting to Catholicism and proclaiming himself king of Baetica. Leovigild's response was greater religious tolerance. In 580 he convoked a council of Arian bishops in Toledo to attenuate dogmatic and sacramental differences between Arianism and Catholicism. Christians could henceforth convert without being rebaptized, but by a simple purification of the hands. And even though he did not accept the doctrine of the Trinity, the king went as far as admitting that the Son was the equal of the Father, but not of the Spirit. From that time on, he ostensibly venerated Catholic shrines and their martyrs. In 581 Leovigild pushed back the Basques, who had come down the Ebro River valley into the

The Creation by the Holy Trinity, tapestry in Saint Just Cathedral, Narbonne

Leogivild, reliquary of san Millán de la Cogolla

Pyrenees and Cantabrian mountains, and founded the city of Vitoria to contain them. Then, managing to avoid an alliance between the Byzantines and his son, he took back Merida from him in 582, and Sevilla and Cordoba the following year. Hermenegild capitulated in 584 and died assassinated in 585. Leovigild then decided to finish dealing with the Suevi. In 583, their king Miro, who had converted to Catholicism, had tried to help the Baetica rebels, but he died shortly afterwards, leaving behind a kingdom torn apart by pretenders to the throne. Taking advantage of the situation, Leovigild seized the Suevi kingdom in 585, but he died in 586. By carrying out the religious reunification of *Hispania*, Leovigild's son, Recared, was to complete the work started by his father. Conscious of the national identity carried by Arianism, Recared knew that religion was the final obstacle to the fusion of his Gothic and Hispano-Roman subjects. He also realized that Arians were a minority within his kingdom and, at the beginning of 587, barely ten months after coming to the throne, he converted to Catholicism. Rebellions in Merida and Narbonensis broke out in response to the conversion, but were rapidly put down. In 589 the king convoked a council in Toledo to proclaim Catholicism as the official religion of *Hispania*. At Recared's death in 603, his immediate successors continued their traditional struggles against the Asturian, Cantabrian and Vascon peoples. But the Byzantine domination of the south-eastern part of the peninsula was the main preoccupation of the Catholic kings of Toledo. Finally, the complete conquest of *Hispania* was the work of

Horseman Stele, Vitoria Museum

19

Landmark Dates

460	Theodore II promulgates a first series of laws
475	Euric has a code of laws recompiled for the Visigoths, the Gallo- and the Hispano-Romans keeping their own laws
506	Alaric II has a new code of Roman laws elaborated, known as Alaric's *Breviary*, with the intention of satisfying the Gallo- and Hispano-Romans worried by the Germanization of laws, induced by Euric's *Breviary*
572	Leovigild, with his *Codex revisus*, creates a national law applicable to all the subjects of the Visigothic kingdom. Among other provisions, the new law authorizes intermarriage between Visigoths and Hispano-Romans.
654	Receswind ratifies the *Liber judicorum*, a compilation of ancient laws (*Leges antiquae*) completed by 186 new laws

King Suintila (621-631), when he definitively expelled the Byzantines from a kingdom that was then at its apex, between 623 and 625. A legal revision of Leovigild's code was necessary after Recared's conversion to Catholicism and was undertaken under the reigns of Chindaswind (642-653) and his son Receswind (649-672). In 654 the latter ratified the *Liber judiciorum* (Book of Judges) that completed Leovigild's 324 laws, described as *Leges antiquae*, with 186 new laws. But starting in 672, the absence of a dynastic principle aggravated quarrels over the succession, weakening an already unstable monarchy. Powerful noble factions, divided into rival clans, fought for dominance and royal power. Elected king in 672, Wamba, a magnate of the court, did not manage to resist a plot hatched by a descendant of Chindaswind's, Ervigio, who took power in 680. Ervigio ensured his own succession and at his death in 687, his son-in-law Egica came to the throne. King from 687 to 702, Egica named his son Witiza as co-regent and, starting in 698, entrusted him with the government of the former Suevi kingdom. Witiza succeeded his father in 702. But at his death in 710, his son Akhila did not manage to establish his power, despite support from several factions, and Rodrigo, a member of the Chindaswind lineage, was elected king. Akhila took refuge in Ceuta with the Byzantine governor, Count Julián, who suggested that Akhila ask for help from neighbouring Moorish chieftains. But in 711 the latter came as conquerors of a *Hispania* that was on the brink of civil war. Mohammed's soldiers put a brutal end to the kingdom of Toledo.

Toledo

VISIGOTHIC ART

Before the Council of Toledo in 587, the Visigoths' artistic production consisted of jewellery or clothing adornments such as belt buckles or fibulae. The conversion to Catholicism of the Arian king and his subjects, the Isidorian renaissance but also the lasting establishment of these peoples in a defined geographic location encouraged the blossoming of artistic development. On the one hand, their artistry continued to be expressed in working objects of stone and precious metals, like the votive crowns in the Guarrazar treasure, discovered near Toledo in 1859. It is likely that these crowns were made to be hung in the Toledo basilica where the councils were held. But this artistic

The crown of King Receswind

renaissance also extended to architecture. Although there are few remnants of civil architecture, some Visigothic churches in the north of the Iberian peninsula have remained in good condition. This state of preservation can be explained by several factors. First of all, except for the crypt of San Antolin de Palencia, they are located in rural areas, which are less likely to undergo upheaval than urban ones. Next, they were built in areas where the Muslim occupation lasted a relatively short time. Finally, as symbols of what had to be reconquered, they certainly profited from the protection of the *Reconquista*'s artisans, and in particular, of Asturian monarchs. They mostly date from the second half of the 7th century. This is the case of San Juan Bautista de Baños, near Palencia, of Sao Frutuoso de Montelios near Braga, of Santa Comba de Bande, south of Orense on the shores of the reservoir of las Conchas on the Limia River, of San Pedro de la Nave near Zamora. As for the church of Santa Maria de Lara in Quintanilla de la Viñas, between Burgos and Santo Domingo de Silos, it was built at the beginning of the 8th century, just a few years before the Muslim invasion. These churches are characterized by their dry-stone bonding. Their layout varies; that of Sao Frutuoso de Montelios is similar to that of the mausoleum of Galla Placidia in Ravenna. The sculpted decorations, which express a decline in figurative art in favour of more abstract designs, cover the pilasters and the columns, the capitals and the fanlights. The sculptors worked in planes, even on the capitals,

where the effect is that of a truncated, inverted pyramid shape. In the church of San Pedro de la Nave, these decorations represent floral or animal designs, such as birds pecking at grapes, but there are also scenes from the Old Testament, such as Daniel in the lion's den or the sacrifice of Abraham, whose graphic representation, getting to its essence, could have been inspired by the lost miniatures of Visigothic manuscripts. The architects used the Moorish arch, generally to a third of its radius, hence making it less closed than the arches used in Hispano-Arab buildings. It also predates them. The triumphal arch that opens onto the apse of Santa Maria de Lara is of this type,

Sun, church in Quintanilla de la Viñas

and it rests on two fanlights supported by columns. On the left fanlight, a man has been carved, topped by a lunar symbol; on the right, a rather feminine face wears a crown of sunrays. Both of them are framed by angels. The former probably symbolizes the Church, the latter, Jesus Christ. Of this church, there remain only sections of the transept and the chevet, which, along their outer circumference have friezes of motifs set in decorated circles. At the foot of the hill of Lara, alternating on the light-coloured stone, we find vine branches, foliage with palm leaves, peacocks, roosters, quail and griffins.

Moorish attack against a Christian fortress, *Cantigas de Santa María*

AL-ANDALUS

Having triumphed over the divisions and the "false prophets" that menaced the cohesion of the young Muslim state, Abu Bakr (632-634) and Omar (634-644), the first two replacements (*khalifa*) of Mohammed, imposed Islam on nearly the entire Arabic peninsula. From then on, the conquests started by the Prophet continued. Attacked by 633, Sassanide Persia was invaded after the victory of Nehawend in 642. Syria and Palestine were subjected starting in 636, after the Byzantine rout on the Yarmuk. Finally, Muslims occupied Egypt and Cyrenaica in 642. At the death of Omar, the supporters of Ali, the prophet's cousin and son-in-law, claimed the caliphate that had passed into the hands of a believer of long-standing, Osman, of the Umayyad clan. After a troubled period, during which the Shiite and Kharijite schisms originated, the Umayyad Mo'awiya, who had been the governor of Syria, was proclaimed caliph in 660. He chose Damascus as his capital. By instituting the caliphate succession in a direct line, he founded the Umayyad dynasty. Begun in 648, the conquest of North Africa did not end until 748; its length and difficulty was caused by fierce Berber resistance.

In 710, the political situation in the Iberian peninsula was anarchic. Perhaps after being called on by Akhila, Musa b. Nusayr, the governor of *Ifriqiya*, launched an expedition towards the peninsula, under the command of a freed Berber, Tariq b. Ziyad, the gover-

SHIITES AND KHARIJITES

When the caliph Osman, the son-in-law of Mohammed, of the Umayyad clan, was assassinated in 656, Ali, his cousin and also Mohammed's son-in-law, took over his succession at the head of the caliphate of Medina. However, Osman's family, convinced of Ali's responsibility in his predecessor's assassination, organized a resistance movement in Syria, led by the Umayyad Mo'awiya, the governor of Damascus. The first confrontation between Umayyades and Alides took place in Ciffin, on the Euphrates River, in the spring of 657. On July 26, Umayyad soldiers, about to give up, attached pages of the *Koran* on the tips of their lances, calling for an end to fratricidal combat and for arbitration by a third party. Ali's consent to

their request provoked the defection of some of his supporters, the *Kharijites*, who considered that only the *Koran*, the word of God, could provide a valid judgement. As purist Muslims, the *Kharijites* called for an elected caliphate regardless of race or tribe. Although he triumphed over the latter at the battle of Nahrawan in 658, for his alleged participation in Osman's murder, at the arbitration in Edroh Ali was deposed from the caliphate in favour of Mo'awiya, at the beginning of the same year. As he was going to the mosque of Kufa, in 661, Ali was assassinated by a young Kharijite. His supporters, the *Shiites*, were to unite into a party (*shia*) demanding a hereditary caliphate, with a member of the Prophet's family at its head.

AT THE SOURCES OF ISLAM

In the south of the Arabian Peninsula, a civilization began to flourish towards the end of the 3rd millenium. From the 4th century BC to the first century AD, it was organized into kingdoms whose caravans followed the incense roads. In the first century, these civilizations disappeared and were replaced by the Himyarites. After the destruction of the Temple of Jerusalem by the Romans in 70, Jews came to populate the south of Arabia and soon, Judaism was adopted by the Himyarite sovereigns. But the Ethiopians, supported by Byzantium, overthrew the Himyarites in 525. The indigenous populations then called upon the Persians, who were to dominate southern Arabia starting in 575. The Yemenites, farmers in the southern oases, and the Qaysites, Bedouins from the northern and central deserts who were nomadic pastoralists and occasional plunderers, were polytheists even though both Judaism and Christianity were implanted in Arabia. In the 5th century, tribes from the north acquired the monopoly of caravan traffic between the Indian Ocean and the Mediterranean Sea and settled in the staging posts of the caravan routes. Pilgrimages were associated with the fairs held there. Hence, in Mecca the tribe of Qoraysh raised around the Ka'aba shrines dedicated to other divinities. According to tradition, the Ka'aba had been built by Abraham and Ishmael who had sealed within it the black stone received from the Angel Gabriel. Mohammed was born about 571. Orphaned at the age of seven, he was taken in by his grandfather, then by a paternal uncle, Abu Talib. Mohammed grew up with his cousin, Ali, the son of Abu Talib. He was twenty-five when he was chosen as a right-hand man by a rich

Meccan widow, Khadija, whom he married. Mohammed often withdrew to the solitude of Mount Hira. Towards 610, the Angel Gabriel appeared to him several times, ordering him to "recite" the divine Word that was transmitted to him. These successive revelations, later gathered in writing, form the Koran (recitation), the word of Allah. Announcing the Final Judgement, Mohammed stigmatized the greed of wealthy Meccans, urging them to purify themselves by alms and prayer, to submit (islam) to Allah. His wife, Khadija, his cousin Ali, Zayd, his adopted son, his close friend Abu Bakr, and Osman his son-in-law, became his first disciples. Affirming the existence of a unique Creator, Mohammed went to war against the pagan divinities worshipped in Mecca, attracting the hostility of the Qorayshite families who earned money from the pilgrimages. In 619, at the death of his uncle, Abu Talib, Abu Lahab, a sworn enemy of the new Islamic religion, took the head of Mohammed's clan, the Banu Hashim. Mohammed, who had also just lost his wife, had to escape to an oasis located 350 kilometres northwest of Mecca, al Madina. Two rival Yemeni tribes, who inhabited the village along with three Jewish tribes, made an agreement with him – he was to re-establish peace in the town and in return, they would welcome his followers. Mohammed and Abu Bakr arrived in Medina on September 24, 622 – the year of the Hegira, from the Arab hijira, emigration, that marks the beginning of the Muslim era. In Medina, Mohammed became the chief of a community, the Ummah, that included Yemeni and Jewish tribes as well as dissidents from Mecca. Joining the Ummah did not

mean joining a new faith. Believing that he would convert the Jews of Medina, Mohammed adopted several measures of their Law, such as fasting on the day of Atonement (Yom Kippur), and prayer in the direction of Jerusalem. But the Jews criticized the contents of the Koran. Breaking with them, Mohammed proclaimed that the only true faith is that of Abraham, the ancestor of his people, neither Jewish nor Christian, but simply monotheistic. From then on, Muslims turn towards the Ka'aba to pray, while collective fasting takes place at Ramadan. In order to provide for the needs of the believers in Medina, Mohammed raided caravans going to Mecca. And in March 624, near the well of Badr, his troops crushed a column of Meccans. In this victory, Mohammed saw the favour of Allah, who supported his fighters against the infidel, and shortly afterwards he expelled the Jewish tribe of Qaynoga'. The following year, the Meccans took their revenge on the slopes of Mount Ohod. Suspected of collaboration, the Jewish tribe of Nadhir fled. In March 627, the Meccan army attacking Medina was pushed back. Mohammed then ordered the massacre of the last Jews of Medina, the Qorayza. His influence grew while the voice of Allah advised him about running a community joined not by blood links, but by faith in a single religion. In 628, Mohammed went to Mecca for a pilgrimage to the Ka'aba. A ten-year truce was concluded. He broke it in 630 and captured the town. He destroyed the idols of the Ka'aba, and obliterated the frescoes of the prophets, except for that of Abraham. Forbidding raids within the Ummah, Mohammed led incursions into Syria. He died suddenly, without naming a successor, on June 8, 632.

nor of Tangiers. In April 711, after having crossed the strait at the head of an army of 7,000 Berbers, Tariq landed in a place that still bears his name, *Djabal Tariq* or Gibraltar. He occupied Cartaya and Algeciras. On July 23, 711, his troops crushed the army of Rodrigo, despite its superiority in numbers, at the battle of Guadalete, to the east of Cadiz. The king was killed during combat, along with a large part of the Visigothic aristocracy. Tariq marched directly on to Toledo, which fell with no resistance, then he continued his incursion as far as Guadalajara, while a detachment of 700 men captured Cordoba. In 712, Musa landed with a contingent of 18,000 men, mostly Arabs. With the help of Akhila's supporters, he broke through any resistance found at Medina Sidonia, Carmona, Sevilla or Merida, before reaching Toledo where he set himself up as a real monarch, having dinars struck to commemorate his victories. Musa went back on the offensive in the spring of 714. He captured Zaragoza, marched on Lerida, then returned through Soria, Oviedo and Gijón. He pillaged Amaya, Leon and Astorga, while Tariq carried out breakthroughs into Aragon. Urgently called back to Damascus to give an account of their conquests, Musa and Tariq fell into disgrace and did not return. The caliph did, nonetheless, confirm Musa's son, Abd al-Aziz, as the *wali* of al-Andalus. The latter continued the conquest by subjecting, in the west, Evora, Santarem and Coimbra, then in the north-east, Tarragona, Barcelona, Gerona and Narbonne. By the time of his death in 716, the Levant and all of Andalusia were under Muslim control. From 716 to 719, his successor, Al-Hurr, completed the conquest of all the peninsula's territory and chose Cordoba as his capital. The remarkably rapid Muslim conquest was facilitated by the relative absence of opposition from the native population. In rural areas, the inhabitants easily adopted the new religion, becoming *Mouwalladun*, while in the cities the *Mozarabs*, Christians who had come under the Muslim yoke, took on the status of *dhimmi*, which, in exchange for tribute, allowed them to keep their goods and freely worship according to their own faith, under the authority of the

Torre del Oro in Sevilla

THE BATTLE OF GUADALETE

On this day of July 23, 711, did the battle take place on the shores of the Guadalete, or of the Guadarranque north of Algeciras, near the lake of La Janda near Cadiz? The Visigothic troops comprised 40,000 men; the Muslim army had 25,000. But the treason of Witiza's two brothers, Oppas and Sisbert, to whom the Visigothic King Rodrigo had entrusted the two wings of his army, reversed the balance of power and gave the victory to Tariq.

The Alcazar in Merida

Detail of the Giralda in Sevilla

The temple of Janus in Autun

A Skirmish

According to tradition, the battle of Covadonga in 718 marks the beginning of the *Reconquista*. It has been established by texts from the end of the 9th century, written by Mozarabs who took refuge in the north of the Iberian peninsula. In these texts, Visigothic nobles elected as their chief Pelayo, the son of Fáfila, a former dignitary at the court of King Egica. Pelayo chose Cangas de Onís as his capital and took the lead in an uprising against the Muslims. Arab troops led by al-Kama, accompanied by Oppas, bishop of Sevilla and brother to Witiza, arrived to put it down. Pelayo and his men took shelter in Santa Maria cave that opens onto the face of Mount Auseba, known as Covadonga. Oppas tried vainly to negotiate the surrender of his co-religionists. Thanks to the miraculous intervention of the Virgin Mary, the Visigoths crushed their adversaries who fled and abandoned the Asturias. The version given by Arab chroniclers is different. Pelayo indeed tried to organize resistance, but at the head of "thirty wild donkeys" who, in no case, could present any sort of threat to Muslim power. In fact, it seems that Covadonga was simply a skirmish between Asturian tribes, attached to their traditions, allied to Visigothic nobles eager for revenge, and Muslims with little interest in such inhospitable territory.

archbishop of Toledo. The first Muslim colonists of al-Andalus, the *baladis*, of Yemeni or Qasi origin, settled in the towns, valleys and plains of the centre, to the detriment of the Berbers who, although numerically superior, were relegated to less fertile regions — in the south, in the mountainous areas of Baetica, and in the north, to southern Galicia and the basin of the Duero River. Towards 720, the new governor of al-Andalus, as-Samh-al-Malik, entered Gaul, but failed in his raid against Toulouse, which ended with the victory of King Eudes of Aquitaine. The Moors nonetheless managed to take Carcassonne and Nîmes, then devastated Autun in 722. In the same year, Pelayo, an Asturian nobleman, inflicted the first defeat on the occupiers of the peninsula, near the grotto of Covadonga, to the north of the Cantabrian mountain range. This was the region in which a movement of Christian resistance began to be organized. In 732, the governor Abd al-Rahmân al Ghafiqi decided to lead another expedition into Frankish territory, heading for the monastery of Saint Martin of Tours, the site of a famous pilgrimage. The Prophet's armies passed through Pamplona, crossed the Pyrenees at Roncesvalles Pass, ravaged Bordeaux, then crushed Eudes' soldiers between the Garonne and Dordogne Rivers. Reaching Poitiers, they had enough time to devastate Saint Hilaire Basilica, before their famous defeat by the Franks led by Charles Martel, on the first day of Ramadan, October 25, 732. Pushed back to the south, the Moors took Arles and Avignon in 734. In 752, Pepin the Short managed to take back Narbonne, forcing the Muslim troops to retreat to the Ebro River and the foothills of the Pyrenees. However, in the Iberian peninsula the Berbers felt more and more wronged by Arab colonists and, in 739, they rose up against the governor Abd al-Malik. To help suppress the uprising, the latter accepted the intervention of the Syrian army sent from Damascus. In the face of this repression, the Berbers from the northern regions took refuge in North Africa, leaving the northern regions of the former Lusitania, the basin of the Duero and the upper valley of the Ebro River deserted and exposed to Christian

Covadonga

incursions. Furthermore, despite an agreement with the governor, the Syrians did not pull back once the situation had been re-established towards 741. Instead, they settled in some of the areas of the centre and the east. This Syrian presence facilitated the accession to the throne of the Umayyad prince Abd al-Rahmân who, having escaped his family's massacre by the Abbasides in 750, had taken refuge in *Ifriqiya*, then come to the Iberian peninsula in 755. Thanks to help from the Syrian *djund*, in 756 he vanquished the governor of al-Andalus, at the battle of Al Musara. Without renouncing the religious authority of the Abbaside caliph of Baghdad, the Umayyad prince thus broke the unity of the Muslim world by proclaiming himself emir. Changing from its status as a satellite province to an Arab caliphate, al-Andalus became a *de facto* independent state. In Cordoba, which he had chosen as his capital, Abd al-Rahmân, nicknamed the immigrant, undertook the construction of the great mosque and of two residences. In contrast to the principal Western Christian states, weakened by feudal division, Abd al-Rahmân's emirate enjoyed centralized administrative structures, organized around the court and placed under the direction of a *hadjib*, who supervised the vizirs of the various ministries. The emir drew his power from the efficiency of his financial and judicial systems, the strength of his army and navy, and the prosperity of his economy. The extension and sophistication of irrigation techniques improved agricultural production and allowed the introduction of new cultures such as rice, sugar cane, asparagus,

The Mezquita in Cordoba

THE ABBASIDES

The Umayyad dynasty ended under Marwan II (744-750), after the insurrection of 747 in the Khorasan by the descendants of Abbas, an uncle of the Prophet. Legitimate Hachemites, the Abbasides furthermore claimed the rights that were allegedly ceded to them in 718 by the son of Mohammed Ibn al-Hanafyia, an illegitimate son of Ali's. Supported by the Shiite movement of the Hanafyia and the local *mawali* who were upset with their status, the Abbaside revolution led by the military chief Abu Muslim, a freed Iranian, soon won over all over Iran, then moved to Iraq, where the pretender Abu Abbas al Saffah was proclaimed caliph in October 749, in the great mosque of Kufa. In January 750, the revolutionary troops crushed the Umayyad army at the battle of the Great Zab, and soon afterwards massacred nearly the entire Marwan family in Damascus. The Abbasides settled in Iraq, making Baghdad the capital of their caliphate. The only survivor of the Umayyad dynasty, the prince Abd al-Rahmân, managed to escape and reach the Iberian peninsula, where in 756 he created an independent emirate with its capital in Cordoba. Far in advance of the western Christian states and rivalling the Abbaside empire in the east, the Umayyad civilization of al-Andalus reached its apex under Abd al-Rahmân III, who took the title of caliph in 929. But the ambitions of several great Arab families and the advances of the Christian reconquest were to undermine the al-Andalus Umayyad caliphate and in the 11th century it was dismembered by the "reyes des taïfas". Soon a new dynasty, the Almoravids from Morocco, took over starting in 1085 and it was integrated as a simple province into a vast Moorish empire centred in Marrakesh.

Glossary

Al-Andalus

Muslim Spain

Baladis

First Arab colonists of
al-Andalus

Caliph

From *khalifa*, replacement:
successor of the Prophet at the
head of the community

Dhimmi

The "protected": non-Muslims
tolerated by the Muslims following
an agreement

Djund

Militias or garrisons spread
throughout the provinces

Emir

Governor of a province, chief of the
police and army

Hajib

Kind of prime minister to the caliph

Ifriqiya

Muslim province of
North Africa

Muwalladun

The "adopted": Iberian populations
who converted to Islam

Mozarabs

From *musta'rib*, Arabized: initially,
Christians who had accepted the
status of dhimmi in al-Andalus

Ummah

Muslim community

Wâli

Equivalent of emir

mulberries and citrus fruit. The variety of raw materials used encouraged the skill of artisans: linen cloth from Zaragoza, silks, crystal and leather from Cordoba, ceramics from Malaga, stimulating exports. Al-Andalus' artisans became masters in techniques of stucco or yeserias, and in woodworking, providing the mosques with superb ceilings. Later, Almohad artists became famous for making *azulejos* (decorated ceramic tiles) that would replace mosaics. Starting in the 10th century, Arabs introduced Chinese techniques for producing paper into the peninsula, and paper soon replaced parchment. The first paperworks of Europe were set up in Jativa, near Valencia. Along the northern frontier, three Marches were created to thwart Christian advances: the upper March, in the east, under the authority of the governor of Zaragoza; the central March, entrusted to the wali of Toledo, and finally, the lower March, in the west, with Merida as its capital. But from the very beginning of his reign, Abd al-Rahmân had to deal with tensions dividing the various ethnic groups that had taken part in the conquest, and with impulses for independence by various local governors. There were several Yemeni and Berber revolts between 766 and 776. In 778, the wali of Barcelona and Gerona called on Charlemagne, promising him easy conquest of the upper March. He hoped to use the Frankish king's forces to eliminate the emir. But the future emperor was defeated before Zaragoza. On their return journey, the imperial forces demolished the walls of Pamplona. In retaliation, the Basques ambushed him at Roncesvalles in August 778. From 797 to 834, in Toledo, Merida and Cordoba, Abd al-Rahmân's successors were confronted with revolts by the *mouwalladun*, who were discontented with their position of inferiority with respect to the old Muslims. In many towns, the Arab aristocracy took advantage of the troubles to govern themselves. Then in the middle of the 9th century, the *Mozarabs* rose up, despite the Muslim authorities' tolerance towards them. In Cordoba, some of them attempted voluntary martyrdom by blaspheming the name of the Prophet and Islam.

The Alcazar in Cordoba

Moorish arch in the nave at Cuxa

GUIFRE THE HAIRY

....

T he *invention* of the *Moraneta*,
the Black Virgin of
Montserrat, or other more or less
legendary facts, are linked to the
personage Guifre the Hairy. He
was born in 852 and is considered
to be the founder of Catalonia.
Charles the Bald who, in 870,
had just given him the fief of
Urgel and Cerdagne, asked Guifre
to help him against the Norsemen.
In the battle Guifre was struck
by an arrow. In the evening, the
Frankish emperor went to the
Catalonian count's tent, where
the count lay on a couch with
his shield, a bare field of gold,
beside him. Charles dipped four
fingers into Guifre's open wound
and traced the four stripes that
appear on the Catalonian coat
of arms, "gold with four pales
of gules". It was at the foot of
Canigou mountain, in Ria near
Saint Michel de Cuxa, that
Guifre the Hairy was born.
He was buried at the monastery
of Sainte-Marie de Ripoll that
he founded.

Meanwhile, throughout the 8th and 9th centuries, Christians consolidated their zones of influence in the Pyrenees and the Cantabrian mountains. Taking advantage of the Berber crisis in 741, Pepin the Short took back Narbonne, then the rest of the former Narbonensis province, also called Septimania, between 752 and 759. To the north-east of Tarraconensis, Charlemagne's army carried out several victorious offensives, capturing Gerona in 785, Ausona and Cardona in 798, and finally, Barcelona in 801. In 806, the Count of Toulouse captured the Pyrenean regions of Pallars and Ribagorza, while a county was founded around Jaca, on the Aragon River. Entrusted to counts of Frankish origin, the conquered territories, Gothic Septimania and north-eastern Tarraconensis, were annexed to the Empire. However, at the end of the 9th century, faced with the ambitions of several Frankish counts, Charles the Bald divided Septimania into two to form, along with the south Pyrenean counties, the Spanish March. Entrusted to Gothic counts, this march, *Gothalonia* or *Catalunya*, comprised, at the beginning of the 10th century, the counties of Ribagorza, Pallars, Urgel, Cerdagne, Roussillon, Vallespir, Besalú, Peralada, Ampurias, Gerona, Ausona, and Barcelona. In 878, at the Assembly of Troyes, the Gothic count Guifre the Hairy, at the head of the counties of Urgel, Cerdagne and Conflent since 870, was invested by Louis II with the counties of Barcelona and Gerona, and received the title of *comes Mercae*, Count of the March, in other words, the military chief whose role was to defend all the counties of *Catalunya*. His brothers, Miro and Radulph received the counties of Roussillon and Besalú, for which they had to take an oath. Subsequently, Guifre's descendants administered the region. In the Cantabrian mountains, Alfonso I (739-757), Pelayo's son-in-law and son of the Duke of Cantabria, united Asturians and Cantabrians in a single kingdom, around the capital of his father-in-law, Cangas de Onís. He captured part of the Basque provinces of Biscay and Alava, the region of Burgos, the eastern part of Oviedo and then, by taking Lugo, part of Galicia. Taking advantage of the Berbers' departure in 741, he led incursions into the Duero valley, attacking Braga, Porto, then Leon, Astorga, Zamora, and Salamanca, which he devastated before bringing Christian clerics and aristocrats back to Asturias. His successors had to face Muslim attacks in Galicia, Alava and Asturias from 757 to 792, socio-political tensions caused by the succession to the throne, and peasant revolts in Galicia and Alava. Nevertheless, Fruela I (757-768) managed to repopulate Galicia as far as Miño, and imposed his authority in the east of the Asturias, in the upper Ebro valley. When he mounted the throne in 792, Alfonso II (792-842) legitimized his power by claiming to be the heir to the kingdom of Toledo and by bringing back its customs: he received the royal unction, surrounded himself with a court composed of secular and ecclesiastical magnates, adopted the *Liber Judicum* and named *comites* at the head of conquered territories. The kingdom's capital was transferred to Oviedo, which was raised to a bishopric, and where the monarch had several churches and a palace built. Finally, it was during his reign that the tomb of James the Greater, the apostle of Spain, was discovered, which was to fire the zeal of the fighters of the *Reconquista*.

CHRISTIANS IN AL-ANDALUS

"Part of the bishops said that Jesus Christ is the adopted son because of his humanity and not adopted by his divinity. The other part says that, in both natures, he is the only Son of God the Father, his own Son and not adopted and precisely in the way that He himself is God, true Son of God. We, Etherius and Beatus, belong to this group, with others who profess the same faith." (*Apologetica* I, 13)

After the invasion of 711, the Christians remaining in the peninsula were able to retain their belongings and freely worship, thanks to the status called *dhimmi* (protected) that Islam accorded to "people of the Book". In exchange, they paid a poll tax, the *jizya*, to the occupier. Numerous in the cities of Toledo, Cordoba, Sevilla and Merida, these Christians subjected to Muslim authority and later called

Mozarabs (from *musta'rib*, Arabized) enjoyed a certain autonomy. They elected the heads of the community (count, censor or exceptor) whose job was to maintain order, and mediate legal disputes and collect the *jizya*. Although they were not allowed to build new churches, Mozarab Christians managed to maintain the ecclesiastical hierarchy and the main episcopal offices that preceded the invasion. The bishops were convoked to regular synods, under the authority of the Metropolitan of Toledo. Until the middle of the 9th century, coexistence with the Muslim occupier went smoothly, and against all expectations, starting at the end of the 7th century the Mozarabs quarrelled with their fellow Christians, who had taken shelter in the northern mountainous areas of the peninsula, and with the Frankish clergy. Indeed, towards 780, in response to the Neo-Sabellianist theses of the cleric Migetius, the archbishop of Toledo, Elipand, began to profess that only the Word issues from divinity and that Jesus, a man among men, had simply been adopted by the Creator

to spread his message among mankind. Was Elipand attempting to make a theological compromise between Christianity and Islam, as his detractors insinuated? In any case, his doctrine called Adoptionism, which was accepted by the Council of Toledo in 784, spread in Galicia, the Asturias, and as far as Septimania, thanks to the action of Felix, Bishop of Urgel. However, a determined adversary soon appeared – Beatus, a monk at the Asturian monastery of San Martín de Liebana who, in 785, in collaboration with the bishop of Osma, wrote an *Apologetica* against Elipand. In the same year, the debate set off by the archbishop of Toledo took on greater proportions and provoked the intervention of the principal religious and political dignitaries of Western Christendom. In 785, Catalonia, included in the March of Spain, became a part of the Carolingian Empire. Learning of the Adoptianist theses defended by the bishop of Urgel, at the request of Pope Adrian I, Charlemagne convoked a council at Ratisbonne in 792, where Felix, condemned, renounced his doctrine. However, having taken refuge in Toledo with Elipand, the bishop of Urgel continued to profess the theses condemned by Rome. In 794, Charlemagne convoked a new council in Frankfurt, at which Adoptianism was declared a heresy. Shortly afterwards, the Pope excommunicated all those who departed from the council's conclusions. Felix nonetheless continued to defend his ideas against Alcuin, who refuted his thesis in seven books, as well as against Paulin of Aquileia. But in 799, the heresiarch was ordered to appear at the council called at Aachen by the emperor and the new pope Leon III. Vanquished by his detractors, who included Leidrade, Bishop of Lyons, Nefrid, Bishop of Narbonne, and Benedict, abbot of Aniane, Felix of Urgel

Former episcopal palace in Braga

was forced to publicly disavow his mistakes. He ended his days in exile in Lyons, where he died in 818. After the council of 799, Elipand remained alone to defend his Adoptionist doctrine, at the head of a very small number of disciples. Despite Alcuin's efforts, the bishop of Toledo refused to disavow his ideas, which he defended until his death in about 808. From the political point of view, the struggle against the Adoptionist heresy, coming at the very beginning of the Christian reconquest of the peninsula, helped to bring the Asturian monarchy closer to the Caroligian kingdom. From the religious point of view, it was to separate the Asturian church from the supervision of the Archbishop Primate of Toledo, whose deviations Beatus had fought against, and favoured its autonomy. Braga soon recovered its status as an ecclesiastical metropolis, while Oviedo rivalled the former Toledan capital. Coming out of the Adoptionist crisis in isolation, the Mozarab church faced new difficulties in the middle of the 9th century, when many of its members who had until then been docile under Muslim domination, rose up against their status which confined them to the suburbs of cities, limited the number and activities of their churches, and forbade all proselytism. Several Mozarab clerics, such as the bishop of Cordoba, Alvarus and the priest Eulogius, also denounced the decline of Latin culture, the lukewarm religiosity and the "arabization" of their peers, who had abandoned the use of Latin and spoke Arabic. Mixed marriages, the attraction of the brilliant and dominant Moorish civilization, indeed provoked the progressive assimilation of the occupier's customs and caused many conversions to Islam among the native Christians. The discomfort of the Mozarab church broke out in Cordoba in June 851, when the monk Isaac, after

having deliberately provoked the authorities by insulting the name of the Prophet, was condemned to death by the emir. Within a few weeks, over thirty Christians, both clerics and secular, men and women, followed his example and died as martyrs. Eulogius and Alvarus of Cordoba, who supported the movement, were imprisoned. In 852, the regional council convoked on the orders of the emir Abd Al-Rahmân II and presided over by the Bishop of Sevilla, Recafred, condemned the martyrs in accordance with the Church's traditional interdiction of suicide. New riots caused by the council's decisions were severely put down. Under Mohammed I, repressive measures against Mozarabs intensified. Nonetheless, Eulogius was freed and he continued his struggle by his writing. His *Liber apologeticus martyrum* and his *Memoriale martyrum*, in three volumes, took on the defence of Christians against the occupiers, while attacking Islam and glorifying martyrdom. Having become bishop of Cordoba, Eulogius was elected archbishop of Toledo in 858

but the Muslim authorities never allowed him to occupy the position. Furthermore, the bishop was soon to experience the martyrdom that he had glorified. In 859, Leocricia, a young Muslim woman whose great-aunt was a Christian, took shelter with Eulogius after renouncing Islam and converting to Christianity. Taking advantage of the situation, the al-Andalus authorities arrested the bishop and accused him of hiding the young renegade. Eulogius and Leocricia were executed in March 859. Both of them were canonized, and their relics deposited, with those of Saint Eulalia of Merida, in Oviedo cathedral by King Alfonso II in 884. A hardening of measures towards Christians provoked by the self-sacrifice of the Cordoban martyrs was soon to cause the exile of many Mozarabs to the Asturias and the March of Spain. The Christian kingdoms in the north were enriched by their culture, which joined their knowledge of Arabic and the wealth of Moorish civilization with the traditions of the Visigothic church founded by Isidore of Sevilla.

Toledo

St James the Greater, miniature of "The Golden Legend" by Jacques de Voragine

THE EVANGELIST OF SPAIN

At the end of the 4th century, a sentence of the treatise *On the Trinity* by Didymus of Alexandria (313-398) attributed the evangelization of Spain to an apostle who could not be Paul. At the beginning of the 5th century, Jerome (345-419), a disciple of Didymus, took up his master's idea in his *Commentary on Isaiah*, and claimed that the fishermen of the Sea of Galilee were sent to preach the Gospel "on the great sea […] as far as Illyria and to Spain". The preachers evoked by Jerome can only be the two sons of Zebedee, James and John. However, in 416, a letter by Pope Innocent discredited the evangelization thesis of the countries of the western Mediterranean by some "non Roman" apostle. "It is obvious", he wrote, "that, in all of Italy, Gaul, Spain, Africa, Sicily and the interlying islands, nobody instituted churches, if not those that the venerable apostle Peter or his successors instituted as bishops." Three years later, during a controversy opposing Augustine, the famous bishop of Hippone, and Hesychius, Bishop of Salona in Dalmatia, the latter maintained that the Gospel had been preached "as far as the end of the Earth" by each of the twelve disciples in person. In a legendary *Life* of the pope Saint Clement (88-97) attributed to him, the Dalmatian bishop even specified that James the Greater was sent by Peter to the Spanish lands to spread the Good Word. However, at the end of the century, an apocryphal work translated from Hebrew into Greek under the title of *History of Apostolic Combat* suggested differing accounts about James. According to its presumed author, a certain Abdias, the first bishop of Babylon who allegedly saw Christ with his own eyes, Illyria was evangelised by Paul, Ethiopia by Matthew, Persia by Thomas, India by Bartholomew, Greece by Andrew, and Palestine by the two Jameses – the brother of Christ, head of the first Church of Jerusalem, and James the Greater, John's brother. Condemned by Pope Gelasius I (492-496), the work was nonetheless tolerated. Towards the end of

Paul, Abbey of Moissac

THE JOURNEYS OF PAUL

Born in Tarsus in Cilicia, Asia Minor, between 5 and 15 AD, Saul received a solid rabbinical education in Jerusalem. As a Pharisee hostile to Christianity, he approvingly attended the stoning of Stephen. Towards the year 36, as he was on his way to Damascus to have some Christians arrested, an invincible force threw him to the ground. Jesus appeared to him and Saul was instantly converted. Thereafter, it was under his Roman name, Paul, that he became one of the most active members of the new Church. During three long journeys, between 44 and 57, he travelled throughout Asia Minor and Greece, evangelizing pagans, the "gentiles" whose apostle he became. Towards 57, in his *Epistle to the Romans*, he announced his intention of reaching Rome, and from there, Spain. However, accused of sedition by the authorities of the Temple, Paul was arrested in Jerusalem in 58. The apostle finally reached the eternal city in 61, but under escort. Under house arrest, he waited for his trial. Freed in 63, Paul, according to tradition, carried out his grand plan of going to the Spanish lands, as is alleged by Clement of Rome and several Apocryphals. He then journeyed to Crete and Greece. But arrested once again, he was imprisoned in Rome. Condemned to perish by the sword, Paul was beheaded towards the year 67.

James's sermon, St James altar in Pistoia

James, brother of Jesus, Silos

APOCRYPHA

....

The apocryphal writings, from the Greek *apocruphos*, secret, hidden, are religious texts that resemble those of the Bible but have not been recognized in the Canon of Writings, that is, in the list of authentic holy books set by the Council of Trent in 1546.

Matthew and James

the 6th century in Gaul, in the literary entourage of bishops Gregory of Tours (538-594) and Fortunat of Poitiers (c. 530-after 600), the *History of Apostolic Combat* was taken up again in Latin in a collection of apostolic stories, known under the title of *Pseudo-Abdias*. James the Greater is mentioned there as the evangelist of Judea and Samaria and, for the first time, he is confronted with the magician Hermogenes. At the same time, in the Byzantine East of the early 7th century, an apocryphal catalogue was circulating, of which the oldest version, written in Syriac, dates from 617. The work, known in its Latin translation as *De Sanctis Prophetis*, tells the faithful to which tribe and which country belonged each of the prophets of the Old Testament, his place of birth, the manner of his death as well as the location of his tomb. Shortly afterwards, a similar catalogue appeared, this time dedicated to the apostles. The different Greek versions of this apocrypha claimed to be based on the highest authorities, among them Dorothy, Bishop of Tyre, Hippolytus of Rome, or Sophronius of Jerusalem, the translator of Jerome into Greek. However, they confuse as the same person James the Greater, son of Zebedee, and James, the brother of Jesus, the presumed author of the Gospel of James, who had himself been for a long time assimilated into James the Less, son of Alphæus. In no version of this Greek catalogue was James given as the evangelist of Spain. As for the location of his tomb, the sources gave either Judea, or Cesarea in Palestine, or even Marmarica, a region located between the western branch of the Nile and Libyan Cyrenaica. In 630, the Visigoths captured from the Byzantines the south-eastern territories of *Hispania*, then in great cultural turmoil. At the time, Isidore was the bishop of Sevilla (600-636). "The glory of Spain and pillar of the Church", the distinguished Latinist, a theologian, exegete and historian, was compiling in his *Etymologies* all the knowledge of his time. In his *De ortu et Obitu Sanctorum Patrum*, he also took over the information of the Byzantine catalogue about the *Lives of the Prophets*, which had probably reached Hispania and been translated into Latin during the Byzantine occupation. A Latin version of the Byzantine apostolic catalogues appeared in the West about 650, with the particularity of attributing the evangelization of Macedonia to Matthew (instead of Ethiopia as in *Pseudo-Abdias*), that of Gaul to Phillip (instead of Scythia), and finally, that of Spain to James (instead of Palestine), although the latter's tomb was still mentioned as being in Marmarica. The most complete and oldest version of this text, contained in the *Brevarium apostolorum*, located the apostle's tomb *in achaia marmarica*; the term *achaia* mentioned in the notice before that of James meaning the place of evangelization, was probably the result of an accidental transposition by the copyist. However, a papyrus from the 2nd century mentions the existence of an *Anchaion* in Marmarica. Most importantly, the two remaining copies of *De Ortu et Obitu Sanctorum Patrum* attributed to Isidore of Sevilla also contain, in a chapter that was probably added to the original work, the information from this Latin version of the Byzantine apostolic catalogues. Thus reassured by a certain authority, the thesis of James the Greater's evangelism in Spain was

James praying to the Pilar Virgin

JAMES AND HERMOGENES

While he was preaching the Gospel in Judea, the Pharisees and the priest Abiathar decided to turn the apostle James away from his faith by calling on the magician Hermogenes. The latter immediately responded by sending one of his young assistants, Philetus, to the Son of Thunder. However, when he returned to his master, Philetus had been converted to the Christian faith. Angered, Hermogenes used magic to immobilize him. Told of the misfortune of his new disciple, James hurried to deliver him by using his shroud. Vexed, Hermogenes called upon an army of demons, ordering them to bring Philetus and James back as prisoners. In vain! The great power of the Spirit protected the apostle

and it was Hermogenes, tied up by his own demons, who appeared before James. Convinced of the superiority of his adversary, the former magician rapidly renounced his dark practices. Armed with the stick given to him by the apostle to preserve him from demonic powers, he ran to get his books of magic so that he could burn them. As the autodafé made the most awful smell, the books were finally thrown into the sea. The story of Hermogenes appeared for the first time at the end of the 6th century, in the collection of *Pseudo-Abdias*. It seems to have been inspired by an episode in the *Acts of the Apostles* in which Peter was confronted by Simon the magician.

THE PILAR

A very ancient and strongly-rooted tradition associates the Virgin of the Pilar of Zaragoza, the patron of Spain, with James the Greater, its patron saint. In the year 39 AD, James was preaching in *Caesaraugusta*, the future Zaragoza. Rather discouraged by the results he was obtaining, the Virgin Mary appeared to him "in mortal flesh", on a pillar, *pilar* in Castilian, of jasper. She encouraged the apostle and asked him to build, at the very place of her appearance, a shrine in her honour, specifying that the pillar had to remain until the end of the world. The same tradition says that the disciples Athanasius and Theodore accompanied James and that they became the first bishops of Zaragoza. The church Nuestra Señora del Pilar de Zaragoza was built at the end of the 17th century. In the chapel dedicated to the Virgin, under a silver canopy, an alabaster statue of the Mother of the Lord is placed on its pillar.

Window showing James and Hermogenes, Bourges Cathedral

35

BEATUS OF LIEBANA

"O very worthy and very holy apostle/Who dazzles as the golden head of Hispania/ Our protector and national patron/ Spare us the plague, be the salvation of Heaven/ Remove all illness, calamity and crime/ Show yourself merciful by protecting the flock entrusted to you/ And kind shepherd for the king, the clergy and the people/ That we may enjoy, thanks to your help, celestial days".
(Beatus of Liebana, *O Dei verbum*)

In this deep valley crossed by the Deva River, overlooked in the south by the eastern ranges of the Cantabrian cordillera and, in the north-west by the Picos de Europa, many monasteries were installed during the 8th century. The most important was that of San Martín de Turieno, which became that of San Torribio, from the name of its traditionally accepted founder in the 6th century. Nothing remains of the original monastery except for the *Cueva Santa,* which was, perhaps, the oratory of Saint Torribio. After the Arab invasion, many relics were transferred from the occupied regions to this area of the Iberian peninsula and it was thus that San Martín Monastery received a piece of Jesus Christ's cross, the relic of the *Vera Cruz.* Numerous Christians followed the same route and one of them, Beatus, settled in the great monastery in the valley of Liebana. Born during the first third of the 8th century, this scholar certainly came from one of the principal centres of Visigothic culture – Toledo, Cordoba, Merida or Sevilla –

bringing his library with him. In 785, he collaborated with Etherius, the bishop of Osma, in drafting the *Apologetica* against Elipand, the archbishop of Toledo preaching Adoptionist theses. But by 776, Beatus had written a first version of his *Commentaries on the Apocalypse.* He wrote a second in 786, and a third shortly before his death in 798. His work is situated within the tradition of the period, when fundamental texts, *Epistles, Acts of the Apostles and the Revelation of St. John*, were accompanied by authorized commentaries. The *Revelation of St. John* had a certain importance in the Visigothic kingdom since the Council of Toledo of 633 had ordered it to be read at masses celebrated on the day of Pentecost. In the Iberian peninsula under the Arab yoke, the contents of the *Revelation* had a particular resonance. The text, probably the substance of the *lectio divina* in many monasteries, assimilated to a condemnation of Rome-Babylon whose destruction it announces, had contemporary importance during the 8th century. The Beast had become Islam, Babylon, Cordoba, and the false prophet, Mohammed. In the same commentaries, Beatus, establishing a correlation between Christianity in Hispania and the son of Zebedee, evoked James as the evangelist of Hispania. "The apostles, even if all were but one, each received his own destination to preach the world. Peter in Rome, Andrew in Achaia, Thomas in the Indies, James in Hispania." And this apostle who had Christianized the Iberian peninsula, freeing it from paganism, why would he not be the one who inspired and led the struggle for liberation? The feast of Saint James, which did not exist in the

Visigothic calendar, was then introduced into the liturgy for which Beatus composed certain texts, particularly the hymn *O Dei verbum.* The acrostic formed by the first letters of each verse sets its composition during the reign of Mauregatus (783-788). With respect to Beatus' preoccupations, it appeared to be especially necessary to invoke Saint James, since this Asturian king, the son of Alfonso I and a Muslim prisoner, colluded with the emir of Cordoba. It was obvious that Beatus played an essential role in the worship of Saint James in Hispania. About thirty years after his death, the tomb of the apostle James was discovered near Iria Flavia. In his time, Beatus of Liebana played an important intellectual, political and religious role. He also had artistic importance, although it was indirect, since, starting in the 10th century, his *Commentaries on the Apocalypse* were copied and recopied and, in most cases, decorated with illuminations showing, among other things, the famous maps of the world attributing an area of evangelism to each of the apostles and, particularly, Spain allocated to Saint James. From the 10th to the 13th centuries, thirty-two manuscripts reproduced this work. Twenty-two are illustrated with illuminations whose wealth and quality prove the inspiration that the *Apocalyse* had on Mozarab artists. Copyists and illuminators in *scriptoria* at San Millán de la Cogolla, San Miguel de la Escalada and Santo Domingo de Silos, produced some of these manuscripts that show, in their colophons, the date at which the work was finished, according to Visigothic counting, thirty-eight years in advance of the Roman rite, as well as the name of the artist.

San Millán de la Cogolla

accredited in the West. In 709, when Aldhelm, abbot of the Anglo-Saxon monastery of Malmesbury, composed poems in the honour of each of the apostles destined to decorate the altars of his abbey church, in the verse dedicated to Saint James, he wrote: *Primitus Hispanas convertit dogmate gentes.* Less than a century later, in the prologue to Book II of the *Commentaries on the Apocalypse*, Beatus, a monk at Saint Martín de Liebana in the Asturias, faithful to the tradition set up since Isidore of Sevilla, also attributed the evangelization of the Iberian peninsula to James the Greater. He also composed a liturgical hymn, *O Dei verbum*, in which the same James is designated as the patron saint of Spain. However, a problem remains. Should not the relics of the evangelist of *Hispania*, like those of Saint Denis of Gaul, or those of Saint Mark, whose mission began on the lagoon of the Lido in Venice, also have been found in his place of evangelism?

TO THE ENDS OF THE EARTH

In *De Ortu et Obitu Patrum*, Isidore of Sevilla wrote: "James, son of Zebedee and brother of John […] preached the Gospel in Hispania, in the western regions, and spread the light of his evangelism to the ends of the Earth. He fell after the blow of a sword by the tetrarch Herod. He was buried in Achaia Marmarica…"

Arcades in Silos cloister

The lamb vanquishing the beast, Apocalypse, Beatus of Liebana

DIFFUSION AND EXPANSION OF CHRISTIANITY

"Go ye into all the world, and preach the gospel to every creature.
He that believeth and is baptized shall be saved; but he that believeth not shall be damned."
Gospel according to Saint Mark

Instituted on the day of Pentecost in Jerusalem, the first Church, directed by Peter, John and James, the brother of the Lord, gathered together at most about a hundred people: the eleven apostles, whom Matthew would soon join to replace Judas Iscariot, the family of Jesus, several women who knew him and some inhabitants of Jerusalem. These "Judeo-Christians" made up a separate community within Judaism. While continuing to observe Mosaic law, they maintained their belief in Jesus, the announced Messiah Israel was waiting for. Every week, the evening of the Sabbath or on the following day, they celebrated together the resurrection of Christ by reproducing his last supper. Luke described this first community as an example. "[they] had but one heart and one soul and none considered as his property any one of his goods; on the contrary, they put everything in common." This Aramaic-speaking group was rapidly joined by Greek-speaking Jews coming from the diaspora. These were the "Hellenists", at whose head seven deacons were installed and Stephen became their spiritual leader. He was also the first martyr, and his stoning ordered by the Sanhedrin towards 35-36 triggered a wave of persecution against the group, which was forced to flee. Speaking the language common in the entire eastern Mediterranean and accustomed to living among pagans, the Hellenists became the first Christian missionaries. Chased from Jerusalem,

they left to preach the Good Word in the synagogues of Judea, Samaria, Phoenicia and Cyprus. They reached Antioch in Syria, the third city of the Empire after Rome and Alexandria. Soon seconded by Barnabas and Paul, delegated by the Church of Jerusalem, the Hellenists found followers among the Jews, but also among pagans, whom they converted without ordering them to first become preachers, hence without circumcizing them. The community grew and the name *Christians* appeared at Antioch for the first time, towards the year 43. In about 45, Paul and Barnabas left on a mission to Cyprus, then went on to Asia Minor and reached Antioch in Pisidia. They preached in Iconium, Lystra and Perga, before joining the port of Attalia from where they sailed for Antioch, towards 47-48, announcing to the members of their community "how [they had] opened the doors of the faith to the pagans". However, the Judeo-Christians in Palestine accepted the presence of these "Gentiles" among them with difficulty, since they were exempted from the prescriptions of the Law. And after an incident that took place during Peter's stay in Antioch, Paul and Barnabas were called to Jerusalem in about 49. Deciding in their favour, the assembly finally agreed to welcome Jews and non-Jews indiscriminately into their churches. Circumcision was no longer imposed on new followers, and entrance into the new Christian community was henceforth by baptism, marking the religion's real start. Confirmed by Peter, "apostle of pagan nations", Paul continued his mission after 49. After having visited the communities already created in Asia Minor, he went to Troy and crossed the sea. In Greece, Paul chose lively, intellectual and commercial cities: he preached in Phillipi, Thessalonika, Athens, Corinth where towards 51-52

he converted Crispus, the head of the synagogue. From there, Paul sailed for Ephesus, stopped in Caesarea and visited Jerusalem before going back to Antioch. His third journey took him to Ephesus, where he remained three years, all the while maintaining constant relations with the other communities, as shown by his *Epistles*. In 57, he left Ephesus for Greece, then continued to Jerusalem, stopping on his way at the islands of Mytilini (Lesbos), Khios, Samos, Kos and Rhodes, and putting in at the ports of Syria, Tyre and Ptolemais (the future St. John of Acre). But in

Üçhisar in Cappadocia

Jerusalem, Paul was arrested for non-respect of the Law. Imprisoned in Caesarea, Paul was finally allowed to sail for Rome in the autumn of 60 in order to be judged. During this new journey, he preached in Syria, Lycia, Crete and Malta, before landing in Pozzuoli in the spring of 61. In Rome, a first Christian community had been formed by a few anonymous missionaries towards the year 30. In 61, according to tradition, Paul met Peter there. Acquitted in 63, the apostle of the nations departed for

Greece, the island of Crete and Asia Minor. Is it possible that he also went to Spain, as he announced in his Letter to the Romans (15,24)? Meanwhile in Rome, after the great fire of 64, to divert suspicion directed at him, Nero (54-68) accused the Christians and started the first persecutions. This was allegedly the moment of Peter's martyrdom. As for Paul, he was arrested in Troas and incarcerated in Rome, where he was beheaded in 67. By the end of the 1st century, the generation of apostles and first missionaries had died out. The communities that had been created were placed under the direction of an *episcop*, assisted by a college of elders, the *presbyterium*. Closer to the faithful, the *deacons* gathered the offerings, took care of the poor, prisoners, widows and the sick. At the beginning of the 2nd century, Christianity was solidly installed in the ports and big cities of the eastern Mediterranean: Jerusalem, Caesarea, Antioch, Ephesus, Phillippi, Thessalonika, Athens, Corinth and Alexandria. After the capture of Jerusalem by Titus in 70, following the revolt of Judea against Rome, the Christian community emi-

grated to Pella in Trans-Jordan. In the course of the second century, Christianity slowly spread eastwards; by about 200, it had reached the city of Dura-Europos, at the border of Roman Syria. The religion progressed more slowly westwards. In the first century, only Rome seems to have been affected. Then, coming from the mother churches in the east, Christian missionaries settled in Gaul during the second century. First of all in Lyons, the capital of the three Gauls, where the members of the community run by the bishop Potheinos (St. Pothin) and his successor Irenee of Smyrna, were mostly arrivals from Pergamum or Phrygia. Martyred in 177 under Marcus Aurelius, some, including Bishop Pothin, the slave Blandine and the young deacon Sanctus, were to remain famous for years. From Lyons, along the trade route following the Rhône-Saône Rivers, the presence of Christianity was attested in Autun, in the middle of Celtic territory, by the end of the 2nd century. In Roman Africa, the first historical evidence of a Christian presence dates to 180, when six members of the community of Scilium in Numidia died from imperial

persecution. However, the new religion spread rapidly on the African continent, with nearly ninety bishoprics in 240. It was in the second half of the third century that Christianity underwent great expansion. Until that time, the threat of persecution had weighed on Christians, who were often accused of terrible crimes. In fact, the message contained in Christianity challenged certain essential aspects of the Roman world. In a polytheistic empire, imbued with sanctity, where the sovereign personified the link between the gods and his subjects, Christianity offered a separation of politics and religion, and refusal of the imperial cult. "Render unto Caesar what is Caesar's, to God what is God's", said Jesus Christ. To strictly hierarchical economic and social structures based on the work of slaves, Paul replied "there are no longer neither slaves, nor freemen, nor man, nor woman". Finally, the prevailing mores (the status of children, cruelty of behaviour at the circus…) were contrary to Christian teaching. Nonetheless, under Gallienus, who in 260 published an edict of tolerance, the "little peace" that the Church enjoyed until 303 favoured its expansion. After the big cities, Christianity reached rural areas in Egypt, Syria and Cappadocia. Starting in 280, Romania was entirely converted. In Gaul, bishoprics appeared in Arles, Toulouse, Marseilles, Narbonne, Vaison and Limoges. Northern Italy, the Danubian regions, Brittany and the Iberian peninsula were also affected. By the dawn of the 4th century, Christianity had spread throughout the Empire, even as far as its most distant provinces. The last decisive step that remained was taken in 313, when Emperor Constantine in Milan proclaimed the peace of the Church and freedom of worship for Christians.

Hadrian's temple in Ephesus

Theodomir discovering St James's tomb

Las Rías Bajas, seen from La Curota west of Padrón, former Iria Flavia

A Strange Brightness

Charlemagne, Aachen

The three most ancient charters of the city of Compostela, successively dated from 829, 844 and 854, without going into details about the circumstances of the event, mention that the body of Saint James was "revealed" under Alfonso II the Chaste (792-842), at the time of the bishop of Iria Flavia, Theodomir (d. 847) on the land of Amaea, today Mihia. Not until 1077 did a more detailed description of the discovery appear. At that time, the construction of the actual cathedral of Compostela forced the removal of the monastery of Antealtares, which until then had been in charge of the tomb. The agreement made on that occasion between the bishop of Compostela, Diego Peláez, and Fagild, the monastery's abbot, known as the *Concordia de Antealtares*, tells that at the time of Alfonso the Chaste, there lived a hermit known as Pelagius in the diocese of Iria Flavia. He was the first to be informed by angels of the presence of James the Greater's tomb, not far from his hermitage on Mount Pedroso, on the territory of Amaea. Shortly afterwards, the faithful of the nearby church of San Fiz de Solovio noticed a celestial brightness showing a specific location. Learning of this, Theodomir, the bishop of the diocese, also noticed the strange nocturnal brightness and ordered a search. This was when the ancient tomb of the apostle James was discovered, hidden under thick brambles covering marble arches.

CAMPUS STELLAE

The name of Compostela appeared only in the middle of the tenth century. Scholarly linguistic studies have shown that one of the ancient names of the location, *Liberum Donum*, Libredon, comes not from the Latin, but from the Celtic *Ilwybr*, "place of passage" and *dunum* "height". This hypothesis would attest the presence here of a centre of ancient Celtic culture, to which medieval accounts relative to the translation of James the Greater, and particularly *The letter of Pope Leon* probably refer, when they mention the very large idol – *vastissimum idolum* – that was to be found near the crypt where the apostle was buried. As for the name of Compostela, popular etymology makes it come from the Latin,

Campus stellae ,"the field of the star", in memory of the nocturnal star that, long ago, showed the faithful of San Fiz de Solovio and Bishop Theodomir the location of the tomb of James the Greater. However, excavations undertaken between 1946 and 1959 below the cathedral of Compostela, have revealed the existence of an ancient necropolis that was used during the first century BC and whose activity suddenly stopped at the end of the 6th century, perhaps with the disappearance of the Suevi kingdom in Galicia. The name of Compostela would then come from the Latin *Compostum* "cemetery", as a word derived from the verb *componere*, which can have the meaning of "to bury".

ON THE DATE OF THE DISCOVERY…

Because of the absence of sources giving a precise date for the discovery of the apostle's tomb, for a long time it was commonly accepted that this had taken place during the lifetime of Charlemagne, who died in Aachen on January 28, 814. The establishment of this link between Charlemagne and the *invention* of the tomb, never recognized, was certainly due to a desire, first of the Carolingians, then of the Cluny monks, to glorify the work and personality of the Emperor. The only indisputable fact is that the event took place during the episcopate of Theodomir, who died in 847. It thus sets the date of its happening in the decade 820-830.

The Translatio, window in Notre-Dame-du-Crann Church

THE TRANSLATIO

The revelations made to the hermit Pelagius were thus verified by the discovery of a tomb that Bishop Theodomir had immediately identified as being that of James the Greater, the evangelist of Spain. How could the body of the martyr executed in Jerusalem by order of Herod Agrippa 1st, in 44 AD, be found about eight centuries later and at the north-eastern end of the Iberian peninsula? In all likelihood, it had been carried there. But the sources concerning the life of the apostle, few in number and with scarce details, mentioned nothing of such transportation. And soon, to resolve the questions raised by the mysterious discovery, legend arrived to remedy the silence of history. The additions to the martyrology of Florus of Lyons, between 806 and 838, taken up in the martyrology of Adon, dating from 860, relate that after the apostle's martyrdom, his relics were transferred to Spain, then buried in its furthermost region: "*Huius beatissimi apostoli sacra ossa ad Hispanias translata et in ultimis earum finibus, vidicet contra mare britannicum, condita*". Two other documents subsequent to the discovery of the apostle's tomb, integrated into the *Codex Calixtinus*, or *Liber Sancti Jacobi*, kept in the archives of Compostela cathedral, provide an answer to these interrogations: the *Translatio sancti Jacobi* and the apocryphal letter of Pope Leon.

Calixtus II

THE SEVEN SAINTS OF ACCI

Between 850 and 870, there were three editions of historical martyrology composed by Adon of Vienna, sometimes called the "Little Roman". This long list of saints and martyrs, placed in the order of the Roman calendar and accompanied by short historical notes, mentions, for the date of May 15th, an ancient cult, predating that of Saint James, about Saint Torquatus of Acci. Torquatus was among the seven bishops ordered to Rome by the apostles and sent by Saint Peter to evangelize the Iberian penisula. He and his companions first stayed in Acci, presently Guadix, east of Granada in the extreme south of the province of Cartagena. But one day the inhabitants, who had remained faithful to their pagan cult,

decided to chase them out of the town. In their flight, the seven bishops crossed a bridge that collapsed during the passage of their pursuers. Seeing this miracle, many followed the example of Luparia, a rich Roman matron, the first to become a convert. Having successfully accomplished their mission in Acci, the bishops disbanded to found other churches in the region, in Granada, Urci, Illturgi. It is obvious that the author of the *Translatio Sancti Jacobi* was inspired by this legend in writing his account, especially concerning the matron Luparia and the collapsing bridge. Furthermore, some of the names he gives to James' seven disciples are the same as those of the saints of Acci.

THE *CODEX CALIXTINUS*

The *Codex Calixtinus*, or *Liber sancti Jacobi*, kept in the archives of the cathedral in Compostela, owes its name to the apocryphal letter of Pope Calixtus II (1119-1124), that serves as its preface. It is divided into five books, composed from texts essential to the history of the pilgrimage and cult of Saint James. The first book offers an anthology of liturgical pieces in honour of the saint. The second mentions the miracles attributed to him. The third contains an account of the translation of the body, as well as an apocryphal letter by Pope Leon. The fourth contains the *History of Charlemagne and Roland* by Pseudo-Turpin. Finally, the fifth is none other than the *Guide for the Pilgrim to Santiago* by Aimery Picaud. This collection was allegedly completed towards the middle of the twelfth century.

N°	James' Miracles
I	The apostle frees twenty Christians held prisoner in Zaragoza by the Saracens. (Second half of the 11th century).
II	The text recounting the sin of an Italian pilgrim, written on the note he had placed on the apostle's altar in Compostela, is erased. (Under the bishopric of Theodomir).
III	A pilgrim's child is brought back to life in the Oca Mountains. (Year 1108).
IV	The apostle takes away the mortal remains of a pilgrim who died at the port of Cize, to Compostela. (Year 1080).
V	The *hanged-unhanged* (Year 1090).
VI	The apostle lends his donkey to a pilgrim from Poitiers who had been robbed by an innkeeper. (Year 1100).
VII	A sailor, attacked by Saracens and fallen into the water with his armour, is brought to the surface by the apostle. (Year 1101).
VIII	A prelate is saved from a shipwreck. (Year 1102).
IX	A knight, first cured by the apostle, escapes from a shipwreck. (Year 1103).
X	A pilgrim fallen into the sea is held up by the apostle for three days until making a safe landing. (Year 1104).
XI	A prisoner escapes by jumping, without damage, from a sixty-meter high tower where he had been imprisoned. (Year 1105).
XII	The goitre of a knight from Apulia is reduced on contact with a seashell brought back by a pilgrim. (Year 1106).

According to the author of the *Translatio Sancti Jacobi*, after the Ascension, James the Greater came to preach in Spanish lands and, from among those he converted, seven accompanied him upon his return to Jerusalem. After his martyrdom, these seven disciples gathered up his body and embarked with it on a small boat without a rudder. In seven days, guided by Providence, it reached the north-western coast of the peninsula. They landed at Iria Flavia, the present town of Padrón, located on the Sar River a few kilometres from the sea. Concerned to find a burial place worthy of the apostle, the seven disciples turned to a wealthy pagan matron of the area, Luparia, who owned a temple on one of her properties. Ill-disposed towards them, Luparia sent them to the king, who had them thrown into prison. Delivered by a miracle, the disciples fled, with the royal guards in pursuit but, just when the latter tried to cross the bridge taken by the run-aways, it collapsed under their feet, drowning them in the river. The disciples returned to Luparia and once again made their request. Pretending to accept, she sent them to Mount *Illicinus* where, supposedly, they would find oxen to hitch up to a vehicle to carry the apostle's body. In fact, the mountain was a shelter for a dragon and untameable wild bulls. But having overcome the dragon and tamed the bulls, the disciples managed to hitch up a wagon and placed the apostle's body in it. They renamed the mountain the *Mons sacer*. Surprised by these prodigious acts, Luparia joined the disciples' faith, causing many conversions among the people. The temple she possessed was emptied of its idols and a tomb was dug there. Three of the disciples decided to remain until their deaths beside Saint James's burial site, while the four others spread out across the country to preach the word of Jesus Christ.

Three other more ancient versions of the apocryphal letter of Pope Leon are known, besides the one contained in the *Codex Calixtinus*. The manuscript of Compostela provides a version of the legend that appears to be in its final stage. Because, although

Wagon carrying the apostle's body, Notre-Dame-du-Crann Church

A scene from the miracle of the *hanged-unhanged*

The doors of Compostela open for Pons de Saint-Gilles

James' Miracles

	N°
A knight, in a bad position during a fight with one of his peers, is saved from harm by the apostle. (Year 1135).	XIII
A merchant robbed and imprisoned by his protector is freed. (Year 1107).	XIV
A fleeing knight escapes certain death. (Year 1100).	XV
A knight, who, on the trail, carried a woman's bag and lent his mount to a beggar, is freed from Hell for proving that he was a real pilgrim.	XVI
A young man who had committed a sin of the flesh before leaving on pilgrimage, convinced by the Devil to castrate himself and commit suicide, is brought back to life by the apostle.	XVII
Pons de Saint-Gilles (1037-1060), Count of Toulouse, sees the doors of the church of the apostle in Compostela opening for him.	XVIII
James appears as a shining soldier to a Greek bishop and announces to him the capture of Coimbra. (Year 1064).	XIX
The sword of a count cannot cut the throat of his vassal, who had implored the apostle to intercede.	XX
A paralyzed man is cured in the cathedral of Compostela.	XXI
A man from Barcelona, made prisoner thirteen times, is freed each time by the apostle. (Year 1100.)	XXII

45

Cape Finisterre

EL PADRÓN

··

Located twenty kilometres from Compostela, close to the Ocean in the angle formed by the rio Ulla and its tributary the Sar, the former episcopal seat of El Padrón used to be known by the name Iria Flavia, with its origin both Celtic and Roman. Its present name comes from the term *el pedrón, the large stone,* the one to which the boat containing the body of the apostle James was attached at the end of its wondrous journey. Shaschek, the secretary of a Bohemian lord, Leon Romisthal, who had travelled througout Spain from 1465 to 1467 and lived in Compostela, told that at the moment of landing, the disciples placed the apostle's body on this stone that, to welcome it more easily, assumed the shape of the body. Today, it is kept under the main altar of Santiago de Padrón church. In fact, it is likely to have been a sacrificial stone, with the cavity in it serving to collect the victims' blood. It has an elliptical Roman inscription, dedicated to some Roman maritime deity. In the Middle Ages, an obligatory addition to the pilgrimage to Compostela was a passage to Padrón. This is attested by the proverb: *Quen va Santiago e non va a Padrón, O faz romeria o non.*

the letter it contains is supposed to come from Pope Leon III (795-816) who would have been a contemporary of the discovery of the relics, everything leads us to believe that the letter was written during the second half of the 11th century, when new excavations were made around the tomb, during construction work on the Romanesque cathedral. In accordance with discoveries made at that time, the number of disciples who remained at Saint James's burial place was only two. It calls them Athanasius and Theodore, and has them buried on the right and the left of the apostle. Furthermore, this letter from Pope Leon eliminates the story of the seven disciples and the matron Luparia. It tells that, after the martyrdom of James the Greater, his disciples stole his body that they carried to Joppe, that is, Jaffa, the present port of Tel-Aviv. Providence having placed a boat at their disposal, they sailed in one go as far as Iria, where they landed. From there, they went to the town of *Libre Don,* eight miles inland. There, not far from a great idol raised for the local cult, they discovered a crypt that seemed suitable as a burial place for the saint. They dug out a vaulted funerary chamber in which they buried the body, after first of all destroying the neighbouring pagan idol. Soon, after converting the inhabitants of *Libre Don,* they decided to pursue their preaching in other Iberian regions. Two of them, Athanasius and Theodore remained as guardians of the apostle's body, beside which, according to their wishes, they were buried after their deaths.

MARBLE ARCHES

Byzantine apostolic catalogues from the 7th century show Marmarica as the location of Saint James's tomb. A Latin version of the text also uses the expression *achaia marmarica,* though the term *achaia* remains quite obscure. Located between the western branch of the Nile River and Cyrenaica, Marmarica is quite a distance from Galicia where the saint's tomb was actually found. But the term reappears – rather clumsily, it is true – on the subject of a Galician tomb, in one of the four versions of the letter of Pope Leon. This is the manuscript at the Abbey of Saint Martial in Limoges, dating from the 10th century, saying that Saint James rests in Galicia, *sub arcis marmoricis,* a reading that the Escurial manuscript zealously cor-rects with *sub arcis marmoricis,* in other words, "under marble arches". Following complicated, if not skilful, slips of the quill, the information from the Byzantine catalogues was thus, and with good reason, transposed to Galicia, *achaia* being changed into *arcis,* and *marmarica* into *marmoricis.* A certificate of donation dated 885 even indicates the future city of Compostela, by the expression Locum Arcis marmoricis, i.e., "the locality of the Marble Arches". If it has disappeared today, excavations undertaken in 1879 under the cathedral's main altar, where the saint's tomb was discovered long ago, have brought to light a small rectangular temple of Roman origin, containing remnants of *loculi,* or funeral seats made of white marble.

St James, façade of Santiago de Compostela Cathedral

2

THE PILGRIMAGE TO SANTIAGO

Ever more pilgrims were coming to Compostela to venerate the tomb of the apostle James. Very quickly, this pilgrimage became one of the most important in Christianity, along with Rome and Jerusalem. Legend took over – it was necessary to explain how the body of Saint James, beheaded in Jerusalem, managed to reach the shores of Galicia. It was necessary too to establish Carolingian power by providing Charlemagne with a role in the discovery of the tomb, a role that the emperor could not have played since he died before the discovery. With the support of Saint James Matamoros, the *Reconquista* regained new strength. And the walkers for God came on. Their faith was immense, and their history was written, and is still being written, on the roads to Santiago.

Statue of St James, cloister of Saint Petri Cathedral, Bremen

THE FIRST PILGRIMS

The first pilgrim to come and honour the tomb of the apostle James was the king of Asturias, Alfonso II the Chaste (792-842). Notified of the discovery by Bishop Theodomir, he immediately arrived with his court, as he recounts himself in a document dated 834. Above the marble sepulchre, he had a small shrine built "of stone and clay". A baptistry dedicated to St. John the Baptist was built a short distance away, as well as the monastery of Antealtares to the east, in the place where the hermit Pelagius had his cell. Twelve monks settled there as guardians of the tomb. Soon, coming from the entire north of the Iberian peninsula, pilgrims began to move in ever-growing numbers. Hardly had a few decades elapsed since the discovery of the sepulchre that a first hospice was offering its services to these "walkers for God" at the Cebreiro Pass, at one of the most difficult places on the route. A town had also sprung up around the Galician shrine – Santiago de Compostela was born. Because of the influx of pilgrims, the modest building set up by Alfonso II had to be replaced. During the reign of his third successor, Alfonso III the Great (866-910), the bishop Sisnando had a triple basilica of marble consecrated on May 6, 899. To the main church dedicated to Saint James, a church consecrated to Mary was attached, as well as another destined for monastic purposes. It was all given the triple name of Holy Saviour, Saint Peter and Saint John. In the following year, 900, the bishops of Iria Flavia established their residence in Compostela. Furthermore, the cult dedicated to the apostle James was rather particular because of the historical context in which it had been started. Beside the depiction of the pilgrim apostle, there appeared in the twelfth century that of the fighting knight, the *Matamoros*, the Moorslayer, lending a helping hand to the Christian armies as they attempted to reconquer the lands occupied by Muslim infidels.

St James Matamoros, Châlons

ANGELS OR PILGRIMS?

The *Chronicle of Silos* recounts that two pilgrims, goldsmiths by profession, introduced themselves to King Alfonso II coming out of Oviedo church. He accepted their services. But these mysterious pilgrims were none other than angels who disappeared the following day, leaving behind the masterpiece that is today kept in the *Cámara Santa* of the cathedral. This legend, which had given its name to the cross completed at the beginning of the 9th century, reflected a historical truth – the arrival in Oviedo of goldsmiths trained beyond the Pyrenees, perhaps sent by Charlemagne to King Alfonso.

The Cebreiro

The Angels Cross, Oviedo

MEDIEVAL PILGRIMAGES

"Get thee out of thy country, and from thy kindred, and from thy father's house, unto a land that I will show thee."
Genesis XII, 1

"Get thee out" are the words of exile that God addressed to Abraham; they are also those of Jesus calling the young rich man to him; as they are also those that the apostles followed, by renouncing their past existence in order to follow him. Making of the *peregrinatio* the symbol of human life that led from the earthly city to the celestial city, the Christian liked to define himself as an exile, a foreigner – *peregrinus* – on earth, a traveller walking towards Eternal Jerusalem, the Kingdom of God announced by Christ in the Gospels. "We have not here a permanent city, but we are in search of the future city." (Epistle to the Hebrews (XIII, 14). Starting in the 3rd century in the East, then in the 4th century in the West, placing their footsteps in those of Jesus Christ and his apostles, monks put into practice this invitation to exile and poverty. But along with the monastic *peregrinatio ascetia*, another form of peregrination, the *peregrinatio ad loca sancta*, developed starting in the 4th century under Constantine. Christians would go into temporary exile to visit the holy places where Jesus Christ had lived and preached. The pilgrimage, in the current meaning of the word, was born. As a form of devotion that engaged the entire being – the body as well as the spirit – the pilgrimage removed from his familiar environment the person who had decided to endure the difficulties and suffering of the road in order to be sanctified. Exiled, a stranger to those he met, the pilgrim's long march was a form of asceticism and penitence, aiming for purification and salvation of the soul, perfected by the contact with holy places. The practice of pilgrimage was thus anterior to the Middle Ages, but it was at this time that it was the most widespread. During the High Middle Ages, the holy places of Jerusalem and the tombs of the apostles Peter and Paul in Rome were the most popular pilgrimage sites of the West. The custom of bringing palm branches back from Jerusalem gave the pilgrims to the Holy Land the name of *palmers*, from *palma*, the palm, while the term *romieux* in France was used for those returning from Rome. The pilgrimage to Saint Martin of Tours also developed greatly during the 6th century. However, after the *invention* – from the Latin, *invenire*, to find – of the relics of the apostle James the Greater in Galicia in the 9th century, Santiago de Compostela became one of the three principal Christian pilgrimage sites during the 12th and 13th centuries. If the practice of pilgrimages became so

Holy Sepulchre Church, Jerusalem

popular during the Middle Ages it was because, for the faithful, it was the principal way to ensure their salvation. To go on a pilgrimage was, above all, to reach a sacred place, sanctified by the passage of Christ, the memory of a saint, or the presence of relics, where divine grace was likely to be manifested more than in any other place, particularly through miracles. The most often, pilgrims came to the place where a saint's remains were kept to pray for his or her intercession thanks to the saving and miracle-working virtues of these relics. This could be spiritual intercession to forgive sins and save the soul, or material help, for a miraculous cure or aid. Many pilgrims also carried out a mission of thanksgiving, for help rendered or a cure. In general, at the end of his journey, the pilgrim tried to come into physical contact with the shrine, to touch the reliquary or to at least come as close as possible. Shrines with an ambulatory and side chapels around the chancel made access easier. In this sacred place, pilgrims placed their votive offerings to

Western façade of Our Lady of Chartres Cathedral

Tomb of St Martin, Tours

thank the saint who had fulfilled, or perhaps would fulfil their wishes – votive candles or, for the wealthier, gifts of silver or gold. Some pilgrims had a copy of part of the body made, to show what had been or was to be cured. For a shrine, possessing relics provided the benefit of divine protection, but also that of receiving offerings from pilgrims. And since there were some who tried to obtain relics at any price, it produced much abuse. Upon their return, pilgrims brought back with them objects that had been in contact with the relics – linens, pieces of stone or wood, oil or water that had run over the tombstone – that were supposed to maintain the protective and miracle-working powers of the relics.

Charlemagne's dream, Great Chronicle of Saint-Denis

THE CHRONICLE OF PSEUDO-TURPIN

The *Historia Karoli Magni et Rotholandi*, also called *The Chronicle of Pseudo-Turpin*, constitutes Book IV of the *Codex Calixtinus* kept in the archives of Compostela cathedral. Most likely compiled in the first half of the twelfth century, this legendary history of Charlemagne's expeditions on the Iberian side of the Pyrenees written in prose to the glory of the emperor, Saint James and the Compostela pilgrimage, was enormously popular during the Middle Ages. Following a relatively common procedure of the medieval period, its author, an anonymous cleric probably of French origin, attributed the authorship of his text to Turpin, a former monk and treasurer of Saint Denis near Paris, who became archbishop of Reims (748-794). It was Turpin who appeared as one of Charlemagne's twelve peers in the *Song of Roland*. The preliminary chapter of the work makes Charlemagne the main character in the discovery of James the Greater's tomb, with the apostle in person charging him with the mission of freeing his country and the road leading to his sepulchre, in order to promote the pilgrimage. "One night", says the text, "the emperor contemplated the sky and saw a path of stars that, leading from the sea of Friesia, continued between Germany and Italy, between France and Aquitaine, crossed Gascony, the Basque country and the lands of Navarre, then, entering Spain, headed straight for Galicia where the body of Saint James remained hidden and ignored." Night after night, the emperor searched for the possible significance of this path of stars until the evening when, having fallen asleep, a figure appeared to him and addressed him in the following terms: "I am the apostle James, a disciple of Jesus Christ [...] who Herod killed by the sword and whose body remains ignored in Galicia, still shamefully subjected by the Saracens. This is why I am greatly surprised that it is possible that you have not liberated my land from the Saracens, you who have conquered so many great cities and nations [...] The path of stars you have been contemplating in the sky means that you should set off with a great army, from these lands as far as Galicia, in order to place the faithless pagans under the yoke and liberate my way and my country and to pay a visit to my basilica and my sepulchre. After you, all the peoples from one sea to another should go there to pray the Lord to pardon their sins and to sing his praises, his power and the wonders he has carried out. And they will make this pilgrimage from your lifetime until the end of the centuries...". And so it was. Charlemagne gathered his army together and led them to Compostela, not without first capturing Pamplona thanks to the glorious help of the apostle. Soon, the entire peninsula was delivered. Charlemagne then raised up from its the ruins the basilica of Santiago, enriched it with loot taken from the Muslims, then returned to France where he founded, in Béziers, Toulouse, Sorde and Paris, churches in honour of Saint James. However, the war started again when the fearsome Muslim king, Agolant, coming from Africa, invaded the peninsula. Charlemagne immediately ordered a second campaign. In the

Archbishop Turpin

THE CAROLINGIANS

Pepin the Short, the son of Charles Martel, overthrew the last Merovingian king, Childeric II, in 751 and founded the Carolingian dynasty, which reached its apex under Charlemagne, who was anointed emperor in 800 by Pope Leon III, and who carved out an empire covering nearly all of western Europe. The accession of the Capetian dynasty in 987 was favoured by the empire's dismemberment under Charlemagne's descendants, further aggravated by the emergence of the feudal system. The key members of the empire's administration, the counts, named and revoked by the emperor, became progressively more autonomous. By the middle of the 9th century, their domains had become hereditary, a situation that was ratified by Charles the Bald in the Capitulary of Quierzy sur Oise in 877. Pepin the Short authorized his vassals to transmit their honours and privileges by inheritance if they died in the course of the expedition he was organizing for his coronation in Rome. The Carolingians promoted a cultural renaissance that influenced the monastic world with the reform of Benedict of Aniane, the world of education, with the creation of rural primary schools, and the arts.

Roland and St Stephen

ROLAND AND FERRAGUT

....

T his episode inspired
Romanesque sculptors and
capitals presenting the scene
can be seen on the façade of
the royal palace of Navarre in
Estella, on the south doorway
of San Andrés Church in
Villamayor de Monjardin, on
the hospital of Saint John of
Acre in Navarrete, and in the
church of San Juan de Ortega.

fields of Sahagún, shortly before the battle, God encouraged his
own and showed his favour by a miracle: the lances that, the previous evening, his warriors had planted into the ground, were green
and blooming with flowers in the morning, before the fight. But
despite the emperor's achievements, the Franks suffered a terrible
defeat and had to return to their homeland, while the reinforce-
ments sent by four Italian marquesses forced the Muslim troops to
retreat into the province of Leon. However, the Saracens went back
on the offensive. Reaching France, they laid siege to Agen, which
fell after resisting for seven months, then arrived in Saintes where,
once again, the miracle of the lances was repeated. Charlemagne
stopped their advance after victorious combat. Pursued by the
Christians, Agolant took refuge in Pamplona. Under the walls of
the city, a long theological debate took place between the chiefs of
the two armies, before the fatal combat in which Agolant met his
death. Two of his allies managed to escape. Beating the Navarre
troops at the battle of Monjardin, Charlemagne continued on to
Nájera, a town held by the giant Ferragut. After a three-day duel,
the giant was finally defeated by Roland. Charlemagne then
marched on Cordoba where he vanquished the two survivors of the
battle of Pamplona. The peninsula was liberated and the emperor
returned to the apostle's city, to which he offered the highest political and ecclesiastical prerogatives. While Turpin consecrated the
cathedral, the former bishopric of Iria Flavia was abolished,
because henceforth it was in Compostela that bishops would

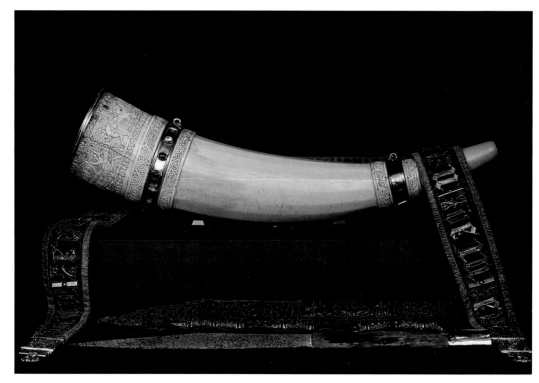

Charlemagne's Horn, Treasure of Aachen Cathedral

Charlemagne and his soldiers, window in Chartres Cathedral

receive their crozier, and kings their sceptre. Raised to being an apostolic seat, second behind Rome, but before Ephesus, the church in Santiago was sovereign. Soon Charlemagne returned to his country. Alas, on the way home, his rearguard fell into an ambush contrived by the kings of Zaragoza, Marsile and Baligant. It was decimated at Roncesvalles. Roland managed to kill Marsile, then put Baligant and his Saracens to flight. Of his one hundred companions, only five survived. Mortally wounded, Roland tried to inform his uncle. In vain he sounded his horn. Slowed by the traitor Ganelon, Charlemagne arrived too late. The emperor had the heroes' bodies carried to shrines in the south of France – in Belin, Blaye, Saint-Seurin of Bordeaux, and the Alyscamps in Arles. He then reached Saint Denis, before returning to Aachen, where a short time later he found peace in death, Saint James having torn his soul away from the grip of devils. Hence, along the path of the pilgrimage, several sites are involved in the epic universe of Carolingian geste. In his *Guide*, Aimery Picaud stops at each of them: Roland rests in Blaye, the valiant knights Olivier, Ogier, Garin and others in Belin. Then come the heights of *Portus Cisere*, on which the cross of Charlemagne stands, then Roncesvalles and Roland's chapel; finally, the fields of Sahagún, location of the miracle of the flowering lances. Nourished by these legends, the pilgrim, in the saving effort of his march, exhausted like his heroes "by hunger, the excessive cold and heat, struck by violence, and endlessly scourged for the love of God", found new strength at each site.

PORTUS CISERE

In his *Guide*, Aimery Picaud wrote: "At the summit of this mountain, there is a place named the Cross of Charles because it was in this place that with hatchets, pickaxes, spades and other tools, Charlemagne going to Spain with his armies cleared his way and first of all, symbolically raised the cross of the Lord and then, bending his knee, turned towards Galicia, addressed a prayer to God and Saint James. Thus, arriving here, pilgrims follow the custom of bending their knee and praying while turning towards the land of Saint James and each one plants his cross like a banner. Up to a thousand crosses can be found. This is why this place is the first station of prayer on the road to Santiago."

The Christian Reconquest of Spain, *Cantigas de Santa María*

THE RECONQUISTA

In 711, when the Muslims swept through Spain, crushing the Visigothic army at the Battle of Guadalete, a Visigothic nobleman, Pelayo, at the head of three hundred warriors, took refuge in the Asturias, where he created the first seat of resistance against the occupier. This was to become the Kingdom of Oviedo. In 718, according to the chronicles, but more probably in 722, the wali of Cordoba sent his lieutenants al-Kama and Munuça against it. Pelayo and his men surprised them in the gorges of the Deva River, inflicting the first defeat of the Moors on Iberian soil. Ascribing his victory to the protection of the Virgin, Pelayo had an altar raised in her honour in the grotto *del Auseba*, which had sheltered him and his companions. The cave would be called the *Cova Dominica*, the grotto of Our Lady, which was to be altered into *Covadonga*. But starting at the reign of Alfonso II (792-842), the eighth successor of Pelayo at the head of the Asturian kingdom, it was the apostle James who stayed beside the Christian fighters against the Muslim enemy. In 834, shortly after the discovery of his relics in Galicia, Alfonso II named him as the "*patronus et dominus totius Hispaniae*", and a few decades later, in the charters of donations to the city of Compostela dated 893, 895 and 898, Alfonso III and his queen Chimena prayed to Saint James for victory. In the meantime, the pilgrims' saint had indeed appeared under the awesome light of the Son of Thunder, transfigured into an intrepid and fearsome *Matamoros*, (Moorslayer), a knight come from Heaven to destroy the enemy with his sword at Clavijo in 844. The Asturian king Ramiro 1st (842-850) had just suffered a severe defeat at Albelda, inflicted by the army of Abd al-Rahmân II (822-852). During a retreat to the nearby hillside of Clavijo to spend the night, St. James appeared to the king in a dream, encouraging him to take up his arms again the following day and assuring him of protection. During the new battle, the apostle himself came to help his protégés, mounted on a brilliant white charger, leading them to victory and freeing from tribute the hundred virgins that the emir had been receiving every year since the reign of Mauregatus (783-788). As a sign of gratitude, on May 25, 844, King Ramiro granted the church in Compostela a tribute renewable annually. After the, most probably, legendary battle of Clavijo, Saint James made his appearance at the side of Christians during victorious combat, ensuring the progress of the *Reconquista* through arms. Under the reign of Ordono 1st (850-866), the Christian advance proceeded decisively: Amaya, Leon, Astorga, Tuy, passed into Christian hands and were immediately fortified. The Asturian monarch used a policy of colonizing conquered territory, putting lands back under cultivation, extending land clearance, and installing monastic communities. Furthermore, he entrusted the administration and re-population of the counties of the upper Ebro valley, in the east of the kingdom, to Count Rodrigo and his son, Diego Rodríguez, who were probably issued from the royal family. The latter took charge of fortifying the region, which, bristling with castles, *castillos*, took the name of Castile. Alfonso III the Great (866-

Landmark Dates	
Christian victory at Covadonga	722
Discovery of the tomb of Saint James	820
Battle of Clavijo	844
Foundation of Burgos	884
Capture of Zamora by Alfonso III the Great	893
The capital of the Asturian-Leon kingdom is transferred to Leon	910
Abd al-Rahmân abandons the title of Emir for that of Caliph	929
Foundation of Medina Azara, west of Cordoba	936
Christian victory at Simancas	939
Al-Mansûr takes full power in Cordoba	978
Al-Mansûr invests and loots Santiago de Compostela	997
Death of al-Mansûr	1002
Break-up of the caliphate	1031
Capture of Coimbra by Ferdinand 1st	1064
Capture of Toledo by Alfonso VI	1085
El Cid takes Valencia	1094
Alfonso VII of Castile and Leon reconquers Calatrava	1147
Foundation of the Order of Saint James	1170
Alfonso VIII is defeated at Alarcos	1195
Christian victory at Las Navas de Tolosa	1212
Cordoba taken by Ferdinand III	1236
Christian victory of Salado	1340
Recapture of Algeciras by the Christians	1343
Fall of the Kingdom of Granada	1492

Pendón of Las Navas de Tolosa

"SANTIAGO Y CIERRA, ESPAÑA!"

T his had become the war cry of the Christians in the *Reconquista*, after the appearance of their respected patron saint, *Santiago Matamoros*, "Saint James, Moorslayer" at the victorious battle at Clavijo in 844. "Saint James and remain steadfast, Spain!" Subsequently, Saint James ensured the victory of his protégés at Simancas in 939, at Coimbra in 1064, Ourique in 1139, Las Navas de Tolosa in 1212, and Salado in 1340. The warrior aspect of the saint had taken on such dimensions that it expanded beyond the borders of the peninsula. In 1214, at Bouvines, after his victory over Emperor Otton of Brunswick and his allies, the Counts of Flanders and Boulogne, all three hired by King John of England, Philippe-Auguste addressed his Flemish prisoners with the following words: "By the lance of Saint James, it was not I who made you prisoners, but the holy patron of Liège whom you have offended." In 1492, the year of the fall of the Kingdom of Granada, that put an end to the Muslim presence in Spain, Christopher Columbus landed on the island of Guanahani, that he named *San Salvador*. And it was with the cry of *Santiago* that the Spanish *conquistadores* launched the attack for the conquest of the New World.

910) continued his father's work by taking Porto in 868, as well as the region located between the Miño and Douro Rivers. Further east, he captured Zamora in 893, then Dueñas and Simancas in 899. During the same period, in 884, the Count of Castile Diego Rodríguez founded the city of Burgos. In 910, Alfonso III was deposed by his three sons, García (910-914), Ordono II (914-924) and Fruela II (924-925), who succeeded each other on the throne and transferred the kingdom's capital to Leon. Starting in 925, the succession to the throne of Leon, coveted by various county factions and complicated by matrimonial alliances, became anarchic. This instability would allow Castile to emancipate itself. Towards 930, Count Fernán González (929-970) united the counties of Lara, Lantaron Cerezo and Alava under his authority and took the title of *comes totius Castellae*. He won renown for his military successes, at Simancas in 939, along with the kings of Leon and Pamplona, then in Sepúlveda, south of the Douro, which he took alone in 940. Eight years earlier, in 932, he had married the widow of King Ordono II of Leon, thus becoming the brother-in-law of two kings of Leon, and the son-in-law of the queen of Pamplona. Indeed, in the future state of Navarre, a local dynasty, that of Inigo Arista, had taken power in Pamplona and founded a Christian kingdom at the beginning of the 9th century, claiming its independence against Frankish and Muslim designs. The Arista dynasty was replaced in the 10th century by that of Sancho Garcés 1st (905-925), which annexed the county founded towards 806 to its own kingdom, following a Carolingian operation in the Aragon valley, near Jaca. At the death of Sancho Garcés in 925, his widow, Queen Toda, exercised a regency in the name of his young son, García Sánchez 1st (925-971) and brought the kingdom of Pamplona out of its isolation by making alliances with its powerful Christian neighbours. She married off her three daughters, Sancha, Iniga, and Urraca, to respectively, Ordono II of Leon (914-924), and his two sons, Alfonso IV (925-930) and Ramiro II (930-950). After becoming a widow, Sancha married the count of Castile, Fernán González. In the east, the Carolingians had established the March of Spain, the future Catalonia where, starting in 870, the Count of Barcelona enjoyed wide-ranging powers. In this way, during the 9th and 10th centuries, new political entities emerged and asserted themselves in Castile, Navarre, Aragon and Catalonia.

However, the accession of Abd al-Rahmân III (912-961) at the head of al-Andalus markedly slowed the progress of the Christian reconquest, which had arrived as far as the Douro. Abd al-Rahmân III used the first years of his reign to restore Cordoba's central authority over all of al-Andalus, which was being weakened by continual uprisings by *muwalladun* and Berbers, on whom the Arab aristocracy had leaned to emancipate itself. Once peace had been re-established within the emirate and his authority stable, Abd al-Rahman III could respond to the Christian offensive. He captured the fortresses of Gormaz, Osma and Clunia, and inflicted the defeat of Valdejunquera on the Christians in 920. In 924, after the capture of Nájera by Ordono II and of Viguera by Sancho Garcés II, he pillaged and burnt Pamplona. Strengthened by this success, in 929 he

Santa María de Naranco Church

THE MASTER OF NARANCO

T he reign of Ramiro 1st (842-850) was troubled because he had to push back the Vikings, who in 844 attacked the north coast of the Iberian peninsula, near La Coruña. He also had to confront a Moorish offensive. But this king also promoted the construction of monuments that are examples of innovative and inspired Asturian architectural art. Hence, a royal palace, still perfectly conserved, was built on the hill overlooking Oviedo, along with other buildings that have since disappeared, and the church of San Miguel de Lillo, of which only the façade and two bays of the nave remain. Their architect is called the Master of Naranco, from the name of the hill. After the transfer of the capital to Leon in 913, the palace was converted into a church, Santa María de Naranco. The Naranco palace and San Miguel de Lillo church are small buildings, conceived vertically, in which beamed arches, allowing stone vaulting, were in general use. This technique was to be developed less than two centuries later by the builders of the Romanesque period. South of Leon, at the foot of the Cantabrian mountain range, near Vega del Rey, the church of Santa Cristina de Lena is a later work of the Master of Naranco, then at the height of his art.

Window in San Miguel de Lillo

San Miguel de Lillo Church

A door in the Mosque of Cordoba

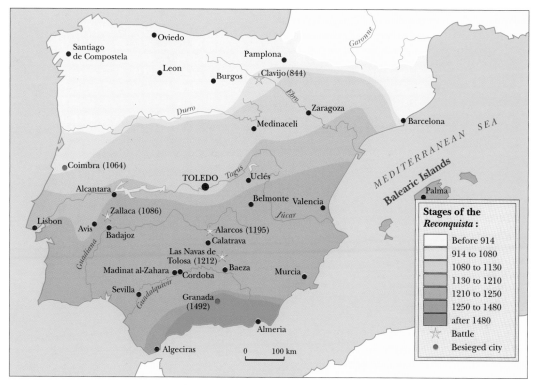

Stages of the Reconquista

Stages of the
Reconquista :

- Before 914
- 914 to 1080
- 1080 to 1130
- 1130 to 1210
- 1210 to 1250
- 1250 to 1480
- after 1480
- ✩ Battle
- ● Besieged city

abandoned his title of emir for that of caliph, and had himself pro-claimed *amîr al-muminîn*, Prince of Believers, thus asserting the religious and political autonomy of his state. The caliphate of Abd al-Rahmân III opened a century of cultural pre-eminence in al-Andalus, whose peak was reached under the reign of his son al-Hakam (961-976). In 936, the caliph founded the city of Medina Azara, west of Cordoba, where he established his residence and which became the capital of the caliphate. He surrounded himself with a court of converts and *Slaves*, i.e., slaves of European origin, to whom he entrusted important positions. At his death, his son al-Hakam II (961-976), then his grandson Hishâm II (976-1009) succeeded him at the head of the caliphate. However, taking advantage of the vulnerability of the under-age caliph Hishâm, the *hajib* Muhammad Ibn Abi Amir, better known under his nickname of *al-Mansûr*, the victor, bestowed full powers on himself in 978. Al-Mansûr brought new life into the holy war. Recruiting entire tribes of Berber mercenaries, he went on the offensive in the north, leading more than fifty campaigns against the Christians, during which towns, villages, fortresses and monasteries were looted and destroyed. Zamora fell in 981, Simancas in 983, Sepúlveda in 984, Barcelona in 985. In 987, Coimbra was sacked, followed by Leon in 988, Clunia in 994, and Compostela in 997. Cervera was attacked in 1000, then it was the turn of the monastery of San Millán de la Cogolla, burnt in 1002. The death of al-Mansûr, in this same year of 1002, did not provide a respite for the Christians, since his son Abd

AL-MANSÛR

At the death of al-Hakam II in 976, his son Hishâm was only 11 years old. With the support of Subh, the favorite of the deceased caliph, Ibn Abî Amir was named vizir and ruled the caliphate. He formed an army of slaves and Berbers, on which he relied to reinforce his power. He launched expeditions against Morocco and in the Iberian peninsula, reviving the flame of the holy war. In 981, he took the title of al-Mansûr Bi Llah, *victorious in the name of God*, and settled in a palace in Medina Azara, where he transferred the caliphate's administration. He then held all the power. According to his chroniclers, he led fifty-seven victorious campaigns against the Christians and destroyed many towns. He died in 1002.

Coimbra

THE TAKING OF COIMBRA

....

C hapter XIX of the *Book of Miracles* tells that Stephen, a Greek bishop who was greatly devoted to the apostle James, made the pilgrimage to his shrine. Arriving in Compostela, opposite the high altar of the basilica, he had a hut of rushes built in which to live a life of fasting, contemplation and prayer. One day, he heard villagers calling on the saint in the following words: "Saint James, good knight, free us from the evils that threaten us today and might threaten us tomorrow." Indignant, Stephen scolded them, "Fools, utter fools, stupid people, you shouldn't call Saint James a knight, but a fisherman!". But the following night, the apostle appeared to him, dressed as a knight, holding two keys in his hand. "Stephen", he said, "you ordered them to call me fisherman and not a knight, this is why I appear to you, so that you will not doubt that God ordered me to fight and be his champion against the Saracens. [...] So that you will firmly believe, with the keys in my hand I will open the gates of the city of Coimbra, that Ferdinand has been besieging for seven years and will deliver it into his power." And the next day, July 9, 1064, his word came true.

al-Malik al Muzaffar, succeeding him as *hajib*, pursued the same politics of devastation. But when Abd al-Malik died suddenly in 1008, perhaps of poison, his brother Sanchuelo committed the fatal error of having himself designated caliph. His assassination started a period of violence and civil war between various Berber, Arab and Slave factions, all struggling for power. This finished off the Cordoban caliphate. In 1031, the last Umayyad caliph was deposed while the caliphate, divided among the different factions, was dismembered into twenty-four rival principalities called *taïfas*. At the time of the caliphate's dismantling, Sancho III the Great (1000-1035), heir of the kingdom of Pamplona, united nearly all the Christian territories under his authority. Through the intermediary of his wife Mayor, he reigned over Castile. As the eldest daughter of the Count of Castile, Sancho García (994-1017), Doña Mayor had received her father's inheritance in 1029, after the assassination of her brother García, who had died without leaving an heir. By the intermediary of his sister, Urraca de Pamplona, the wife of Alfonso V of Leon (999-1028), Sancho the Great also dominated the Asturian kingdom. At the death of Alfonso V in 1028, Urraca exercised the regency in the name of her young son, Bermudo III (1028-1037), who died without leaving an heir. Furthermore, Sancho had annexed the counties of Sobrarbe and Robagorza to his Pamplona kingdom. However, at this death in 1035, he divided his possessions among his sons: the eldest, García, (1035-1054) received Pamplona; the second, Ferdinand 1st (1035-1065), Castile, Gonzalo, and the counties of Sobrarbe and Robagorza; and his illegitimate son, Ramiro 1st (1035-1063) received Aragon. Ferdinand 1st, the heir to Castile, had married Sancha, the sister of Bermudo III of Leon. At the death of the latter, in 1037, he joined his Castilian heritage and the kingdom of Leon, laying the foundations of a new kingdom in which Castile would be pre-eminent over Leon. From 1065 to 1072, his sons – Sancho II the Strong of Castile (1065-1072) and Alfonso VI of Leon (1065-1109) – fought for dominance, but then after 1072, Alfonso VI ruled alone over Castile and Leon. After recovering from the devastation caused by al-Mansûr, the Christians took up the offensive again starting in the middle of the 11th century and reached the Tagus River. Wealthy but divided, the taïfas could not stand up to them. In 1064, Coimbra was recaptured, followed by the region between the Mondego and Douro Rivers in 1065. But when Alfonso VI entered Toledo in 1085, before continuing his eastward advance to Zaragoza, the taïfa kings called on the Almoravid Berbers of North Africa. Landing in Algeciras, they defeated the Christians at Zallaca, in the area of Badajoz, in 1086, stopping their advance. It was at this time that a certain Rodrigo Diaz de Vivar, known thereafter by his nickname *El Cid*, won fame for protecting the kingdom of Valencia, that he captured in 1094, and defended until his death in 1099. Nonetheless, after the defeat of Alfonso VI at Consuerga in 1097, Valencia fell in 1102, followed by Uclés in 1108. The only heir of the king of Castile and Leon, Sancho was killed in the course of his last combat. During the first half of the 12th century, it was Aragon that went on the offensive, under the lead of Alfonso 1st the Warrior (1104-1134), the great-grandson of

Sancho II the Great (1000-1035), through the intermediary of his illegitimate son Ramiro 1st of Aragon (1035-1063). With the help of French knights, the Warrior occupied the fertile Ebro valley, taking Zaragoza and Tarragona in 1118, before capturing, upriver and on the river's tributaries, Tudela and Tarazona in 1119, and Calatayud in 1120. Despite his marriage in 1109 with the Infante of Castile, Urraca, the heiress of Alfonso VI the Warrior died without descendants in 1134, bequeathing his kingdom to military orders. Refusing this will, the Aragonese elected as their king his brother Ramiro II (1134-1137), whose daughter Petronilla in 1137 married a Templar knight, the Count of Barcelona Raymond Beranger IV (1131-1162), thereby partly fulfilling the wish of her uncle and especially, uniting the destinies of Aragon and Catalonia. This union facilitated the reconquest of Fraga and Lerida in 1147. In the west of the peninsula, in 1095, Alfonso VI had given the *portucalense* territory, south of Galicia, to his vassal Henry of Burgundy, the husband of his illegitimate daughter Teresa. Their son Alfonso Henriques (1112-1185), who defeated the Muslims at the battle of Ourique, north of Faro, in 1139, emancipated himself from Castile by proclaiming himself king of Portugal in 1140. He installed his capital in Coimbra, before recapturing Santarem and Lisbon in 1147. In the same year, Alfonso VI's grandson, Alfonso VII of Castile and Leon (1109-1157) managed to reconquer the fortress of Calatrava, south of Toledo, which was defended by the Knights Templar. However, at this death in 1157, the monarch divided his kingdom between his two sons; Sancho III, the eldest, received Castile, while his brother Ferdinand II (1157-1188) inherited Leon and Galicia. Dying a year after coming to the throne, Sancho III of Castile was replaced by his son Alfonso VIII the Noble (1158-1214), then aged three. This new division, joined to Alfonso VIII's minority, was the source of tension between Christian monarchs who fought for possession of border territories, especially in Navarre, where Sancho VI the Wise (1150-1194) captured the area of Rioja that had previously been annexed by his Castilian neighbour. But during this second half of the 12th century,

Orange tree Court in Cordoba

Uclés

BELLS FOR COMPOSTELA

At the end of the 10th century, when the fervour of crowds marching to the tomb of Saint James in Compostela rivalled that of pilgrims to Mecca, the apostle was seen both by Christians as well as Muslims as the anti-Mohammed, the hero of the reconquest. Al-Mansûr was aware of this when he chose Compostela as his target in 997. The city was ravaged, and before setting the basilica on fire, the warrior had the doors and bells torn away and carried to Cordoba by Christian captives. There, they were stored in the great mosque. The event was to strike imaginations; the same bells were carried by other prisoners, this time Muslim, to Toledo, at the taking of Cordoba by Ferdinand III, King of Leon and Castile, in 1236.

Military Orders

Hospitallers

In 1113, Pope Paschal II recognized this order serving a hospital in Jerusalem. It was transformed into a military order in about 1135 – the Hospitallers of Saint John of Jerusalem. After the fall of Acre in 1291, the Hospitallers went to Cyprus, then conquered Rhodes in 1309. They were chased out of Rhodes in 1522 by Suleiman II. They settled on the island of Malta with the agreement of Charles V in 1530, hence becoming the Knights of Malta.

Templars

In 1120, Hugues de Payens founded the brotherhood of the Poor Knights of Christ to protect Christian pilgrims in the Holy Land. They settled in Al Aqsa Mosque, on the site of the Temple. After Acre, the Templars left for Cyprus. Philippe le Bel organized their arrest in 1307. In 1312, the order was dissolved by Pope Clement V. Molay, Grand Master of the order, died at the stake in 1314. The order's goods were transferred to the Hospitallers. In Portugal, with the support of King Dinis, in 1319 the Templars founded a new Order of Christ.

Calatrava

With the help of Raymond, abbot of the Cistercian abbey of Fitero, Sancho III installed an army corps at Calatrava, facing the Almohad threat. The soldier-monks formed the Order of Calatrava, approved by Pope Alexander III in 1164.

Avis

Founded in Evora in 1162, in 1211 this order invested Avis in Portugal, which became the seat of the order.

Alcantara

The military order of San Julián del Pereiro was created in 1176. The fortress of Alcantara was attributed to them in 1218 by Alfonso IX.

Calatrava Castle

the Almohads, who had replaced the Almoravids and taken power in North Africa, extended their domination to Muslim Spain starting in 1146. Faced with this new threat, the Christian sovereigns called on foreign military orders, Templars and the Knights Hospitallers of Jerusalem, and at the same time, forming Iberian orders: Calatrava in 1158, Avis in 1162, Santiago in 1170, and Alcantara in 1183. By this time, the Christians had once again gone on the offensive south of the Tagus and were in a position of strength. Alfonso II the Chaste (1162-1196), successor to Raymond Beranger at the head of the Aragon kingdom, and Alfonso VIII of Castile, joined forces and took Teruel in 1170, Cuenca in 1177, Cáceres in 1184, while making incursions into the valley of the Guadalquivir. Contemplating victory, they shared out their future conquests in 1179: the kingdom of Valencia, east to Alicante, would

Templars, Villalcázar de Sirga

BERBER DYNASTIES

....

Towards the middle of the 11th century, on a Senegalese island, Berbers founded a fortified monastery, *ribât* in Arabic, from which they took their name – *el-morabitum*, Almoravids. Yusuf ibn Tashfin, the dynasty's founder, took their head in 1077, conquered Morocco and made Marrakesh his capital. Appealed to by the taïfas, he intervened in the Iberian peninsula a first time in 1086, then returned in 1091 to capture al-Andalus in less than twenty years. In 1147, another Berber dynasty, the Almohads, put an end to Almoravid domination. Their name came from *el-mowahiddun*, those who believe in divine unity. Their defeat at Las Navas de Tolosa in 1212 by Christian armies was the beginning of the dismemberment of their empire, which was completed by the fall of Marrakesh in 1269.

THE ORDER OF SANTIAGO

In 1170, Ferdinand II of Leon (1157-1188) entrusted the protection of Cáceres, just recaptured from the Muslims, to Pedro Fernández and his twelve brothers in arms who had helped him take the town. Wishing to found a knightly order modelled on the prestigious ones created for the defence of Christianity in the Holy Land, in May 1170 Pedro Fernández concluded an agreement with the prior of the canon monastery of Santa María de Loyo in Galicia, near Portomarín, in the presence of the king and the archbishops of Toledo and Compostela. Subjected to the spiritual authority of the Augustinians of Loyo, the "Congregation of the Brothers of Cáceres" assured the protection of hospices run by canons along the pilgrimage route, such as Portomarín or San Marcos de Leon. At the beginning of 1171, faced with the threat of the Muslim army, Ferdinand II convoked the master of the new militia to Leon to prepare the gathering of his forces. On this occasion, February 12 1171, the archbishop of Compostela, Pedro Gudesteiz, solemnly pre-

sented Pedro Fernández with a red banner with, in its centre, the Son of Thunder, brandishing his sword in one hand, holding a cross and the reins of his white horse in the other. From then on, the Brothers of Cáceres would serve under the name of Saint James. Having become the *Caballeros de la Espada* "*Knights of the Sword*" in memory of the sword brandished by the apostle, they made up the "Militia of Christ and Saint James" against the soldiers of Mohammed. But after losing their seat at Cáceres, retaken by the Muslims in 1173, and quarrelling with Ferdinand II of Leon, the knights decided to move to Castile, where Alfonso VII (1158-1214), surrounded by the Master of the Order of Calatrava and the Grand Prior of the Order of Saint John of Jerusalem, welcomed them with great honours. In January 1174, the Castilian monarch gave them the town and the fortress of Uclés, held until then by the Hospitallers of Saint John. The next year, Pedro Fernández went to Rome to Pope Alexander III who, in July 1175, ratified the bull of approval of the religious and military order of Santiago.

Castle of the Order of Santiago in Belmonte

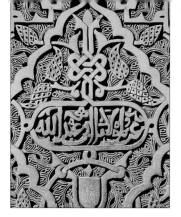

Arabesques, Granada Alhambra

THE MOOR'S LAST SIGH

I n 1237, Mohammed ben Yusr ben Nasr, taking advantage of the troubles affecting the Almohad empire, captured Granada and founded the Nasride dynasty. The kingdom of Granada also included the regions of Almeria and Malaga. Through a complex set of alliances, with the Merinides of Fez, the kings of Castile and Genoa, between wars and truces, sometimes at the price of weighty tributes, *parias*, and despite endemic internal dissensions linked to the absence of rules governing succession, the kingdom of Granada was able to maintain itself for nearly three centuries. A brilliant civilization developed with the construction of the Alhambra, the *red citadel*, decided by Mihamad 1st, and of the Generalife, the hanging gardens, renovated at the beginning of the 14th century by Ismail 1st. There was also the presence of an important *madrasa*, or religious school, founded by Yusuf 1st, towards 1350. But in 1483, the Catholic kings launched a new offensive against the kingdom of Granada. Malaga fell in 1487, Almeria in 1489 and, after two years of siege, Granada fell on November 25, 1491. And legend has it that Boabdil, the defeated emir, turning towards what used to be his capital from the summit of the pass south of Granada, sighed, hence giving it the name of *Suspiro del Moro*. And that his mother said to him, "Do not cry like a woman over this kingdom that you were not able to defend like a man."

belong to Aragon; Castile would receive the rest. But the Almohad response was rapid. Landing in Tarifa in 1195, the armies of the new caliph Abu Yusuf Ya'kub crushed Alfonso VIII's army at Alarcos, pushing back the Christian troops north of the Tagus. Sancho VII of Navarre (1194-1234) and Alfonso IX of Leon (1188-1230) preferred to give up the fight, and finally Alfonso VIII negotiated a truce in 1197. After the death of Abu Yusuf in 1199, the truce was officially broken in 1211, when a new Almohad invasion entered the peninsula. At the request of Pope Innocent III, who encouraged them to carry on a crusade against al-Andalus together, the Spanish monarchs joined their forces for a decisive battle. Peter II of Aragon (1196-1213), Sancho VII of Navarre, Alfonso VIII of Castile, the vassals of Alfonso IX of Leon and of the King of Portugal, took the head of the army, mainly consisting of Spanish knights, that left from Toledo on June 24, 1212. The Christians were victorious at the battle of Las Navas de Tolosa, south of Calatrava. After a pause, James 1st of Aragon (1213-1276) continued the offensive and conquered the Balearic Islands between 1229 and 1235, then the kingdom of Valencia in 1238. In 1230, Ferdinand III (1217-1252) permanently united the crown of Castile, that he had from his mother Berenguela, daughter and heiress of Alfonso VIII, to the kingdom of his father Alfonso IX of Leon. Helped by his son Alfonso X (1252-1284), Ferdinand III advanced on Andalusia. After Cordoba in 1236 and Sevilla in 1248, Cadiz fell in 1263, while the kingdom of Murcia became a Castile-Leon protectorate in 1243. In the west, Alfonso III of Portugal (1247-1279) completed the conquest of Algarve by taking Faro in 1249. In 1340, an army of Castilians, Portuguese, and Aragonese, under the command of Alfonso XI of Castile-Leon (1312-1350) defeated Muslim troops at Salado, before taking Algeciras in 1343 with the help of Navarre. Christians were thus assured of controlling the Strait of Gibraltar. Alone, the Kingdom of Granada was to remain for nearly a century and a half. Granada fell only in 1492, during the reign of the Catholic Kings Isabelle of Castile and Ferdinand of Aragon.

Lions Court, Granada Alhambra

St James Matamoros, Raxoi Palace, Santiago de Compostela

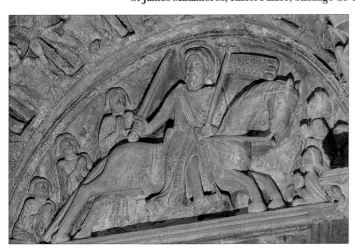

St James Matamoros, Compostela Cathedral

MATAMOROS

Towards the middle of the 12th century, along with depictions of Saint James as an apostle or pilgrim, those of Saint James the warrior, an ardent *Matamoros*, Moorslayer, on his white steed, brandishing a sword against the armies of al-Andalus appeared in Spain. This is how he appeared among the fighters of the *Reconquista* during the mythical battle of Clavijo in 844. One of the first depictions of the Matamoros decorates the tympanum of the door to the treasure in the southern arm of the transept in the cathedral of Compostela.

The monk Gómez of St Martin d'Albelda giving Godescalc the manuscript of "De virginitate beatae Mariae"

THE RISE OF THE PILGRIMAGE

Starting in the tenth century, the first foreign pilgrims set off on the road to Santiago de Compostela. A blind monk from Reichenau was perhaps the first non-Hispanic to accomplish the pilgrimage in 930. At Puerto de Ibañeta, coins dating from Charles the Simple (898-922) and others from the time of the English king Aethelred II (about 980) were also found – signs of the passage of pilgrims in this place. Most certainly martyrologies, widespread in the western churches, contributed to spreading the news of the discovery of Saint James's tomb at the far end of Galicia, in a place then considered as "Finisterra", the "end of the world". The first certain mention of a foreign pilgrim concerns the bishop of Puy, Godescalc, who went to Compostela in 950. His trace would perhaps have been lost if he had not stopped on his way at the monastery of Saint Martin of Albelda, in Rioja, and ordered a copy of *De virginitate beatae Mariae* by Ildephonse of Toledo. The bishop took possession of his book on his return in 951; the pilgrim's way, the road to Santiago was hence also, from its very beginnings, a means of communication and cultural exchange. Several years later, about 959, the abbot Caesarius of the Catalonian monastery of Saint Cecile of Montserrat set off for Compostela. Arriving in Santiago, he asked the Compostela church's apostolic authority to restore in his favour the former

Saint-Michel d'Aiguilhe, Le Puy

A SCRIBE'S WORK

At the end of a manuscript, there sometimes appeared the scribe's name, age, the date of his work. This information is called the colophon. In that of *De Virginitate*, copied for Godescalc in 951, Gómez, a monk of Albelda, wrote the following: "The very holy Bishop Godescalc carried this little book from Hispania to Aquitaine during the winter, in the first days of January…"

Saint Cecile of Montserrat Monastery

Cloister, Santo Domingo de Silos

MOZARAB LITURGY

....

M ozarab liturgy, the direct heir of Visigothic liturgy, presented notable differences with the Roman rite. Among other things, the Visigothic calendar was thirty-eight years ahead of the Roman, and during Mass, nine prayers were recited and three passages from the Gospels were read. Both rites used communion.

The arms of Cluny

metropolitan dignity of the church in Tarragona. Just like the popes, the bishops of Iria-Compostela thus took the title of bishops of the *apostolic seat* of Compostela. However, this effrontery was unacceptable to Peter's successors in Rome, at a time when Compostela was attracting pilgrims in ever greater numbers. Soon the archbishop of Reims, Hugues de Vermandois, came in person to visit the Galician shrine, as attested in *The Life of the Hermit Simeon of Armenia*, which recounts that he stayed in Santiago and freed the daughter of a king of Galicia from demons. But a pilgrim's journey was not without danger and, in 961, Raymond II, Count of Rouergue and Marquis of Gothia, was assassinated on the road to Santiago. Then in 966, Norsemen attacked the Galician coast. Sisnando, the bishop of Compostela, died defending his city, despite its fortifications. The Norman threat was soon supplanted by the *hâjib* of Cordoba, al-Mansûr, who blocked the routes leading to Compostela by invading Leon and Navarre. He then attacked the apostle's city, which was pillaged and burnt in 997. But once the immediate terror caused by "the greatest barbarian" had passed, as described by the author of the *Chronicle of Silos*, a monk from Silos abbey which too was destroyed by al-Mansûr, the pilgrimages took on renewed vigour. Pilgrims' lodging was organized within abbeys and hospices in the various regions they had to cross, while towns began to grow near bridges, crossroads and hospitals along the way, living from trade and guaranteeing the safety of pilgrims. Faced with Viking raids, the bishop of Compostela, Cresconius (1037-1066), surrounded his city with a larger wall, defended by Honesco Castle, and added two towers to the basilica. Nonetheless, relations between Rome and Compostela worsened in the first half of the 11th century. The irresistible expansion of the pilgrimage, the title of bishop of the *apostolic seat* of Santiago the Compostela bishops were so proud of, led the popes to fear that Compostela would overshadow Rome's spiritual authority over the Western churches. In 1049, the Council of Reims excommunicated Cresconius for daring to use the title reserved for the successors of Saint Peter. However, neither Cresconius, nor his successor, Gudesteiz, stopped using the rank and title. The situation did evolve during the second half of the century. Favoured by the reigns of Ferdinand 1st (1035-1065) and especially Alfonso VI (1072-1109) of Castile and Leon, the establishment of Cluny, a fervent supporter of the papacy in France, spread beyond the Pyrenees into Spain. Even if they did not join the order, many of the monasteries along the pilgrimage route adopted the customs and rules of the famous abbey in Burgundy. The peninsula was open to French influence in architecture and art, and this influence was visible in the shrines along the road. In 1080, Alfonso VI decided to replace the Mozarab liturgy by the Roman rite, and ten years later, Carolingian writing replaced Visigothic script. These measures, aimed at bringing the Hispanic church closer to Rome, were applied even more effectively because bishops of Cluniac origin were promoted as heads of the principal bishoprics in the peninsula. Dalmace, a former Cluniac, was elected as bishop of

SANTO DOMINGO DE SILOS

Monks settled in the valley of Tabladillo in the 7th century. Could they remain during the Arab occupation? In any case, as soon as the region was freed from the Muslim yoke, their *scriptorium* was active. A copy of *Commentary of the Rule of Saint Benedict* was copied there in 945. In 954, Fernán González, the first hereditary count of Castile, granted the monastery its autonomy and the right to render justice. At the end of the 10th century, the followers of al-Mansûr destroyed it. It was in 1040 that Domingo, who would give his name to the monastery, was named abbot of Silos by King Ferdinand 1st of Castile (1035-1065). He was to occupy the post until his death in 1073. Domingo was born in Cañas, north of Suso where he became the prior. Because of conflict with King García "el de Nájera", he had to leave Suso in 1040 and join Silos. During his thirty years as abbot, he made Silos into a great monastery and developed the activity of its *scriptorium*. He may also be the origin of the Romanesque cloister project. During the 11th, 12th and 13th centuries, copyists and illuminators of Silos were known by the amount and quality of their work. Among their works, the *Commentaries of the Apocalypse* by Beatus of Liebana are richly illustrated with Mozarab illuminations. Some members of the community were themselves writers, such as *El Silense*, an anonymous monk, the author of the *Chronicle of Silos* in the 12th century. The lower northern and eastern galleries of the cloister were built from the end of the 11th to the middle of the 12th centuries. The western and southern galleries, as well as the upper cloister, were built from the mid-12th to the beginning of the 13th century. In the northern and eastern galleries, at the beginning of the 12th century, a genial sculptor worked on the six reliefs showing the Ascension, Pentecost, the two Marys before the tomb, the descent from the Cross, the doubt of Saint Thomas and the disciples of Emmaus. On the latter, Jesus wears a scallop shell attached to his pouch, an obvious symbol of Saint James. By the bearing and faces of the characters, these masterpieces remind the visitor of the carvings of Isaiah in Souillac and Jeremy in Moissac. In the sculpted programme of the cloister of Silos, some see the same master, while others claim that another equally gifted sculptor worked simultaneously. Still others consider that they are the work of Moorish artists. Today, these light-coloured stones accompany monastic meditation and extraordinary Gregorian chants. There are places that seem condemned to beauty in all its forms.

The unbelief of St Thomas, Santo Domingo de Silos cloister

Cluny

THE PALLIUM

P apal insignia since the 5th century, the pallium was a thin white scarf decorated with black crosses, woven in Rome by nuns of Saint-Agnes-Beyond-the-Walls from wool of lambs blessed by the Pope on St. Agnes' Day.

Iria and settled in Compostela in 1094. His action with Pope Urban II in favour of the independence of the Compostelan mitre was of great importance. Even though the bishop's seat of Iria, suffragan of Braga, had been transferred to Compostela long before, this transfer had never been recognized by the papacy. It was only in 1095, at the Council of Clermont, that, at Dalmace's urging, Pope Urban II ratified the transfer of the bishopric of Iria to Compostela and withdrew it from Braga's supervision. A short time before, the bishop of Compostela had attended the ceremony consecrating the grandiose abbey church of Cluny III by the Pope, and dedicated one of the radiating chapels off the ambulatory to the apostle James the Greater. Starting in 1095, Compostela received increasing privileges. In 1104, Dalmace's successor, Diego Gelmírez (1100-1140) travelled to Rome and received the right of *pallium* from the Pope. This was the symbol of union with the Roman church and its head, a source of jurisdiction. Then in 1120, at the request of Pons de Melgueil, Abbot of Cluny, (1109-1122), Pope Calixtus II (1119-1124) raised Compostela to an archibishopric, to the detriment of Merida. At the same time, the new archbishop was named pontifical legate in the ecclesiastic provinces of Merida and Braga. At the end of the 12th century, the construction of the present Romanesque cathedral of Saint James was completed. And it was in ever increasing numbers that crowds of pilgrims crossed its threshold at the door of Glory and crowded around the apostle's sepulchre.

Vestiges of the narthex at Cluny

ALFONSO VI, BENEFACTOR OF CLUNY

On September 11, 909, the Duke of Aquitaine William III founded a Benedictine abbey on his lands of Cluny, in the diocese of Mâcon. He entrusted the direction to Bernon, the abbot of Baume-les-Messieurs. Placed under the patronage of Saints Peter and Paul, and the direct protection of the Holy See, the new foundation adopted the reform of Benedict of Aniane, who, according to the monastic ideal of perpetual prayer, greatly prolonged the length of offices and time of prayer initially conceived by the rule of Saint Benedict. The quality of the first abbots, all canonized by the Church, and papal protection, ensured rapid prosperity for Cluny. Laying down the bases of Cluniac spirituality, its second abbot, Odon (927-942) provided Cluny with the role of exceptional reformer. In 931, Pope John XI allowed it to take charge of any monastery at the request of a lay cleric, and to accept within its ranks any monk whose monastery refused the reform. After the direction of the abbot Aymard (942-954), Cluny expanded even further under Maïeul (954-994) and Odilon (994-1049). In 981, on the occasion of the consecration of the second abbey church, Cluny II, the abbot received the relics of Saints Peter and Paul. In 998, Pope Gregory V granted it the privilege of exemption, hence ensuring its autonomy by removing it from the jurisdiction of episcopal authority, a measure extended by John XIX in 1024 to the entire Ecclesia cluniasencis, in other words, all the reformed establishments. The Cluniac order could henceforth be legally constituted. The abbot of Cluny was the most important position. As abbot of all the order's houses, he chose the priors at their head and, even if some

Cluniac abbeys retained their own abbots, like Vézelay or Moissac, the latter were subject to his approval and had no more power than a prior. An eminent dignitary of the Church, the abbot of Cluny had not only religious, but also political influence. In the framework of the Gregorian reform, he advocated the purification of morals and the institution of the Peace of God. Sovereign lords on their abbey lands, the monks in black habits considered their principal duty to be the celebration of the holy office, prayer for the salvation of the dead, charity, and hospitality. Established under Odilon in Burgundy, Auvergne, Provence and Italy, the order spread to the edges of Europe under Hugues de Semur (1049-1109). By the time of Peter the Venerable (1122-1156), the Cluniac order consisted of 1,200 dependencies, inhabited by about 10,000 monks. It was at the initiative of Sancho the Great (1000-1035) that the Cluniac reform arrived in the north of the Iberian peninsula. Having learned of the expansion of Cluny, in 1025 Sancho sent a religious delegation led by Paterne, whose mission was to find out about monastic perfection as it was practised there, and to come back to apply it at monasteries on the Iberian side of the Pyrenees, after the suffering caused by al-Mansûr's incursions. Thus, the abbey of San Juan de la Peña, at the opening of Somport Pass, then the abbey of Oña, in the upper valley of the Ebro River, adopted the customs applied at Cluny while maintaining their autonomy. Sancho's three sons, García, King of Navarre (1035-1054), Ramiro 1st, King of Aragon (1035-1063) and Ferdinand 1st, King of Castile and Leon (1037-1065) continued the policies of monastic reform begun by

their father. García founded the monastery of Santa María la Real de Nájera in 1052, but did not subject it to Cluny, while Ferdinand developed solid ties with the Burgundy abbey and instituted an annual tribute of a thousand ounces of gold in its favour. This friendship was consolidated under the reign of his son Alfonso VI, King of Leon in 1065 and of Castile in 1072, who married Constance of Burgundy, the niece of Hugues de Semur. In 1073, Alfonso offered the monastery of Palencia to Cluny, and then, after annexing Rioja in 1076, offered the monastery of Nájera. In 1090, he doubled the amount of the annual tribute instituted by his father, thus financing the construction of the grandiose abbey church Cluny III, the largest Western church before Saint Peter's in Rome. In an attempt to bring the Hispanic church closer to Rome, Alfonso opened the route of Compostela to Cluniacs. The abbot, Peter the Venerable, returned the favour with the fine posthumous homage dedicated to him at the end of his first Book of Miracles. "This king was a great friend and benefactor of Cluny. I will not mention the countless pious works that he bestowed on our abbey, but must say that this magnificent and glorious king made himself with his kingdom, for love of Christ, the debtor of the poor of Christ… He built two abbeys in Spain, authorized other founders to build more and contributed to their construction. He established there Cluniac monks, multiplied generosities so that they may serve God according to their rule. He restored the fervour of monasticism, nearly dead in Spain, and by such zeal prepared for himself the eternal kingdom after that on earth."

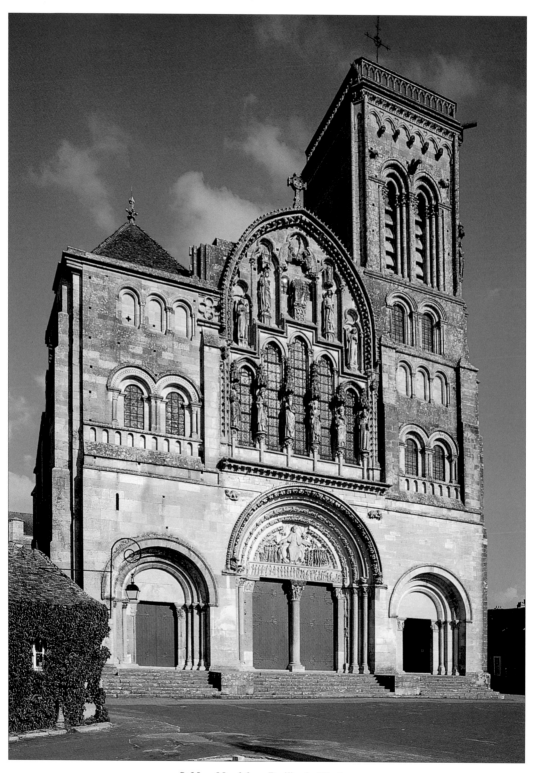

St Mary Magdalene Basilica in Vézelay

ON THE ROAD TO THE STARS

Christ, Saint Sernin, Toulouse

During the second half of the 12th century, men and women of all social classes, of all nationalities, left their country, their city or their village and set out, on foot or on horseback, to follow the pilgrimage road to the Galician shrine. The fervent pilgrim and presumed author of *The Pilgrim's Guide to Santiago de Compostela*, Aimery Picaud, a monk from Parthenay-le-Vieux in Poitou, defined the four main roads that made up the framework of a network of multiple tributaries, bypasses and variations that crossed France and, in Spain, joined a single road, rapidly called *Camino francés*, leading to Compostela. "There are four roads that, leading to Santiago, join into a single road at Puente la Reina, in Spanish territory; one passes through Saint-Gilles du Gard, Montpellier, Toulouse and the Somport Pass; another by Notre-Dame du Puy, Sainte-Foy de Conques and Saint-Pierre de Moissac; another crosses Sainte-Marie-Madeleine of Vézelay, Saint-Léonard in Limousin and the city of Périgueux; still another goes through Saint-Martin de Tours, Saint-Hilaire de Poitiers, Saint-Jean d'Angély, Saint-Eutrope de Saintes and the city of Bordeaux. The route that passes through Sainte-Foy, that which crosses Saint-Léonard and that which goes through Saint-Martin join at Ostabat and after crossing the Cize Pass, in Puenta la Reina they join the road that crosses the Somport; from there a single road leads to Santiago." The shrines at the starting points of these four routes, themselves objects of pilgrimage, were the rallying points for pilgrims. The route going through Toulouse, or *via Tolosa*, started in Arles at the resting place of Saint Trophime. This road was taken by pilgrims coming from Italy, Switzerland or Central Europe, as well as the "Romieux" who, after Rome, were going to Compostela, or vice versa. They had come after crossing the Alps at Montgenèvre Pass, or by the road along the Ligurian coast. The road leaving from Notre-

Conques

THE PILGRIM'S GUIDE

The *Pilgrim's Guide* is the last book of the *Codex Calixtinus* or *Liber Sancti Jacobi*. Its drafting is usually attributed to Aimery Picaud, a monk or priest from Parthenay-le-Vieux in Poitou, who was also one of the principal organizers of the entire *Codex*. After having described, in the first three chapters, the four main routes "that are only one" from Puenta la Reina until the tomb of James the apostle, Aimery informs his readers, potential pilgrims, about "good or bad waters" met on the road. His book, written in a lively style, then indicates the "characteristics of countries and people" that any pilgrim is likely to meet and "the holy bodies" that should be "visited along the way". After describing the "characteristics of the city and the church of Saint James", Aimery ends his book by encouraging charity towards pilgrims, that everyone should "receive and lodge with good will".

Medieval Pilgrims

1125	Matilda, daughter of Henry 1st of England and widow of the German emperor Henry V
c.1130	Aimery Picaud, author of *The Pilgrim's Guide*
1137	William X, Duke of Aquitaine. He died on April 9 in Compostela, in front of the apostle's altar
1138	Alfonso VII, King of Galicia
1140	Alphonse Jourdain, son of Raymond IV of Saint-Gilles, Count of Toulouse and nephew of Alfonso VI
1147	English and German crusaders, whose ship had put in at Vivero on the way to the Second Crusade
1154	Louis VII, King of France
1180	A Swedish duke
1192	Guillaume, Archbishop of Reims
c.1200	Saint Dominic
1211	Alfonso IX, King of Leon, who attended the consecration of Compostela cathedral
1213	Saint Francis of Assisi

1217	Dutch and German crusaders, whose ships had put in at La Coruña on their way to the Fifth Crusade
1224	Jean de Brienne, King of Jerusalem
1244	Sancho II, King of Portugal

Dame du Puy, or *via Podiensis*, was that of Santiago pilgrims from the centre of France and Eastern Europe. Pilgrims from Germany, Lorraine, Champagne and Burgundy could follow the route leaving from Vézelay and passing through Limoges, called the *via Lemovicensis*. Finally, the road called *magnum iter Sancti Jacobi*, taken in particular by pilgrims from northern France and Europe, Denmark and the Low Countries, passed through Paris and Orléans, but really started at Saint-Martin de Tours, giving it its name of *via Turonensis*. The English, as well as some Hanseatic and Flemish pilgrims, joined this fourth route by sea. However, pilgrims who were curious or wishing to satisfy a special devotion could pass from one route to another by taking bypasses or side-roads. In fact, whatever itinerary was taken, stage by stage, the pilgrim accomplished a series of pilgrimages, recounted by Aimery Picaud in chapter VIII of his *Guide*, where he enumerates the "holy bodies that rest along the road to Santiago and that pilgrims should visit". Some Santiago pilgrims did not hesitate to detour through famous pilgrimage sites more or less distant from the route, such as Mont Saint Michel, Rocamadour or Montserrat. Others, having meditated at the tomb of Saint James, crossed Spain and the Straits of Gibraltar to reach Jerusalem, or else, following the *via Tolosana*, reached Italy and Saint Peter's in Rome. The pilgrims' motivations varied. Naturally, in the best case, the pilgrimage was freely accomplished from pure devotion and religious fervour. In its most

MONTSERRAT

In the heart of Catalonia, the Montserrat range stretches its ridges bristling with rocky peaks aimed at the sky along the wide strip of land edged by the Llobregat River and its tributary the Anoia, between Vallès and Penedès. Very early on, man considered this gigantic mineral sculpture as a sacred place. By the 8th century, hermits found solitude there and, in 888, the existence of Saint Mary's hermitage was attested in the document about its donation to Ripoll monastery. In 959, Caesarius, a monk from Saint Cecilia of Montserrat, travelled to Compostela. But it was only in 1025 that Oliba, Bishop of Vic, abbot of Ripoll and Cuxa, settled a stable community at Saint Mary's. The monastery acquired great importance, and towards the end of the 12th century it received a statue of the Virgin, which still stands on the main altar of its church. The patina of time and smoke have turned the statue black, giving it the name *Moreneta*, but it is worshipped by Catalonians who con-

The Black Virgin of Montserrat

sider her their patron saint. Devotion to the Virgin of Monserrat, to whom Alfonso X dedicated six of his *Cantigas*, spread throughout the world because of pilgrims going to Santiago joining the *Camino francés* at Logroño, through Lerida and Zaragoza; because of military operations in the Mediterranean and the east by the Catalonian-Aragonese crown during the 14th and 15th centuries; and finally, thanks to the action of Bernat Boil, former hermit of Montserrat who, in 1492, accompanied Christopher Columbus to America. Today, fervour for *Moreneta* is still passionate, and, twice a day, pilgrims can listen to the Escolans, little singers from the Escolania, whose existence dates back to the 13th century.

Montserrat Sierra, seen from El Bruc

Pilgrims songs in the Codex

ULTREÏA !

....

A long the road, it often happened that Santiago pilgrims sang while they walked. In their songs, they evoked all the moments of their pilgrimage, from the day of departure until their return, passing through various towns, visiting shrines and, of course, the arrival in Santiago de Compostela, throughout spontaneously expressing their faith, their joy and sadness and their fears. And when they were simply tired of walking, starting up a song diminished their fatigue, strength and enthusiasm revived, and, for travellers in unknown lands, their solitude became less burdensome. "E ultreïea! E sus eia! Deus aïa nos!" (On further and again, God helps us!), was one of the choruses that was sung as a rallying cry, encouraging the hearts of the fervent pilgrims.

perfect, and most rare, form, it was a totally gratuitous act, corresponding to a real spiritual quest. To go on a pilgrimage, leave one's social condition, the warmth and comfort of home, was to renounce worldly goods in accordance with the evangelical ideal of poverty and humility, and rob the old man to "nakedly follow the naked Christ". In the difficult asceticism imposed by walking, the thirty kilometres repeated every day, in the heat or the cold, hunger and thirst, the many dangers and uncertainty of finding lodging, the pilgrim relived some of the sacrifice of the Cross. Upon his return, he might become a monk. The *Song of the Spiritual Pilgrim*, from the register of the Confraternity of Saint James of Senlis, paints the portrait of the perfect pilgrim: "Always following the good Jesus Christ/ In his suffering/ A great heart is needed to imitate him/ And great patience/ The good pilgrim renders service/ Without self-interest/ And does not take his exercise / In what he enjoys./ To do much and talk little/ Is his motto/ To die for oneself to live for God/ His undertaking."

However, the majority of those who chose this voluntary exile did so in the hope of obtaining a material or spiritual favour at the end of their pilgrimage. In the first case, it was often the curing of an illness or an infirmity; arriving in Compostela, the faithful prayed to the miracle-working gifts of Saint James. Starting in the mid-13th century, the sick invoked the saint at home, promising to undertake a thanksgiving pilgrimage once they were cured. These pilgrimages were hence akin to those carried out after a vow pronounced in a moment of dire peril. In the second case, the pilgrimage was a means of ensuring the salvation of one's soul, to do penance, as in the *Song of the Pilgrim's Duty*: " To satisfy God / for the evils that I have committed/ I wish to make a vow/ despite my enemies, to Saint James the apostle/ honoured in Galicia/ where our Lord God/ is adored in him." At the end of the Middle Ages, the desire to see other lands, to visit foreign courts were added to the devotion that caused nobles and men in high places to carry out the pilgrimage. Other valiant knights even found the opportunity to organize tournaments and the passage of arms, or to simply prove their military prowess. In 1402, Jean de Werchin, seneschal of Hainaut, declared with his public announcement of his route from Coucy to Compostela that he would accept the challenge of fighting with blunt arms made by any knight met on his way, on condition of not having to go more than twenty leagues out of his way.

However, if these pilgrims decided to leave for various reasons, others were forced to do so. During the 11th and 12th centuries, expiatory pilgrimages were among the canonical penances, and there were many who put on the pilgrim's cloak after being condemned for more or less serious crimes by ecclesiastical tribunals. Iron rings, sometimes forged from the crime weapon, encircled arms, the neck or the torso of murderers walking the pilgrimage route. In the 14th and 15th centuries, the Inquisition imposed pilgrimages on condemned heretics and the same sentence was occasionally used by some civil tribunals in France and, especially, in the Low Countries. In these conditions, once they

PILGRIM CONFRATERNITIES

The first pilgrim confraternities appeared in the 12th century and developed mostly during the 14th and 15th centuries. There were many of them in France, Switzerland, Germany and the Low Countries. Admission conditions varied from one confraternity to another, but moral criteria always played an important role. Most of them accepted Santiago pilgrims who had accomplished the pilgrimage in person and without constraint, through sheer devotion. Others also admitted pilgrims by delegation, or even those who were on the point of leaving, or sometimes people who had not made the pilgrimage but who were particularly devoted to the saint. Upon joining, the new brother had to swear to observe the rules and to behave charitably towards other members. In many ways, the brotherhood constituted a new family, a spiritual family for the former pilgrim. The correct working of activities planned by the confraternity's rules was ensured by an elected board, including a master, provosts, deans and other rectors. Sometimes clerks were added, as well as treasurers charged with obtaining the annual dues from members. The brotherhood's activities were particularly obvious during religious ceremonies, especially Saint James' Day, celebrated either on the day itself, July 25th, or the first Sunday following. The day started with a high mass in the morning. After pronouncing a tribute to the saint, the brothers lit up the church with candles that they had sometimes made themselves. Coming out of the church, wearing their Santiago emblems or symbolic objects of the pilgrimage, they walked in procession, re-enacting for a short time their previous journey. On this occasion, some confraternities showed off their honorary staff, topped with a statue of the saint. Next, the brotherhood met for an assembly, during which the new direction was

Santiago pilgrims

elected and, if necessary, new members were admitted. The day ended with a great banquet marking the mutual solidarity that united members of pilgrim society. Confraternities also organized theatrical activities, mystery plays on the occasion of religious feasts, or simply with an educational purpose, with the subject of the representations often linked to the saints' cult. Brotherhood life implied solidarity and help among members of the association, but also towards other pilgrims, the sick and the poor. Hence, some confraternities ran hospitals for pilgrims. Brothers' duties were also to accompany pilgrims leaving for Compostela. They attended the departure mass, then accompanied them to the start of the route. At the death of a member, the brothers attended his funeral and had funeral masses said in his memory. Often, the deceased was buried in his pilgrim's costume, with his pouch decorated with a scallop shell, his wide-brimmed hat and his staff at his side.

Book of the St James Pilgrim Confraternity of Senlis

Scallop shell and staffs, Santiago

THE SPREAD OF IDEAS

....

S ome heretics were condemned to making pilgrimages. Others, false pilgrims among the real ones, travelled along the pilgrimage routes, thus trying to remain incognito and sometimes, to spread their ideas. Lombardy was an area favoured by the Patarins, reserved dualists who had considerable contact with the Cathars of Languedoc, convinced dualists. The *via Tolosana*, linking Northern Italy and Galicia via Languedoc, certainly played an important role in this relationship. And it was the reason for which, in the first half of the 13th century, the city of Leon saw vigorous development of dualistic ideas.

reached Santiago, pilgrims obtained a certificate of confession and communion, called a *compostela*, testifying that they really had accomplished the journey. Furthermore, a new category of pilgrims developed during the Middle Ages – proxy pilgrims, who carried out the journey for somebody else. Many towns, overwhelmed by public calamities, like the plague in the 14th century, sent delegations of pilgrims to beg for the intercession of Saint James. During the Middle Ages, it also became frequent that a dying person bequeathed his vow of pilgrimage to his heir, or provided in his will for sending one or several people on a pilgrimage to ensure the salvation of his soul. To these posthumous pilgrimages, there were soon added vicarious pilgrimages, like the Countess Mahaut of Artois, who had at least six pilgrimages to Compostela made for her between 1312 and 1328. Hence real professional pilgrims appeared, paid to accomplish the journey, such as Yvonne Warguier, who called herself a "poor varlet", forced to go on pilgrimage "to earn her poor living". However, whatever their reasons, upon becoming pilgrims, all of them abandoned their own social structure and group to integrate a new and similar community.

This separation was marked by precise rites. On the day of departure, after attending Mass and confessing in one's parish church, the pilgrim knelt in the chancel, with his two indispensable companions for the road, the satchel or scrip (called *pera* in Latin, *escharpe* in Old French, then in the modern period, *malette*) and the staff, lying on the altar. The priest blessed these two distinctive insignia of the pilgrim, before solemnly handing them to their owner while pronouncing specific invocations. Recognizable because of these two possessions, which thus acquired a symbolic and sacred dimension, after receiving benediction, the pilgrim found himself placed in the safekeeping of the Church and the Peace of God. At the end of the ceremony, the clergy and the people accompanied him in a procession as far as the beginning of the road, singing litanies, before leaving

Blessing staffs and scrips

PILGRIMS' ATTRIBUTES

By the High Middle Ages, the scrip and the staff, blessed before the great departure, comprised the two characteristic attributes of pilgrims, allowing them to be recognized as such. The staff was originally shorter than the walker, and with a single knob. Subsequently, it was pictured as being bigger than its owner, and with two knobs. The sermon, *Veneranda dies*, integrated into the first book of the *Codex Calixtinus* (towards 1137) defined its two main functions: to help in walking "like a third foot", and to defend the pilgrim, physically "against the wolf and the dog", but also symbolically, against traps set by the devil. A weapon of salvation through penitence, it became "the staff of hope/ tipped with charity/ covered with constance,/ love and chastity" in the *Song of Pilgrims' Duty*. The scrip, or pouch, that contained the pilgrim's meagre rations, was called *escharpe* in Old French, through alteration of the Frankish *skerpa*, bag slung across the shoulder. In the 16th century, this term was replaced by *mallette* (valise), until the word *panetière* (shepherd's bag) became used in the 19th and 20th centuries. The *Veneranda dies* sermon gives it powerful symbolic value. It is narrow because, in order to survive, the pilgrim puts his faith in God and not in his own resources; it is made of leather to remind him that he must mortify his flesh; finally, it is always open, to give as well as to receive. Starting at the end of the Middle Ages, other accessories were added to these two attributes. A gourd, made of a dried and emptied marrow or a recipient of the same shape, contained the pilgrim's drink. Sometimes it was attached

to the staff by a hook placed between the two knobs. A short time later, appeared a certificate box containing authorizations, safe-conducts, letters of recommendation, passports and other confessional letters that pilgrims needed, starting in the 15th century. Finally, at this time the use of the pater-noster or rosary became general. The pilgrim's costume was functional above all else. In the Middle Ages, saints walking were usually depicted dressed in a tunic, always long for women, but that could stop at the knees for men, and a surcoat, a looser piece of clothing, usually shorter, of coarser material, sleeveless and slit at the sides. The hood, extended by a collar covering the shoulders, and a hat, first of all conical in shape, later with a wide brim, completed the outfit. In the 15th century, a pelerine, or large cape covering the walker to the ankles, increasingly replaced the surcoat. The use of a round hat, with a brim turned up in front, became common. The hood's collar became longer, until it developed into a separate piece of clothing called a mantlet. Covering the shoulders, it was sometimes made of leather and by the 18th century, had become the most characteristic item of the pilgrim's outfit, to the extent that it was one of the pilgrims' attributes. Above all, by the first half of the 12th century, the pilgrim going to Santiago was distinguished by the emblematic scallop shell. In the waters off the Galician coast live molluscs with a bivalve shell, belonging to the genus *Pecten*. Their ancient dedication to Venus gave them their Spanish name of *concha venera*. Santiago pilgrims used to gather these Galician *veiras*, wide

shells whose shape is similar to a hand, on the shore and then sew them onto their hats, as a sign of their travels when they set out on the journey home. The author of the *Venerande dies* sermon saw in the shells the symbol of good works flowing out of an open hand. Legends turned the scallop shell into the sign of Saint James's miraculous power, saving a prince from the stormy waves into which his bolting horse had thrown him. On the point of drowning, the knight called on the saint for help and soon his body came miraculously ashore, covered with scallop shells. It was also a scallop shell brought back from Compostela by an Italian pilgrim that, according to the *Liber sancti Jacobi*, made an enormous goitre on a knight from Apulia disappear, by simply being applied to it. In the 13th century, the bishops of Compostela conceded to the shopkeepers on the Saint James Cathedral square the exclusive rights to selling reproductions of the famous scallop shells, made of lead or tin. However, the success of the Compostela shell was such that its use became general and it became the common insignia of all pilgrims. Between the 15th and 18th centuries, Santiago pilgrims also brought back two other kinds of objects – "bourdonnet", from the French word for staff, *bourdon*, and *azabaches*. The bourdonnets were small sticks carved to look like the pilgrims' staffs, and like the shells, were attached to hats or cloaks. The azabaches were a speciality of Compostela until the 17th century. They were small religious objects, such as medallions or statuettes of Saint James, carved from the jet mined in Asturias and Leon.

Pyrenean cirque in Gavarnie

AT THE COURT OF THE GREAT KHAN

I n the 13th century, the renown of Compostela seems to have spread beyond all borders. Its echo even reached Asia, as attested by the Flemish Franciscan Guillaume de Rubruck, who was sent on a diplomatic mission to the Mongols by King Louis IX (St Louis). In 1254, Rubruck was north of the Gobi desert, at the camp of Khan Mongka (1251-1259), the grand-son of Genghis Khan. Following the Mongol ruler as far as Karakorum, the empire's capital since 1235, among the sovereign's entourage he met Sergius, a former Armenian weaver who had become a hermit near Jerusalem before coming to the Empire of the Steppe. This Sergius seems to have been very embarrassed about having promised the Mongol chief to convince all the Western peoples to obey him, Mongka Khan, in return for ending a dispute that had arisen between them. Realizing the difficulty of carrying out such a promise, Sergius asked the Franciscan missionary whether he thought the Pope would lend him horses to get to Compostela, where he would pray Saint James for help.

him facing his destiny. Some Santiago pilgrims chose to accomplish their penance all alone. But there were many more who travelled in a group. When tiredness led to discouragement, they mutually encouraged each other, to the rhythm of pilgrims' songs. True pilgrimages were supposed to be done on foot, nonetheless some, particularly among the privileged nobles or clerics, travelled on horseback. Starting in the 12th and 13th centuries, pilgrims had a special judicial status, the *Lex Peregrinorum*, which protected them from arbitrary arrest, attacks and economic exploitation, exempted them from certain taxes and tolls, and also assured the safety of belongings left behind upon departure. There were also various provisions in case of death. Because nature and the surroundings were still wild, many dangers had to be faced on the way there and back. Bandits and thieves haunted the forests, robbing and even murdering. Some of them, known as "*coquillards*" from the shell, or *coquille*, of St James, hid their true identity under a pilgrim's costume, deceiving the devout intentions of real Santiago pilgrims. To these human dangers were added the threat from packs of wolves and natural obstacles. The heights of the Pyrenees mountains impressed the *Guide*'s author. To cross the pass at Roncesvalles, "there are eight thousand to climb and as many to descend. [...] He who ascends believes that he can touch the sky with his own hand." The plains too were to be feared. "To cross the Landes near Bordeaux, three days are necessary for people who are already tired. It is a bare country, where everything is missing. [...] If you cross [them] in summer, take care to keep away from your face the enormous flies that proliferate over there [...]; and if you do not watch your feet carefully, you will go as far as your knees in marine sand." Crossing streams and rivers was still another hardship. Bridges were few and far between in the Middle Ages, fords unstable, and rivers often dirty, as mentioned in Chapter VI of the *Guide*, which lists "the good and bad rivers along the road to Santiago". Hence, according to Aimery Picaud,

Pilgrims on foot and horseback, Hours of the Duchess of Burgundy

Wolves attacking pilgrims, Roncesvalles Museum

Woman with skull, Santiago

VOW OF PILGRIMAGE

....

T he first defining notion of a
voluntary pilgrim was the vow,
that is, the promise made to God
of going to a specific shrine. Once
this vow was taken, it had to be
accomplished and, in case of
absolute impossibility of carrying
it out, only a bishop could dispense
the pilgrim. According to 13th
century canons, only a man who
was free, of age, not subject to
paternal authority, unmarried,
not having professed religious
vows and not having received
holy orders, could freely make a
vow of pilgrimage. This definition
excluded many individuals,
who had to ask someone else's
authorization before being allowed
to depart. They included serfs
obtaining permission from their
lords, minors from their parents,
married men or women from their
spouses, monks and nuns from
their superiors, and clerics from
their bishops. In addition, the
pilgrimage of women was the
object of much criticism. In the
14th and 15th centuries, texts of
comic literature outdid each other
in developing the theme of women
pretending to go on pilgrimage
and instead meeting a lover or
going on an adventure. This
misogynous mentality persisted
in the vocabulary of the 15th and
16th centuries, where a *coquillarde*
(from the shell, *coquille*) meant
an adulterous woman.

"all the rivers one meets from Estella until Logroño have water
that is dangerous to drink for men and horses, and their fish are
fatal to those who eat them. […] You must not eat them because,
without a doubt, either you will die shortly afterwards, or you will
fall ill." Passers and toll keepers did not hesitate to try to profit
from the distress of pilgrim travellers, demanding large sums for
access to bridges and passages. "Many times too", writes the
Guide's author, "after receiving the money, the passers make
such a large group of pilgrims get on board, that the boat tips
over and pilgrims drown; and then the boatmen rejoice nastily
after grabbing the clothes from the dead." But despite the tribulations of the *peregrinus* condition, of being a stranger continu-
ously confronted with the unknown and disorientation, prey to
the meanness of the locals, despite hunger, thirst, cold or heat
that made up their daily lot, in the holy tombs and relics in
shrines along the route, the pilgrims found spiritual comfort,
enthusiasm and the strength to continue on their chosen path.
At nightfall, surprised in the wooded solitudes of isolated mountains, a ringing of bells providentially guided the pilgrim's steps
to a hostel along the route.

Hospitals, the "houses of God", at the same time "comfort of
holy pilgrims, rest for the poor, consolation for the ill, salvation
for the dead and help for the living", lined the pilgrimage routes
starting in the 11th century. Many of them, like those in Aubrac,
Saint Christine at Somport or Roncesvalles, were served by
canons of Saint Augustine. Upon arrival, before being offered a
meal, linen and a bed, the pilgrim was greeted with the traditional washing of the feet, a relief after a long day of walking. A
purifying rite commemorating Christ's action with his disciples
before the Last Supper, it was also a sign of charity and humility,
signifying the pardoning of sins. Besides the reception provided
in hospitals or hostels attached to Benedictine monasteries, pilgrims could count on the hospitality of holy hermits, some of
whom became famous. Towards the middle of the 11th century,

The Aubrac Domerie

THE CALL OF THE JUBILEE

The institution of a holy year of grace and remission every fifty years, or a jubilee year, entirely dedicated to Yahveh, is part of the prescriptions written in Leviticus in the Old Testament. The opening of this holy year was announced to the sound of a trumpet made of a ram's horn, and it is probably from the Hebrew *yôbél*, meaning ram, that the word *jubilee* has its origin. During the Jewish jubilee year, measures applicable during a sabbatical year, in other words, the last year in a period of six, came into force: lands that could be ploughed were left fallow, their fruits being reserved for the needy and for animals; slaves were given their freedom; all debts were postponed; and last of all, everyone was to be charitable to his neighbour. Furthermore, during the jubilee year, the one starting after seven sabbatical years, goods acquired in the course of the forty-nine previous years had to be returned to their owners or their heirs. Subsequently, Christianity emphasized the spiritual meaning

of the jubilee year. At the beginning of the 7th century, Isidore of Sevilla defined it as "a year to pardon sins", prefiguring "rest without worry in perpetual beatitude". The first Christian jubilee year was instituted only in 1300 by Pope Boniface VIII, who conferred complete indulgence on whomever visited the basilicas of Saints Peter and Paul in the course of the year starting at Christmas 1299. At Christmas 1300, the closing papal bull conferred the same indulgence on those who, for lack of time, had not been able to complete their pilgrimage. The practice of indulgences developed over the Middle Ages. In the pardoning of sins, if confession could erase the moral error, in no case could it remit the temporal penance, which remained to be done either in purgatory, or in this world, by expiatory acts such as fasting, long prayers, pilgrimages or alms. The granting of an indulgence remitted some of the penance by partial indulgence, or else all of it, by full indulgence of the temporal penance caused by sins already

pardoned. If the granting of partial indulgences was widespread, until the 13th century full indulgence was much more rare. But to stimulate crusaders' enthusiasm, in 1215 at the Lateran Council Pope Innocent III had granted full indulgence to every knight at his departure for the Crusades. When he instituted the first jubilee year in 1300, Pope Boniface VIII had set its periodicity at one hundred years. Then, given the success of this new institution, the frequency of jubilee years increased. Clement VI (1342-1352) set them every fifty years, and also added Saint John of Lateran to the two Roman basilicas to be visited. Pope Urban VI in 1389 set the jubilees every thirty-three years, and finally Paul II in 1470 set them every twenty-five, where they remain to the present day. Starting in 1500, the faithful also had to honour the basilica of Saint Mary Major. Tradition attributed to Pope Calixtus II (1119-1124) the institution, in 1122, of the first jubilee of Saint James. However, it was starting only from the early 15th century that full indulgences seem to have been associated with him. The first historically attested Compostelan holy year dates from 1428. In Compostela, the jubilee year is always celebrated when July 25, the date commemorating the apostle's martyrdom, falls on a Sunday. The jubilee lasts one year starting from the opening of the Holy Door on December 30. This door is only opened for the Compostelan jubilee year, which happens four times every twenty-eight years, according to a periodicity of 6, 11, 6, and 5 years.

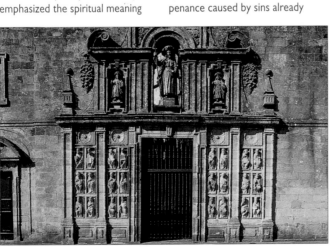

The Pardon Doorway, Santiago de Compostela Cathedral

Doorway detail, Las Platerías

A LIFE OF PILGRIMAGES

....

A lthough most pilgrims carried out only one pilgrimage in their lives, others renewed the experience. After going to the Holy Land at the age of thirteen, Bona of Pisa, d. 1207, made nine pilgrimages to Compostela, wearing an iron chain as a belt. During the same period, Facio of Cremona allegedly went to Rome eighteen times, and as often to Compostela...

Compostela cathedral also provided other relics for Santiago pilgrims to worship. From 1102, at the instigation of Bishop Diego Gelmírez, its treasure was enriched with the remains of Saint Suzanne, Saint Fructuoso, and the martyrs Sylvester and Cucufat, confiscated from the church in Braga, and even with the head of Saint James the Less, brought from Jerusalem by Bishop Maurice of Braga and offered to Gelmírez by Queen Urraca, along with fragments of the True Cross. Over the centuries, relics of other saints were added: Lucy, Pauline, Barbara, Severine, Marguerite, and Teresa of Jesus, John the Baptist, Clement, Zephyrin, Benedict, Vincent, Anthony, Dominic, Christopher and Felix... On the cathedral square in Compostela, pilgrims hurried to buy, from the *concheros* who had a monopoly on the business, the precious and emblematic scallop shells, whose acquisition was strictly regulated and which they attached to their cloaks or to the brim of their hats. Before setting out on the return journey, many went to Padrón, the former Iria Flavia, on the banks of the Ulla River where Saint James's boat had stopped after reaching the shores of Galicia. According to tradition, it was on *Monte Santiaguino*, the hill of Padrón, that the apostle preached at first. Upon their return, after rejoining the community which they had temporarily left, many former pilgrims continued to show their devotion to Saint James within the confraternity of their town or their parish.

Galician shore

THE CULT OF RELICS

Relics are either the bodily remains of men or women considered as saints, or else objects sanctified by their contact. The cult of relics was essentially born along with Christianity which, believing in the resurrection of bodies, particularly worshipped some of the chosen who were certain to come back to life at the Last Judgement. The worship of martyrs' bodies, and later, of those of other saints, thus focused on their tombs, around which the faithful gathered on the anniversary date of their death, celebrated as a second birth. The proximity of their remains further perpetuated the presence of the dead within the community, a presence made glorious because of miracles, and cures carried out by their powerful intercession. Starting in the middle of the 4th century in the East, certain martyrs' remains began to be moved, in order to better respond to the veneration of the faithful. Then the Byzantine church authorized the division of relics, hence multiplying the number of pilgrimage shrines. During the Carolingian period, the translation of holy bodies and the distribution of fragments of their remains became general in all of Western Europe. Such operations were supposed to be carried out with a bishop's authorization, but soon non-authorized translations, commerce, even stealing of relics, an importance source of revenue for the shrines, became common. If the authenticity and efficiency of relics thus exposed to the worship of the faithful were occasionally called into question during the Middle Ages, they were nonetheless important catalysts of medieval piety.

Reliquary foot of St James, Treasury of Oignies Priory, Namur

Reliquary of the True Cross, Saint Sernin Basilica, Toulouse

St James, high altar of Santiago de Compostela Cathedral

THREE CENTURIES OF SCEPTICISM

At the dawn of the 16th century, critical thought born out of Christian humanism began to question the meaning of pilgrimages, by placing the essential spirit of the faithful not in external acts but in the spirit of charity and every person's heart. Excesses, superstition and credulity produced by these pilgrimages were roundly criticized. Furthermore, under cover of devotion, were there not some who were interested in debauchery and wandering? Erasmus was one of the first to denounce the superstition and abuse surrounding their practice. In his second book of *Colloquia* (1518), using a English pilgrim named Ogyge who, covered with scallop shells and medals of tin and lead, showing off necklaces of straw and snake eggs, returns from Compostela, where he had gone to accomplish a vow by his mother-in-law. The humanist from Rotterdam satirizes the rather suspicious rituals of the walkers for God, denouncing vicarious pilgrimages, through which "without moving, one imposes a task on others", not without implying that offerings made to the poor are much more useful than those enriching Compostela cathedral. In addition, Ogyge has no choice but to realize that "good Saint James feels much less well than usually" since "new ideas circulating all over the world mean that he is being saluted much less often than before". A few years later, Rabelais went further in his *Gargantua* (1534). In chapter XLIII, Grandgousier addresses a group of pilgrims from Berry in France. "And from now on, do not fall easily into these pleasant and useless journeys. Support your families, each work according to his vocation, educate your children and live according to the teachings of the good apostle Saint Paul. In doing so, you will be safeguarded by God, his angels and his saints. And there will be neither plague nor evil to harm you." To the scepticism of the humanists were added the bitter verbal attacks of the Protestant reformers. "No-one knows whether what

Detail, Pardon Doorway, Santiago

ERASMUS

Born in Rotterdam about 1469, Erasmus, an illegitimate child orphaned at the age of 14, entered the convent of the Augustinians at Steyn, near Gouda. He continued his studies in Paris, at Montaigu College, then left for England where, becoming a tutor, he studied with the theologian Colet and became friends with Thomas More. On his return to Paris, Erasmus wrote his *Adages* in 1500, then stayed in Italy from 1506 to 1509, where he studied Greek. In 1509, he taught at Cambridge and wrote *In Praise of Folly*. Returning to his native land, he published in Basle, in 1516, a translation of the New Testament from the Greek text, and *Institution of a Christian Prince*, dedicated to the future Charles V, whose councillor he had become. His *Colloquia* appeared in 1519, then in 1521, his *Essay on Free Will*, where he opposed Luther's doctrine. Luther responded with *Tract of the Serf Arbiter*. Erasmus died in Basle in 1536.

Pilgrim's mantlet from the 16th century, La Rochelambert Castle

INQUISITION

Instituted by the Catholic Kings with the agreement of Pope Sixtus IV in 1478, the first Spanish Inquisitors were charged with watching converted Jews – mostly after persecutions – and punishing any relapses. Sixtus IV's criticisms of the pitiless cruelty of the General Inquisitor Tomas de Torquemada (1485-1494) did not prevent the inquisitorial jurisdiction from being enlarged. This followed the policy of religious unification pursued by the Spanish monarchs and aimed at all Jews who, starting in 1492, had to choose between baptism and exile. In 1501, the same measure was applied to Moors from the former kingdom of Granada, and in 1502, was extended to the mudejars of Castile, then those of Aragon and Catalonia. The inquisition then concentrated all its attention on the Moriscos – converted Muslims, and even more on the Marranos – converted Jews, regularly called to appear during *autos da f*e (trying and sentencing a heretic). Starting in 1525, the Spanish Inquisition began proceedings, ending in moderate condemnations, against Erasmians and visionaries who preached a more personal form of devotion. However, when Protestant communities were discovered in Sevilla and Valladolid at the beginning of Philip II's reign, autos da fe were once again organized in these two cities, making dozens of people perish and totally eliminating Protestantism from Spain. The fear of any religious deviancy also led the Spanish inquisitors to pursue the most famous representatives of mystical thought, such as the reformers of Carmel, Saint Teresa of Avila (1515-1582) and Saint John of the Cross (1542-1591). The Spanish Inquisition was officially abolished only in 1823.

lies [in Compostela], in the apostle's tomb is a dead dog, or a dead horse", wrote Luther about the Santiago pilgrimage, "so forget it and do not go there...let him who wants to travel there, but you, stay at home". Harmed by the supporters of modern devotion, pilgrimages suffered during the religious persecution of the second half of the 16th century. In Spain, the Inquisition – the secular wing of the Catholic church – reorganized after 1542, was raging, encouraged under the reign of Philip II (1556-1598). Condemning the least suspect with neither scruples nor mildness, especially if the suspect in question was German, the Inquisition contributed to a drop in attendance at the Galician shrine. In 1559, three Bavarian pilgrims who had left Compostela without going to confession had been arrested, taken back to Santiago, imprisoned and severely interrogated over a period of six weeks. In the Netherlands, then under Spanish domination, Philip II tried to apply the same terror regime but came up against the hostility of the Gueux, who rebelled starting in 1566, supported by Queen Elizabeth I of England (1533-1603). The struggle between the two monarchs broke out in 1577, when Francis Drake's pirates attacked and looted three Spanish galleons near Callao, Lima's port, taking considerable booty in gold, silver and precious stones, including splendid emeralds that the queen had set in her crown. She also named Drake a knight, on the deck of his ship, upon his return to Plymouth in 1580. Galician coasts were not spared from attacks by English pirates. In 1589, after the bitter

LUTHER

An Augustinian monk and priest, Martin Luther (1483-1546) taught theology at the university of Wittenberg, in Saxony. A fiery and tormented spirit, it was while reading *Saint Paul's Epistle to the Romans* that Luther found an answer to the great question about the soul's salvation. A sinner, in accordance with the doctrine of original sin, man has no influence on his own salvation; all his good works are in vain; God, in his immense mercy can freely and arbitrarily grant him the grace of *faith*, alone able to justify him. Indulgences prescribed by Pope Leon X to whomever gave alms to pay for St Peter's basilica in Rome, gave Luther the opportunity to rise up against the practice of indulgences and pontifical author-

ity by publishing his ninety-five theses. Called to explain himself, Luther soon rejected papal infallibility and all the traditions of the Roman Catholic church. According to him, Scripture was the only authority for a Christian, who must find God's will in it by himself. Excommunicated by the pope in 1521, he took refuge with the prince of Saxony, where he worked on the first German translation of the New Testament. Starting in 1522, he was busy organizing the new religion, based on preaching holy Scripture. Baptism and the Eucharist were the only two sacraments of the Lutheran reform, which also rejected the cult of saints. Luther died in 1546, leaving behind a rapidly developing movement.

Buckland, Drake's former manor

defeat of the invincible Spanish Armada, Drake launched an expedition against La Coruña. Disembarking, the English buccaneers profaned churches, threatening the apostle's city. It was probably on this occasion that the ecclesiastical authorities of Compostela decided to hide the saint's relics in a place kept so secret that they were not found again before the end of the 19th century.

However, between 1545 and 1563, the Council of Trent responded to the Wittenberg reformer by reaffirming dogma and reorganizing the Catholic church, after the most flagrant abuses had been rooted out. The cult of saints' bodies and the value of indulgences were completely rehabilitated in December 1563. In addition, taking up for itself the criticisms made by Erasmus and his contemporaries, the Catholic Counter-Reformation, while attempting to abolish certain practices judged superstitious, gave new impetus to pilgrimages, emphasizing above all their spiritual and moral meaning. In his *Pilgrim of Lorette* (1604), the Jesuit priest Richeôme reminded the reader that the only point of religious travel was to honour God and his saints, to do penance by "patiently enduring the work and inconvenience of the way" and to increase one's devotion by the desire to imitate "the beautiful examples of the saints one visits". To go, and to meditate from the bottom of one's soul, as Jesus did during his pilgrimage on this earth, was, in the eyes of the post-Tridentine clergy, the real meaning of pilgrimage and the duty of all Christians. It was not neces-

WHAT IS YOUR NAME?

French pilgrims going to Compostela were called jacquets, jacquots, jacquaires, jacotes or jacobipètes, i.e., *those who will ask Saint James (Jacques).* Some of these names have provide common surnames. Besides the JACQUES, JACQUET, and JACOB present in all of France, the name JACQUOT is popular in Lorraine and the Vosges, JACQUEMARD in Burgundy, Jura and Savoy, JACQUELIN in the central regions of the country, JAMET in Normandy and Brittany, JAMMES in Languedoc, JAUME in Provence and Catalonia, and GIACOMO and GIACOBI on the Mediterranean coast. And finally, BOURDON (staff) and PELLERIN (from Pelerin, Pilgrim) present in the north, through their surnames also pay tribute to their ancestors who, long ago, went to pray in Compostela.

St James, Leon Cathedral

DOMENICO LAFFI

....

D omenico Laffi, a priest from
Bologna in Italy, went to
Compostela three times: in 1666,
1670 and 1673. He wrote an
account of his second voyage,
published under the title *Viaggio in
Ponente a San Giacomo di Galitia e
Finisterrae per Francia e Spagna.*
Leaving from Bologna, he went
through Milan, Turin, Mont-Cenis,
Briançon, Tallard, Carpentras,
Avignon, Nîmes and then joined
the *via Tolosana*, but avoided the
Somport Pass, preferring to cross
the Pyrenees by the Puerto de
Ibañeta, before following the usual
route of the *Camino francés.*

Maison Carrée, Nîmes

sary to make an actual voyage. But this spiritual pilgrimage, this
interior voyage preached by official Christianity, was confronted
with the daily reality of walkers for God. Very often, the pilgrim
who had come to beg for a cure, a miracle, or some other favour,
only dreamed of touching the statue, only making this ritual
motion through which he would enter into direct contact with the
sacred, which was not that of clerics trained in a seminary. And
though in France the Santiago pilgrimage regained popularity at
the beginning of the 17th century, under the reigns of kings
Henry IV (1589-1610) and Louis XIII (1610-1643), churchmen
were ever more reticent about allowing their flock to leave. Once
again, the pilgrimage of crowds was seen as a suspicious practice,
an escape from social and familial duties, and an encouragement
of laziness and wandering. At the end of the 17th century, the
rationalist thinking of the Enlightenment was not compatible with
the miracles and legends surrounding the cult of saints. It was no
longer the time of medieval marvels. Irrevocably condemned by
French philosophers and enlightened German despots, the pilgrimage was simply "a voyage of badly understood devotion" in the
terms of the authors of the *Encyclopedia* (1735). "There is no

Pilgrims fleeing from wolves, Roncesvalles Museum

longer this willingness to go and visit distant places, to receive
from Heaven aid that one can more easily find at home by good
works and enlightened devotion. In a word, this kind of travel is
only for professional travellers, rogues who, from superstition, laziness or debauchery, go to Our Lady of Loretto, or Santiago de
Compostela in Galicia, asking for alms along the way." This suspicion weighing on the pilgrims was not only that of clerics or
philosophers. Soon, civil authorities went to war against the holy
walkers, generally considered as "disreputable wanderers". In
France, after a series of restrictive measures, after 1738, any departure for a pilgrimage was subjected to the double approval of the
bishop and the king, and those who could not show their official
permit were threatened with permanent galley duty. And along

the routes, many hospitals were forced to close their doors by royal decree. Nonetheless, pilgrimages retained many of their followers, as attested by the registers of the Saint James confraternities, that show a sustained number of departures until the French Revolution. In Compostela, the 18th century saw the development of Baroque architecture dear to the Counter-Reformation. The sumptuous façade of the Obradoiro, the master work of the architect Fernando de Casas y Novoa, was superimposed onto the Romanesque façade of the cathedral. However, pilgrimages were not exempt from the religious persecution that followed the Revolution, nor by Napoleon's reign, during which they were strictly regulated, if not forbidden. Reduced to the condition of survivals of the past, scorned, denounced or persecuted, pilgrimages lost ground at the beginning of the 19th century. But soon, the Romantic movement once again encouraged "popular devotion" along the roads to Compostela, offering them a revival.

St James, Santiago

AMOROUS FEASTS

At the end of the 17th century and during the 18th, pilgrimages became an artistic and literary theme. In his tale *The Little Dog who Shook Silver and Precious Stones*, Jean de La Fontaine was one of the first to present a lover dressed as a pilgrim to meet his lady friend. Received at the academy as the painter of amorous feasts, Watteau contributed to the development of this artistic fashion, with his famous painting *Pilgrimage to the Island of Cythera*. Important people like President Mollé, the Marquise de Pompadour or even Louis XV were painted in pilgrims' costumes.

Louis XV, adolescent, in costume for "Pilgrim to Cythera"

Clock Tower, Santiago

Portico of Glory, Santiago de Compostela Cathedral

SANTIAGO TODAY

After the ordeal of wars and persecution, pilgrimages slowly increased in number during the second decade of the 19th century. If holy places attracted some illustrious travellers of the Romantic century, fascinated by the East and the Mediterranean, such as Chateaubriand or the poet Lamartine, the most popular pilgrimages were Marian, following the appearances of the Virgin in 1830 in the Rue du Bac in Paris, in 1846 at La Salette in Dauphiné, and finally, at Lourdes in 1858. On December 8, 1854, the Marian cult was reintroduced by Pope Pius IX, who proclaimed the dogma of Immaculate Conception, according to which the Virgin, raised above all the other saints, was conceived without original sin. At the time, the pilgrimage to Compostela was at a low. On July 25, 1867, only about forty pilgrims were present for the apostle's feast. Hidden at the end of the 16th century because of the threat of Drake and his pirates, Saint James's relics remained in an unknown location and seemed completely forgotten. In 1878, during restoration work on the cathedral, Cardinal Payá y Rico, archbishop of Compostela (1874-1886) decided to carry out excavations underneath the basilica, in order to definitively settle the question of the holy relics. After fruitless digging in five different places, it was decided to look under the high altar. The searchers brought to light the primitive tomb of Roman origin, that had been discovered by Bishop Theodomir, but no trace of the apostle's relics. Then, remembering a tradition according to which holy bodies were supposed to lie behind the high altar, the canons Labin and López Ferreiro, who were in charge of the excavation, decided to dig at the back of the chancel near the ambulatory. During the night of January 28-29, 1879, at a depth of one metre eighty, they discovered a small roughly made recess under the medieval pavement, containing the mixed-up and deteriorated bones of three

Virgin with Child by Botticelli

LOURDES

The route along the Pyrenees piedmont, a detour of the *via Tolosana*, passed through Lourdes, overlooked by its fortress. The latter had been besieged by Charlemagne in 778 when it was occupied by the Moors. Famine was threatening the besieged troops when an eagle dropped a trout at the feet of the chief, Mirat, who had it taken to the Frankish king to make him believe that they still had reserves. Charlemagne was about to lift the siege when the bishop of Puy accompanying him proposed to Mirat to surrender to Our Lady and not to Charlemagne. And so the Muslim chief laid down his arms at the feet of the Black Virgin of Puy and converted, taking the name Lorus, at the origin of the town's name of Lourdes. The town's coat of arms shows an eagle "holding a silver trout in its beak". In a surprising twist of history, after the Virgin appeared eighteen times to Bernadette Soubirous, between February 11 and July 16, 1858 and announced at the sixteenth appearance, "*Que soy era Immaculada Councepciou*", Lourdes became, and remains today, one of the great pilgrimage centres in the world, annually welcoming over five million pilgrims.

Fortress of Lourdes

Pilgrims today

different skeletons, probably buried in great haste. The enquiry to authenticate them, led by the archbishop of Compostela and then by the Congregation of Rites in Rome, lasted nearly five years. Finally, after comparing with the right mastoid apophysis, taken from Saint James's skull in 1138 in Compostela to be offered to bishop Atto of Pistoia, the canonical trial concluded that the remains discovered in 1879 were indeed those of James the Greater and his two disciples, Athanasius and Theodore, who had been worshipped in Santiago during the entire Middle Ages. The judgement was confirmed by the bull *Deus Omnipotens,* promulgated by Pope Leon XIII (1878-1903) on November 1, 1884. But during a period when positivism prevailed, the pontifical decision rapidly drew criticism from eminent historians of the Church's origins, such as Monseigneur Duchesne (1843-1922) who, in a memorable, cutting article, published in 1900 in the *Annales du Midi,* ruined the historical foundations of Saint James's evangelism in Spain. After meticulous analysis of the texts upon which Compostelan tradition rested, the religious scholar concluded, "From all that is said about Saint James's preaching in Spain, the translation of his remains, and the discovery of his tomb, only one fact remains – the Galician cult. It dates back to the first third of the 9th century and is addressed to a tomb from Roman times, which was then believed to be that of Saint James. Why was this believed? We know nothing about this." Besides, as the article's author discreetly insinuated, was not this tomb discovered by Bishop Theodomir rather that of the bishop of Avila, the Priscillian heresiarch, who was beheaded in Trier along with two of his disciples in 385, and whose body was brought back to Galicia to be buried? Much ink was spilled in discussing this thesis. Despite everything, the second *invention* of Saint James's relics in Compostela had indeed restored pilgrims' spirit. While scholars and professors such as Joseph Bédier or Emile Mâle praised the cultural impact of the Santiago pilgrimage in the rise and expansion of literary and architectural styles of the medieval period, some set out on the holy road, in the steps of the first pilgrims. After the strife of the two world wars, the phenomenon continued to develop. In 1950, on the anniversary of the millenium of the pilgrimage by Bishop Godescalc of Puy, Jean Babelon, head librarian at the French National Library, founded the "Society of Friends of Santiago de Compostela", with the purpose of promoting "the study of artistic, literary, religious and social movements caused in Europe by devotion to Saint James the Greater, particularly demonstrated by the great pilgrimage to Compostela". In 1987, the Council of Europe officially proclaimed the roads to Santiago "European cultural itineraries". The flood of pilgrims walking to Compostela continues to increase: in 1985 there were 619, 1,800 in 1986, 2,905 in 1987, 3,051 in 1988, and 5,760 in 1989, the year in which Pope John-Paul II went to Santiago de Compostela for the fourth World Youth Day. Many thousands more went to Santiago in 1999, during the last jubilee year of the 20th century.

BEACON BETWEEN TWO WORLDS

The thesis according to which the relics found in Galicia in the 9th century were in fact those of Priscillian and two of his disciples was insinuated in 1900 by Monseigneur Duchesne and revived by several scholars and historians, faced with the rarity of documents attesting the evangelization of Spain by James the Greater. Even film makers ventured into the field, such as Buñuel in The *Milky Way.* But twentieth century scepticism has not prevented pilgrims, in their thousands and in ever increasing numbers, from taking the road to the stars. So, to respond to the arguments of the sceptics of the Santiago tradition, perhaps the best is to let Saint James himself answer, in *The Satin Shoe*: "I, a beacon between the two worlds, those that the chasm separates have only to look at me to find themselves together. I take up too much space in the sky for any eye to be mistaken... The happy and the satisfied do not look at me. It is pain that makes the great hole in the world through which my semaphore is set."

The Botafumeiro, Santiago de Compostela Cathedral

2

ROADS

1

THE EUROPEAN ISTHMUS

Coming from the British Isles, the Scandinavian or Germanic countries, Bohemia, Italy, France or Spain, pilgrims from all of Europe, nourished by the same fervour, walked towards Santiago de Compostela. Leaning on their staffs, drinking from their gourds, by various paths they joined one of the four great roads crossing France, that joined to make one in Spain, as far as Santiago. On this "European isthmus", so-called by René de la Coste-Messelière, stand churches, hospitals, monasteries, redoubts, towns and cities – witnesses of more than a millennium of artistic expression. Above all, a European conscience was forged here. And Goethe wrote: "Europe was born in a pilgrimage and Christianity is its mother tongue."

St James, church in Lübeck

CRUEL DILEMMA

....

S aint Vaast d'Arras Abbey was
proud of its long possession
of James the Greater's skull,
once offered by a king of France.
But such a precious relic attracted
the greed of a certain Robert,
provost at the chapter of Aire,
who, with his friend Philip,
Count of Flanders, conceived
a plan to acquire it. Hence,
the count went to Arras, grabbed
the skull and brought it to the
church in Aire, which was solemnly
consecrated shortly afterwards,
to the great displeasure of the
abbot of Arras. The latter,
bitterly defending his rights,
stirred up such a conflict that
Pope Alexander III was forced
to intervene. Following a biblical
example, the pontiff found a
solution to the conflict in 1172
by having the alleged apostle's
skull cut in half. The forepart
remained in Aire; the rear section
was returned to Saint Vaast.
Following these events, Count
Philip left for Santiago de
Compostela, in order to make
sure of the relic's authenticity.
He came back very disappointed,
because the only real skull of Saint
James was indeed in Santiago.
Picked up by his disciples along
with the rest of his body after his
beheading in Jerusalem, it had
arrived in Galicia in a small boat
guided by Providence.

Jesus Christ, 10th c. runic stone at Jelling in Denmark

Münster Cathedral

FROM ALL OF CHRISTIANITY

The pilgrimage to Compostela acquired international fame during the 12th century. Britons, Flemings, citizens of Hanseatic towns, Scandinavians, Germans from the Rhinelands or the southern lands, Swiss, Italians, Poles, Hungarians, Bohemians – all, as pilgrims coming from all of Christian Europe, arrived by numerous, varied routes, by land and by sea, and rejoined the four great roads, *Tolosana, Podiensis, Lemovicensis* and *Turonensis*, that all became one – at Puente la Reina, to form the *Camino francés* leading to the tomb of the apostle James, in Santiago de Compostela. The Germans, the *Guide*'s "Teutons", many of whom in the 12th century took the *via Podiensis*, later preferred to follow the *Oberstrasse* like the Swiss, pilgrims from Central Europe or some Northern Italians. This road led from the Benedictine abbey of Einsiedeln, Bern and Geneva to Valence and continued to Pont-Saint-Esprit, until it joined the *via Tolosana* in Saint Gilles, or in Montpellier via Aigues Mortes. On their way home, German pilgrims willingly took the *via Turonensis* and the *Niederstrasse* which, leaving Paris, reached Cologne through Aachen, Brussels, Valenciennes, Arras and Amiens. Gathering at Lübeck, Danes and other Scandinavians could join the *Niederstrasse* via Hamburg, Bremen, and Münster. From Haarlem or Utrecht, the Dutch crossed towards Brussels and Paris through Antwerp, then

St James, Amiens Cathedral

THE ABBEY OF EINSIEDELN

Founded in 934, on the spot where Saint Meinrad, a monk of Reichenau, had been assassinated in 861, the abbey of Einsiedeln, enjoying numerous royal privileges, was an active centre of monastic reform during the 10th and 11th centuries.

Map of principal roads to Santiago de Compostela in Europe

- Niederstrasse
- Oberstrasse
- Via Francigena
- Ruta de la Plata
- Via Turonensis
- Via Lemovicensis
- Via Podiensis
- Via Tolosana
- Camino francés
- Other road
- Other site

0   200 km

The principal roads to Santiago de Compostela in Europe

A canal in Bruges

A White Lie

Founded in 1015, the abbey of Saint James in Liège was originally dedicated to James the Less. But in 1056, the monks from Liège who had been sent to Santiago did not hesitate to tell a white lie by claiming that their abbey was dedicated to James the Greater. After many discussions, they managed to receive important relics of the saints Pancras and Sebastian, and especially, a fragment of an arm belonging to Saint James the Greater. And towards 1078, after the foundation of a hospice called Saint James in Liège, the abbey definitely changed the patronage of the Less to the Greater.

through Bruges, Ghent, where a church dedicated to James the Greater was built in 1093, or Lille. The Flemings met the *Niederstrasse* at Arras or Amiens. Leaving from Aachen, a road led to Paris more directly through Liège, Namur, then Reims or Soissons. Similarly, leaving from Frankfurt or Koblenz, there was a road passing through Trier and Arlon, joining the *via Lemovicensis* via Châlons, Troyes, and Auxerre, or else there was the *Oberstrasse* through Metz, Toul, Dijon, and Lyons. Furthermore, the Scandinavians, Dutch and Flemish often travelled by sea, like the English and Bretons. Hanseatic merchants, embarking at Reval (Tallinn), Lübeck, Hamburg or Bruges, took advantage of their business travels to accomplish the pilgrimage. Embarking at Sandwich, Winchelsea, Brighton or Portsmouth, English pilgrims reached the Normandy coast in Dieppe, and through Rouen joined the *via Turonensis* at Chartres. Embarking in Plymouth, they reached the bay of Mont Saint Michel then joined the *via Turonensis* either at Poitiers via Angers, or at Saint-Jean d'Angély, via Rennes and Nantes. Others landed at La Rochelle, Soulac or Bordeaux. However, during the Hundred Years War, they sailed directly to La Coruña.

As for Italian pilgrims, there were many who had embarked at ports on the Tyrrhenian Sea, landing in Barcelona or Tarragona, then followed the roads of the great Marian shrines of Montserrat and Zaragoza, before joining the *Camino francés* in Logroño. Overland, there were two possible routes towards the *via Tolosana* in Arles or in Saint-Gilles via Avignon. The coast road along the Ligurian coast, following the old Roman *via Aurelia* that joined Civitavecchia to Arles, or the Alpine way through Montgenèvre Pass, taking the *via Francigena*. Born during the High Middle Ages from the reconstitution of ancient Roman roads by the Lombards, the *via Francigena*, crossing the principal Italian cities, was the traditional route, and that most often taken by Italian pilgrims to Santiago. Leaving from Rome, it gathered pilgrims from regions in the centre and the south, then, via Viterba and Acquapendente,

Nave, St James Church in Liège

The Porta Nigra in Trier

Saint James Tower in Namur

CARTA ITINERARIA EUROPAE
....

D rawn between 1470 and 1511 and dedicated to Emperor Charles Quint, the *carta itineraria Europae* showed the principal communication routes of the time, which were also those taken by pilgrims going to Santiago. Placing the north at the bottom and the south at the top, it is orientated contrary to modern maps, which explains the Germanic names of *Oberstrasse*, "the upper way", and the *Niederstrasse*, "the lower way".

Angel Gabriel, Reims Cathedral

AACHEN

At the end of the 8th century, Charlemagne (747-814) set his residence in the north of the Eifel range, in the location of the antique *Aquae Grani*, a spa well-known for its hot water springs, abandoned by the Romans in about 375. Of the vast palace built starting in 790, only the *Aula*, the reception room, and the chapel containing Charlemagne's tomb remain. Built between 796 and 805, the chapel's plan associated a central octagon, surrounded by aisles, with an exterior periphery with sixteen sides. In the west, a square porch flanked by two staircase towers provided access to the galleries where the emperor sat on a throne filled with relics, constructed on the model of King Solomon's throne. From there, he overlooked the high altar on the ground floor, dedicated to the Virgin, and faced the Christ of the Apocalypse, shown on the mosaics of the dome, and the altar of the Holy Saviour. Columns of porphyry, Corinthian capitals of white marble, and mosaics decorate the entire building. By his coronation in Aachen in 936, Otto 1st (912-973) started the tradition according to which Germanic sovereigns had to be crowned in the Palatine chapel, then in 1165, on the occasion of Charlemagne's canonization, Frederick de Barbarossa (1122-1190) raised Aachen to a free city and capital of his empire. In 1175, Aachen received a fortified wall, and in 1267, the municipal council had a city hall built on the location of the *Aula palatina*. Starting in 1349, pilgrimages were organized every seven years to worship the numerous relics in the chapel (the Virgin's tunic, the Infant Jesus's swaddling clothes,…) and also in 1349, an annual fair attracted many merchants into the city.

Reliquary of Charlemagne, treasure of Aachen Cathedral

Bargello Palace in Florence

THE ALTOPASCIO ORDER

....

Towards the middle of the 11th century, several Luccan nobles decided to found a hospital to receive Santiago pilgrims and travellers on the *via Francigena*. Built near a small stream, the Teopascio, the foundation was at first called by the Latin terms *ad Theupascium* "near the Teopascio". However, the first Italian texts attached the preposition to the noun, creating the name *Altipasso*, which became *Altopasso*, then *Altopascio*. Soon, a real hospitaller network grew out of this hospital, multiplying its dependencies along the *via Francigena* and throughout all of Europe. In 1226, Gallico, rector and grand master of Altopascio, undertook the organization of what had become a hospitaller order. He enlarged the hospital, fortified the town born beside it, and wrote the rule of the Hospitaller Order of Saint James of Altopascio, approved by Pope Gregory IX in 1239. In Europe, the order was commonly called by the approximate literal translation of *Altopascio*, giving in France, *Haut-Pas*, in Spain, *Alto-Paso*, and in England, *High Gate*.

reached Siena with its hospital *dei pelligrini* and its two churches dedicated to Saint James. Crossing the hills of the left bank of the Elsa, through San Giminiano it reached the shores of the Arno near San Miniato al Monte, then took the direction of Altopascio, seat of the hospitaller's order of the same name, to arrive in Lucca, a town with many hospitals, where the crucifix of the Holy Face, attributed to Nicomedus, allegedly coming from Palestine in a ship without a crew, was the object of great devotion. However, by the 13th century, pilgrims preferred a different, easier itinerary along the right bank of the Elsa, via Piggibonsi and Castelfiorentino, an itinerary located on Florentine lands and that Florence, in its expansionist policies, reinforced and provided with establishments to receive travellers. Hence, many pilgrims made the detour through the Tuscan capital, the site of many hospitals, including that of Saint James of Oltarno, founded in 1300, then took the time to visit Pistoia, the city to which the archbishop of Compostela, Diego Gelmírez, had offered an important relic of the apostle James in 1140. The old itinerary of the *via Francigena*, once past Lucca, took the direction of Sarzana, then following the course of the Magra River, crossed the Apennines at Cisa Pass, to reach Parma and Fidenza, cities at which pilgrims arrived from Apulia, after following the Adriatic coast by Pescara, San Benedetto and Ancona, to take the *via Emilia* in Rimini as far as Bologna. Those who had detoured by Florence and Pistoia, then crossed the Apennines at Poretta Pass in the direction of Bologna,

Santa Maria a Piè di Chienti in the Ancona Region

PISTOIA

St James, altar of Saint Zenon Cathedral, Pistoia

In 1140, the bishop of Compostela, Diego Gelmírez, offered to the blessed Atto, Bishop of Pistoia, the right mastoid apophysis from the skull of James the Greater. Kept in a silver altar, carved and hammered by the most renowned silversmiths of Siena, Pistoia and Florence, from 1287 and until the 15th century, the relic was placed in a chapel specially built in honour of Saint James, in the right aisle of the city's *Duomo* or cathedral. With its six hundred and twenty-eight figures, the altar, mentioned by Dante in his *Divine Comedy*, presents, in its upper section, Christ in majesty with, below him, Saint James seated and surrounded by a procession of saints. The lower section evokes biblical scenes, as well as the apostle's life. Among the hospital institutions in Pistoia, the actual Palace of Tau contained the convent of the Antonine hospitaller order. The façade of the *Ospedale del Ceppo* was given, in the 16th century, a porch with arcades on columns, decorated with a remarkable frieze in enamelled terracotta, illustrating works of mercy practiced in the hospitals for the ill, travellers and pilgrims.

Detail of frieze of the Ospedale del Ceppo, Pistoia

113

also rejoined the *via Francigena* at Parma. After Fidenza, the *via Francigena* reached the shores of the Po River and the city of Piacenza, an important crossroads for pilgrims arriving from Veneto and the Balkans, but also those coming to Italy from southern Germany through the Brenner Pass. Following the river's course as far as Alessandria, it continued towards Turin, then crossed the Suze valley, where many Benedictine and Cartesian monasteries were installed, before crossing the Alps at Montgenèvre Pass, taking the historical itinerary taken long ago by Julius Caesar to invade Gaul, and before him, but in the opposite direction, Hannibal of Carthage with his elephants to attack Italy. Once the Alps were crossed, the pilgrims reached Briançon, and not far away, the chapel of Saint James of Prelles, decorated with frescoes showing the legend of the *hanged-unhanged*. After going along the course of the Durance River through Embrun, Tallard, and Sisteron, once past the Cluniac priory of Ganagobie, they turned their steps westwards in the direction of Apt. Passing not far from Gordes and the Cistercian abbey of Senanque, they then joined the *via Tolosana* at Arles, coming from Cavaillon. However, beginning in the 14th century, Avignon, the seat of the papacy from 1309 to 1377, became one of the most important cultural and artistic centres in Europe. It contained a large colony of Italians and, to the detriment of Arles, attracted many Italian Santiago pilgrims who gathered there before joining the *via Tolosana* at Saint Gilles. In Avignon, the pilgrims of the *via Francigena* met up with those who had taken the itinerary along the Ligurian coast, whose principal stages after Sarzana were Genoa, Savona, Ventimiglia, and Nice, then inland, Grasse, Draguignan, and Saint-Maximin-la-Sainte-Baume, before reaching Aix and Arles or Avignon. Shorter and less difficult than the traditional itinerary, the coast route was taken starting in the 13th century, once the *via Aurelia* had been restored in the region of the Bracco range, but never rivalled the importance of the *via Francigena*.

Fresco in Prelles Chapel

Chevet of Senanque Abbey

Mosaic in priory of Ganagobie

Sisteron

Papal Palace in Avignon

St James Chapel in Cavaillon

MONT SAINT MICHEL

Originally a forest covered the ground at the foot of granite rocks. Then the sea expanded and the rocks became small islands. One of them, standing nearly eight metres high, had been inhabited ever since the 7th century by hermits, who were attracted by the solitude of the peak emerging out of the fog, surrounded by the danger of the waters. Favourable for meditation and prefiguring spiritual elevation, the place was known by the name of Mount Tomb – a name perhaps derived from the Celtic, or from the Latin *tumba*, with the double meaning of tumulus and tomb. It was one of the first western shrines dedicated to Saint Michael the Archangel. The protector of Israel and the synagogue, then of the church, "prince of the people of God", and "prince of the angels", Michael, whose name, from the Hebrew *Mi/ka/el* meaning "who (is) like unto God?", had been mentioned in the 2nd century BC in the *Book of Daniel*. An emanation of the supreme principle, as an Archangel Michael belonged to the next to last choir of the celestial hierarchy of nine choirs, established in the 5th century. In the literature of Revelation, he was the warrior angel, fighting the Evil of the fallen angel, of the Devil embodied in a dragon. The dispenser of justice, Michael was also the psychopomp who led and weighed the souls on the day of the Last Judgement. In 314, Emperor Constantine had the first shrine dedicated to him built in Constantinople. Then in the 5th century, devotion to Saint Michael, eastern in its origins, came westwards through Italy. In 492, the Archangel appeared on Monte Gargano in Apulia, then, in 590 in Rome, where the mausoleum of the Emperor Hadrian containing a church took the name of Castel Sant-Angelo.

The *Revelatio ecclesiae sancti Michaelis*, written in the middle of the 9th century tells that, according to oral tradition, in 708, Aubert, bishop of Avranches, in a dream saw the Archangel Michael, who asked him to build an oratory in his honour, on the north slope of Mount Tomb, on the place a lost bull had trampled. After two more appearances, the bishop was convinced and had a first shrine dedicated to the Archangel built, with the miraculous help of a child who, all alone, rolled enormous stones by simply touching them with his foot, to clear and flatten the area. Several years later, the name of the island was changed to Saint Michael's Mount, or Mont Saint Michel. On the altar of the new shrine, Aubert placed two relics that his messengers had gone to get from the Italian monastery of Monte Gargano: a piece of the red coat that the Archangel was wearing during one of his appearances, and a piece of the stone on which he had placed his foot. Twelve canons were installed as guardians of the hill sanctuary, which was destined to become one the principal pilgrimage destinations of Christianity. In 927, William Long-Sword, son of Rollon, the first duke of Normandy in 911, granted important donations to Mont Saint Michel's canons. But his successor Richard 1st, Duke of Normandy from 942-996, was to chase them out, probably to better establish his authority in a place lastingly influenced by Breton domination. They were replaced in 965 by twelve Benedictine monks from Fontenelle Abbey, later named Saint Wandrille, under the leadership of their Flemish abbot Maynard. The arrival of the Benedictine monks gave a new impetus to the cult of Saint Michael, consecrating the spiritual and architectural birth of the abbey.

The original church was then rebuilt, before becoming a crypt, known today as Notre-Dame-sous-Terre (Our Lady under ground), for the abbey church raised on the rocky summit in 1023. It contained a nave with seven triple-elevated bays, a transept, and a sanctuary that collapsed in 1421, to be replaced in 1466 by the current chancel in Flamboyant Gothic style, with its flying buttresses, its pinnacles and balustrades. In the 11th century, the Cluniac reform, spread in Normandy by Guillaume de Volpiano (962-1031), was introduced in Mont Saint Michel. But the choice of its abbots was nonetheless subject to the approval of the dukes of Normandy, and when the mount's monks freely elected Ranulphe de Bayeux to replace abbot Raoul de Beaumont, named by William the Conqueror (1027-1087), the new abbot was sure to send Duke William, who had meanwhile become king of England after his victory at Hastings in 1066, six ships loaded with gifts as a sign of respect and submission. The duke-king responded generously, offering Ranulphe four English monasteries, among which was the Cornwall replica of Mont Saint Michel. However, this interference of ducal power created grave problems, like that from 1149 to 1153 opposing abbot Robert de la Manche, the pope's cousin, whose nomination had been ratified by the Holy See, and abbot Robert Hardi, elected with the approval of Henry II Plantagenet (1133-1189). The quarrel ended only with the death of the two protagonists and the arrival, in 1154, of the great abbot Robert de Thorigny, former prior of Bec-Hellouin, whose intellectual prestige left a lasting imprint on the Mount abbey. Under his leadership (1154-1186) the abbey reached the peak of its influence. Robert welcomed Henry II to the Mount three times, once, in 1154, with his adversary the king of France, Louis VII (1137-1180). He provided the abbey's scriptorium with a decisive impetus, making Mont Saint Michel the "city of books", whose history was written in verse in the vernacular by a young monk-poet,

Guillaume de Saint-Pair. Robert also tried to increase the renown of the Mount's pilgrimage, attracting a growing number of pilgrims whose offerings allowed the construction of new buildings. Robert's death, then the conquest of Normandy in 1204 by Philippe Auguste (1180-1223) turned a page in the history of Mont Saint Michel,

henceforth placed under the protection of the kings of France, such as Saint Louis (1126-1270) and Philippe le Bel (1285-1314) who presented the abbey with donations, leading to the completion of the Gothic "Wonder". Raised on three levels, on the northern slope of the mount, and supported by powerful buttresses, it was begun in 1204. On the upper level, that of the church, it contains the refectory and the cloister. The middle level contains the guests hall and the knights hall, originally reserved for monks who came to work there and to warm up. However, tradition has it that the Royal Order of Saint Michael, instituted by Louis XI, held its first chapter there in 1470. Finally, the pilgrims' almshouse and the cellar occupy the lower level. During the Hundred Years War (1337-1453), Mont Saint Michel was the seat of a garrison and was transformed into an impregnable citadel. As the patron saint of armies, during those troubled times the Archangel Michael enjoyed great popularity in France and soon appeared to a young girl in Lorraine, Joan of Arc. Starting in 1333, the "shepherds crusades", ardent processions of children and adolescents, also came to pay him homage. But in the 15th century, the commendatory system brought on the decline of an abbey that was to suffer further during the Wars of Religion. The Maurist reform in 1662 could not stave off the inevitable, and in 1789 the Revolution chased out the last of the monks. Transformed into a prison, the abbey sheltered rebellious priests, chouans or royalist rebels from Western France, then in the 19th century, political prisoners such as Barbès or Blanqui. Classified as a historical monument in 1874 by Mac-Mahon, its restoration was undertaken and completed in 1965 with the arrival of monks from Saint-Wandrille and Bec-Hellouin.

Mont Saint Michel

Saint James Tower in Paris

Via Turonensis

Gathering Santiago pilgrims coming from northern and north-eastern Europe in Paris, the "great road to Santiago" led, through Orléans or Chartres, to the famous shrine of Saint Martin of Tours, hence giving it the name *via Turonensis*. After the Poitou, loved by Aimery Picaud, and the marvellous Romanesque churches of Saintonge, epic heroes took on a new life at the shrines of Bordeaux, Blaye and Belin, giving pilgrims the strength to affront the arid crossing of the moors and the heights of Cize and Roncesvalles passes before finally reaching the land of the apostle James and rejoining, via Pamplona, the *Camino francés* at Puente la Reina.

Paris

Entering Paris by rue Saint-Martin or rue Saint-Denis, the seat of a hospital founded by the city's Saint James confraternity at the beginning of the 14th century, the pilgrims attended mass at Saint-Jacques-de-la-Boucherie church, on the site of which a chapel dedicated to the apostle had already existed in 1079. Of this building, enlarged over the centuries, only the tower remains. Raised in the early 16th century in Flamboyant Gothic style, it was the starting point of the four hundred leagues separating the pilgrims from the cathedral in Santiago de Compostela. After a detour by Notre Dame, entering rue Saint-Jacques after crossing the Seine River by the little bridge, the pilgrims passed Saint-Severin church, the residence of the abbots of Cluny, whose façade is decorated with many scallop shells, and the Jacobin convent located near Saint-Jacques gate on Montagne-Sainte-Geneviève. This Dominican convent was installed in a pilgrims' hospice, founded in 1206 by a doctor of theology who, in 1218, offered it to Saint Dominic's spiritual heirs, who had arrived in Paris a year earlier. With the encouragement of Queen Blanche of Castile (1223-1252) and her son, Saint Louis (1226-1270), this hospital and its Saint James's chapel were enlarged, to become the first *studium generale* of the Order of the Preaching Brothers, from then on commonly called Jacobins. In his collection of anecdotes, the friar Etienne Bourbon told how the bishop of Paris, Guillaume d'Auvergne, had long before urged Blanche of Castile, wishing to go to Santiago on pilgrimage, to use the money for her journey for other purposes: "Take your purse, Madam", he said, "go to the Friars of Saint James and buy back their debt." Crossing the Philippe Auguste ramparts, the pilgrims followed the faubourg (suburb) of Saint Jacques, at whose entrance the Italian hospitaller order, the *Altopascio*, High Gate, present in Paris since the 13th century, had founded a commandery in 1322. Before leaving Paris in the direction of Etampes, pilgrims threw a ritual stone at the Issoire Tomb, which provided the name of the present street. It was there that the pious William, temporarily leaving his desert of Gellone, had come to aid King Louis and gave the fatal blow to the Moorish giant Isoré who wanted to take the city.

Stages	Kms
Paris	925
Orléans *	808
Cléry-Saint-André	794
Tours *	700
Châtellerault	635
Poitiers *	599
Melle	543
Aulnay	514
Saint-Jean-d'Angély *	498
Saintes *	467
Pons	447
Blaye *	391
Bordeaux *	345
Belin-Béliet *	306
Saugnacq-et-Muret	291
Vieux-Richet	282
Saint-Paul-lès-Dax	190
Sorde-l'Abbaye	164
Sauveterre-de-Béarn	145
Saint-Palais	133
Gibraltar Stele	130
Ostabat	120
Saint-Jean-Pied-de-Port	102
Saint-Michel □	98
Puerto de Ibañeta	73
Roncesvalles *	71
Viscarret-Guerendiain □	59
Pamplona □	24
Puente la Reina	0

References from the *Guide* by Aimery Picaud:
□: Stages
*: Presence of "holy bodies"

Tomb of Louis XI in Cléry

THE MIRACLE OF SAINT EUVERTE

···

O ne day as St Euverte celebrated the holy sacrifice in Holy Cross Cathedral in Orléans, the hand of God appeared above the altar, blessing the bread and wine with the priest. Pilgrims and faithful could ask to take communion from this precious chalice.

To Tours via Orléans

Departing from Paris, the road to Etampes started with Saint-Jacques de Montrouge. Leaving behind Artenay, the pilgrims reached the shores of the Loire River and the fortified city of Orléans. A prestigious episcopal seat during the Carolingian period, the city, rich in relics where pilgrims following the *Guide* were supposed to go and worship the wood of the Cross at the cathedral, and the knife of the Last Supper at Saint Samson Church, displayed particular devotion to one of its first bishops, Saint Euverte, the object of a special miracle reported by Aimery Picaud. The Augustinian abbey of Saint Euverte, located beyond the city's ramparts, held the relics of its holy patron that pilgrims did not fail to visit before continuing on their way. On the way out of Orléans, some made a detour to the east, in order to go and pray at the sacred relics of Saint Benedict, kept since 673 by the Benedictines at the abbey of Fleury-sur-Loire. But the main road continued in the direction of Notre-Dame de Cléry Basilica, a shrine of Marian pilgrimages since 1280. Destroyed during the Hundred Years War, Louis XI (1461-1483), a fervent pilgrim of Our Lady, had it rebuilt in Flamboyant Gothic style, before being buried there in 1483. Continuing their route, the pilgrims reached the fortified city of the powerful counts of Blois, where they were welcomed by the monks of Saint Lomer Abbey, of which Saint Nicholas Abbey Church survives, before arriving in Tours via Amboise.

Chevet of Fleury Abbey Church, Saint-Benoît-sur-Loire

PARIS TO TOURS VIA CHARTRES

T he alternate route to Tours via Chartres was taken by many pilgrims, especially those coming from England and the provinces of western France. Leaving Chartres, they reached the shores of the Loir River and Saint Florentin de Bonneval Abbey, and from there, by way of Marboué, the fortified town of Châteaudun, the former capital of the Counts of Dunois. At Cloyes, their next stage, they could find shelter at the Trinity hospital and pray in Saint George's Church at the beautiful polychrome stone statue of Saint James. In 1212, a young shepherd had left Cloyes for the Holy Land, taking with him twenty thousand children, who all disappeared. Following the Loir valley, the pilgrims soon reached Vendôme, where the Benedictine monks of the powerful Trinity Abbey welcomed them. It had been founded in 1053 and affiliated to Marmoutier. A pilgrimage shrine – possessing one of St George's arms and a Holy Tear of Christ – the abbey received the unique title of cardinal abbey, its abbots being named cardinals automatically, by decision of Pope Alexander II. The pilgrims could make a detour by Saint James Chapel in Vendôme, before heading in the direction of Saint-Genest de Lavardin Priory. Its fine church, dating from the end of the 11th century, is decorated with remarkable wall paintings, the oldest of which, located in the choir, show the baptism of Christ and the Tree of Jesse. The priory chapel of Saint-Gilles in Montoire, the next stage of the route, also has very fine frescoes in the apse and the transept. From Montoire, the pilgrims reached Tours directly or through Saint-Jacques-des-Guérets, whose church contains another remarkable set of frescoes, including one showing the beheading of Saint James.

Chevet of the Trinity Abbey Church in Vendôme

Fresco in Lavardin Priory

Fresco in Saint-Jacques-des-Guérets

121

CHARTRES, PILGRIMAGE SITE

Leaving from Paris, some pilgrims reached Tours by going through Chartres, a famous Marian shrine. The Virgin had been particularly worshipped in Chartres very early on. A *Life* of Saint Béthaire, bishop of Chartres in the 6th century, claimed that at that time a church dedicated to the Virgin already existed in the town on the Beauce plain. Loved by the Carolingian monarchs, especially Pepin the Short who provided donations before 768, the church Saint Mary of Chartres was to receive from Charles the Bald in 876 an extremely important relic, formerly offered to Charlemagne by the emperor of Byzantium – the Holy Tunic worn by Mary at the time of the Annunciation, during the conception of the Word. Carefully enclosed in a cedar-wood reliquary, it was supposed to attract numerous pilgrims and place the Chartres shrine under its protection. Unfurled like a banner by Bishop Gantelme at the New Gate in 911, did it not set to flight the Norsemen besieging the town?

James the Greater, fresco in the crypt

Converted, their chief Rollon hastened to honour the venerable church with his gifts. Soon, Chartres became the most famous centre of Marian pilgrimage north of the Loire River. And to maintain all the purity of the Virgin's shrine, its pavement was set at a slight angle so that it could be easily washed following feast days, after the departure of the crowds of pilgrims. No-one was allowed to be buried there, and the chapter's acts were sealed with pure wax. Several buildings, each larger than the previous one, succeeded each other before the construction of the present cathedral, begun in 1194 after fire had destroyed the Romanesque cathedral. Of the latter, there remain the crypt and the triple carved western doorway, called the "royal door", built starting in 1144, framed by two high towers. The boldness and innovation of the master builder in 1194, evident in the plan and the architecture of the new Gothic cathedral, marked the development and command of the style. Chartres became the model for cathe-

Reliquary of the Virgin's Veil

drals in Reims, Amiens, Beauvais, and others. Its plan is comprised of a nave with six bays, with side aisles continuing along the arms of the transept, taking on the appearance of a veritable transverse nave. The chancel, with four bays, is encircled by an ambulatory with seven decorated chapels, alternately shallow and deep. The master of Chartres decided against roofing in six parts, as used by his predecessors, for four-sectioned roofing that allowed him to eliminate alternating supports

Notre-Dame Cathedral

St James preaching in a synagogue, window in Notre-Dame Cathedral

James the Greater and James the Less

and to have a bay of the central nave correspond to a lateral bay. Perfectly mastering the art of flying buttresses, he eliminated galleries, a buttressing element that had become useless, to complete an elevation of three storeys, with great arches, triforium and high windows. Finally bay and rose windows were decorated with a remarkable set of stained glass, made during the first third of the 13th century. The pilgrim choosing to make a detour through Chartres, before rejoining the *via Turonensis* at the shrine of Saint Martin, found in the cathedral of Our Lady of Chartres multiple representations of the apostle he had sworn to go and worship in Galicia. From the cathedral crypt, where he appears on the fresco with its centuries old colours in Saint Clement's chapel, dressed in a coat spotted with white shells, to the brilliant high stained-glass windows in the nave and chancel, to those in the side chapels of the ambulatory. At the central door-

way of the southern façade, where he stands sculpted in stone, carrying the sword of his martyrdom and the scrip of the eternal pilgrim, James the Greater still comforts the soul of walk-

ers, and his presence illuminates the shrine raised to the glory of the Virgin Mary. Was it not to the great bishop of Chartres, the very holy Fulbert (1006-1028) that tradition ascribes the composition, in honour of Saint James, of four liturgical pieces contained in the first book of the *Codex Calixtinus*?

Column-statues of the Royal door in Notre-Dame Cathedral

Charlemagne's Tower in Tours

Tours

As a major stage along the way, the city of Tours gave its name to the *via Turonensis* leading to Santiago de Compostela. A bishopric from the 4th century on, it remained famous for the pilgrimage to the tomb of its second bishop, Martin (371-397). Under the episcopate of Perpetuus (458-488), the Martinian pilgrimage greatly developed. A basilica replaced the modest chapel built in 437 over the saint's tomb, and his miracles, gathered in a collection, spread the fame of the "apostle of the Gauls". Along with the crowds of anonymous pilgrims, Clotaire 1st (558-561), preceded by Clovis (481-511) and his wife Clotilde, but also religious figures such as Saint Genevieve and the Fathers of the Jura came to worship at Saint Martin's tomb. Eloi provided it with superb gold plate, at the instigation of Dagobert 1st (629-639). The abbey that had sprung up around Saint Martin's Basilica adopted the Benedictine rule in the 7th century, before becoming a collegiate church in the 9th century. Alcuin was its abbot from 796 to 804, and in the 10th century, with its two hundred canons, it contained the largest community in the kingdom. Around the year 1000, given the increase in the number of pilgrims, the construction of a larger basilica was undertaken. This was replaced at the end of the 11th century by a building of enormous proportions, about a hundred metres long, provided, like the great pilgrimage churches, with an ambulatory permitting easy circulation around the chancel, comparable to the basilica of Santiago de Compostela, according to Aimery Picaud. "One should [...] visit, on the shores of the Loire, the venerable body of Saint Martin, bishop and confessor. [...] The reliquary where his precious relics rest next to the city of Tours, shine with the profusion of gold, silver and precious stones, it is rendered illustrious by frequent miracles. Overhead, an immense and venerable basilica has been magnificently raised in his honour, in the image of the church of Saint James." However, the troubles of the Wars of Religion were

A capital in Saint Martin's Basilica, Tours

THE BENEDICTINE RULE

Born in about 490 in Nursia, in the Umbrian Appenines, the young Benedict was sent to study law and rhetoric in Rome. But it was to absorb "learned ignorance" that he decided to retire to the desert of Subiaco, in the upper valley of the Aniene River, where he forced himself to follow an extremely ascetic regime. As his fame grew, he founded twelve small monasteries gathering together the local hermits before settling, in 530, on the summit of Monte Cassino, where he became the abbot of a community for which he wrote, starting in 534 and probably until his death in 547, a "short rule for beginners", the fruit of his long experience. Taking inspiration from the rule of a master who has remained anonymous, Benedict defined a completely cenobitic way of life. Grouped around the abbot, to whom they vowed obedience, the monks also made vows of chastity and stability, lived in mutual humility, silence and charity, dividing their time between moments of prayer, the *lectio divina*, and manual work. Clear, relatively short, and of moderate asceticism, the Benedictine rule did not immediately become accepted in western monasteries, despite its qualities, its sense of moderation and its realism. Under the impetus of Pope Gregory the Great (590-604), a fervent admirer of Saint Benedict, it was adopted in Anglo-Saxon monasteries and, from there, it expanded into Germanic lands, especially through the action of Saint Boniface. At the same time, the reconstruction of Monte Cassino in 718, and the support of Carolingian monarchs contributed to its rise, so much that the synods meeting in Aachen, from 816-819, within the framework of the religious reform of Benedict of Aniane, imposed it as the unique and only rule in all Carolingian monasteries.

MARTIN, SOLDIER, MONK, BISHOP AND SAINT

Martin was born in the first half of the 4th century in Sabaria, today identified as Szombathély in Hungary, into a modest pagan family. No doubt the profession of his father, a tribune in the imperial army, provided the newborn with the name of Martin, placing him under the protection of Mars, the god of war. After a childhood spent in northern Italy, at the age of 15, under Constantius II (337-361), he was enrolled in the imperial guard, in accordance with contemporary rules imposing long military service on veterans' sons. However, Martin was a catechumen, and his gentle, sober and kindly disposition distinguished him from the other soldiers. On a particularly severe winter day, while his garrison was in Amiens, seeing a poor man freezing with cold at the city gates, Martin cut his cloak in two to give him half. And the following night, in a dream, it was revealed that the man he had warmed was Jesus Christ. Speeding up his baptism, Martin understood that the time had come for him to carry out his true vocation. In 356, the Caesar Julian the Apostate (355-361) had gathered his troops at Worms, on the Rhine, in order to push back the barbarians. The evening before the battle, refusing the *donatium*, an imperial bonus destined to strengthen the fighters' courage, Martin proclaimed himself to be a "soldier of Christ" and claimed the right not to fight any more. Called a coward and immediately thrown into prison, he demanded to go to the front lines, weaponless, under the sole protection of the sign of the cross. And when his superiors forced him to carry out his plan, the enemy asked for peace. From then on, Martin had no trouble obtaining his demobiliza-

tion and, henceforth free to devote his life to God, he found a spiritual master in the bishop of Poitiers, Hilaire. Martin worked beside him as an exorcist. However, in this same year of 356, the Council of Béziers having adopted the Arian ideas of Emperor Constantius II, Hilaire, a faithful defender of the Nicaean *symbol*, was forced into exile in Phrygia. Martin then undertook a long voyage preaching in northern Italy, where he converted his mother, and as far as Illyria. Returning to the area of Milan after being chased out of the northern Balkans, where Arianism was triumphant, he retired in solitude to the island of Gallinaria, off Genoa, about 358-359, before rejoining Hilaire, back in Poitiers from exile, in 360. Martin, who had found his vocation in eremitic life, set up a new hermitage a few kilometres south of the city at Ligugé, on the left bank of the Clain River. Disciples soon arrived to share the asceticism of his existence, thus establishing Gallic monastic life. Soon the miracles and cures operated by Martin spread his fame. And during the summer of 371, several worthies

St Martin sharing his coat

from the Touraine region came to find him, allegedly to have him cure the wife of a certain Rusticus. But upon his arrival in Tours, where Bishop Litorius had just died, Martin the hermit, who was not even a priest, was acclaimed by crowds to succeed him. This election was contested by the high clergy, who reproached the new bishop his scruffy appearance and his poor clothing. However, Martin carried out his new functions perfectly. As a missionary, he covered the region on donkey-back, dressed simply, making idols and pagan cults disappear through numerous miracles, replacing them with chapels and hermitages. He travelled, going to the imperial palace in Trier on several occasions. But he never abandoned his humility and remained faithful to his first vocation – being a monk. Three kilometres upriver from Tours, on the right bank of the Loire River, he settled in the desert of Marmoutier where he felt best, sharing his existence with his disciples in poverty, asceticism and prayer. And in 384, when the council of Bordeaux condemned the theses of Priscillian, Martin took his defence and went personally to Trier to plead in his favour to the usurper Maxim. But it was in vain. Favourable to the detractors of Priscillianism, the emperor had the heresiarch and his disciples executed in about 385-386. Martin developed great contempt for politicians. Death came to the bishop of Tours while he was travelling in Candes, at the confluence of the Vienne and Loire Rivers, on November 8, 397. Carried in a boat as far as Tours, his body was buried on November 11 in the common cemetery of the town.

to deal a fatal blow to the Martinian pilgrimage. The basilica was destroyed in 1562, its relics burned. Of course, the canons carefully gathered some ashes and rests of the tomb, but the fervour and enthusiasm of the former crowds had disappeared. Becoming a parish church during the Revolution, Saint Martin's basilica became a stable before being completely razed in the 19th century. It was rebuilt in Romano-Byzantine style starting in 1886. The clock tower that flanked the southern side of the façade, and Charlemagne's tower, formerly raised at the far left of the transept, above the tomb of Luitgarde, the emperor's wife, remain from the Romanesque collegiate church,

After worshipping the relics of Saint Martin, pilgrims coming from Orléans or Chartres always went to Saint Gatien Cathedral in Tours before continuing on their way, in the direction of Poitiers via Montbazon, Sainte-Catherine-de-Fierbois, Sainte-Maure and Saint-Jacques in Châtellerault.

Clock tower in Tours

SAINT JAMES IN CHÂTELLERAULT

Consecrated in 1066 by Isembert II, bishop of Poitiers, the church of Saint James in Châtellerault contains a fine 17th century wooden, polychrome statue of Saint James dressed as a pilgrim.

Saint Gatien Cathedral in Tours

Saint James, Châtellerault church

Poitiers

Arriving between the Clain and Boivre rivers, the pilgrims reached Poitiers, the capital of Poitou county since the Merovingian period, and an important administrative, religious and intellectual centre during the entire Middle Ages. Starting in the 10th century, the powerful counts of Poitou, whose lands extended from the Berry to the Atlantic, also became dukes of Aquitaine. The heiress of the Duchy of Aquitaine, Eleanor, brought Poitiers to her husband, the king of France Louis VII in 1137, then to her second husband, Henry II Plantangenet, king of England in 1154. Possessed by Richard the Lionheart, then King John, the city was finally annexed to the kingdom of France by Philippe Auguste in 1204. Entering Poitiers from the north by the Paris Gate, the pilgrims were welcomed by the monks of the Cluniac abbey of Saint-Jean-de-Montierneuf, founded towards 1070 by William VII of Aquitaine. Then, in the heart of the city, Notre-Dame-la-Grande was waiting for their prayers. Completed between 1120 and 1150, its façade is one of the masterpieces of Romanesque art. Flanked by two columned towers topped with a tholos, it has a single doorway decorated with voussoirs, framed by two blind archways with Gothic arches, above which a remarkable frieze is sculpted with bas-reliefs. On the middle level, two series of arcades shelter apostles and bishops around a Romanesque bay window, itself topped with a gable decorated with a mandorla, containing Christ in majesty. After a

St Peter, Notre-Dame-la-Grande

ORDERED CHARITY

....

The *Guide* tells us that in Poitiers, two pilgrims asked for hospitality in rue Saint Porchaire, but that only a poor man living at the end of the street, near the church, offered it to them. During the night, through divine vengeance, a violent fire destroyed all the houses in the neighbourhood, sparing only the one where the pilgrims had been taken in.

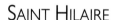

SAINT HILAIRE

The life of Hilaire de Poitiers, born in about 315 into a rich pagan family of landowners, is known only through his writings. His conversion was probably due to his reading of the Bible. Becoming a catechumen, he was baptized and in around 350. When the chief of the Poitiers Christian community died, the voice of the people acclaimed Hilaire bishop. After spending five years organizing his diocese, Hilaire was renowned enough that a certain Martin, a former soldier of Hungarian origin, chose him as a spiritual master. Deep sympathy arose between the two men. But in 356, the Arian council convoked in Béziers by Emperor Constantius II (337-361) condemned Hilaire to exile in Phrygia. Hilaire had been a

faithful defender of the *symbol* of Nicaea, imposed by the council of 325, presenting the Son of God as consubstantial with the Father. Exiled, ceaselessly pursuing his struggle for the re-establishment of orthodoxy, Hilaire gathered a collection of documents relative to the Trinitarian question in his *De Synodis*, at the same time working on his major work, *De Trinitate*. After participating in the Arian council at Seleucia in 359, and vainly trying to rally Constantius to his cause, he managed to return to Gaul, where Julian had usurped power in about 361. Publishing his pamphlet *Against Constantius*, Hilaire had no difficulty in obtaining a meeting of an orthodox council in Lutece in 363. Dedicating the rest of his life to writing, Hilaire died in Poitiers in 367.

Detail of St Hilaire's reliquary

Façade of Notre-Dame-la-Grande

Capital of Sainte-Radegonde

THE BATTLE OF POITIERS

....

Called by the powerful Duke Eudes of Aquitaine, the mayor of the palace, Charles Martel (684-741), defeated the Muslim army near Poitiers in 732. On the strength of his victory, Charles extended his power by taking Bordeaux then, taking advantage of Eudes' death, he was sworn fealty by the new duke. Intervening in the Rhône valley and Provence against the Muslims, he subjected these regions to his authority. He then settled his sons in Burgundy, thus preparing the accession of the Carolingian dynasty.

Chevet of Saint-Hilaire

visit to Saint Peter's Cathedral of Poitiers, a Gothic building constructed starting in 1162, the pilgrims could go and pray at the tomb of Radegonde. A former captive of Clotaire 1st (558-561), who made her his wife, she was consecrated a deaconess at Noyon by the bishop, Saint Medard. In Poitiers, she founded the abbey for the nuns of the Holy Cross, where she introduced the rule of St Césaire of Arles. Since 587, Radegonde's tomb lies in the church bearing her name. Rebuilt over the course of the centuries, it contains Romanesque sections – the porch-belltower, the polygonal apse of the chancel with its ambulatory and radiating chapels – united by a single nave, from the 13th century. But pilgrims gathered most often around the tomb of Saint Hilaire, the first attested bishop of Poitiers (350-367). Built on the site of the saint's sepulchre, Saint Hilaire's Basilica received, according to tradition, the visit of Clovis in 507. Abd al-Rahmân burnt it in 732, before his defeat by Charles Martel. After the Norse attack in 833, it was rebuilt in the 11th century. Served by a community of canons, it was placed under special protection by the Holy See in 1074. Vaulted in the 12th century, it suffered during the Wars of Religion, then, sold as national property at the Revolution, it became a stone quarry. Restored in the 19th century, it contains a nave flanked by side-aisles, a transept opening onto two chapels, and a chancel with an ambulatory and radiating chapels. It possesses remarkable sculpted capitals, as well as fine 11th century frescoes. Its crypt still contains the saint's relics.

Sainte-Radegonde and St Peter's Cathedral in Poitiers

Tower and chapter house in Charroux

A PARALLEL ROUTE

Leaving from Poitiers, some pilgrims left the main road through Saintes and headed for the powerful abbey of Saint-Saveur in Charroux. According to tradition, it was founded in 783 by Charlemagne and Count Roger de Limoges. Four councils were held in its abbey church, the first, in 989, prepared the institution of the Peace of God. A stage appreciated by pilgrims, it contained at least seventy relics, among them Holy Blood, and fragments of the True Cross. Passing the priory of Saint Nicolas in Civray, the pilgrims continued the road along the Charente River valley, and, via the Benedictine abbey of Saint-Amant-de-Boixe, they soon reached Angoulême and Saint Peter's Cathedral. The main work on the cathedral had been done between 1101 and 1130 by Girart II, the city's bishop and papal legate from 1107 on. In 1118, while the Christians of the *Reconquista* were recapturing Zaragoza from the Moors of al-Andalus, Girart had two sculptors brought from the building site of Saint-Sernin in Toulouse. He entrusted them with carrying out the decoration of the five tympana on the ground floor of his cathedral's façade. And hence the pilgrims could admire, on the right of the central doorway, the "frieze of Roland", mortally wounding Marsile, the treacherous Moorish king of Zaragoza. Leaving Angoulême for Saint-Gilles de Puypéroux Abbey and the Templars commandery in Cressac, whose chapel is decorated with remarkable frescoes showing scenes from the Crusades, the pilgrims crossed the Dordogne River for a stage at Sauve-Majeure Abbey. They next rejoined the *via Turonensis* and the road through the Landes area in Barp, near Belin, if they had not decided to join the *via Lemovicensis* at La Réole.

St Nicholas Church in Civray

Celles-sur-Belle Abbey

Saint-Hilaire Church in Melle

The Poitou

After leaving Poitiers, the pilgrims reached the shores of the Feuillarte River and Notre Dame de Fontaine-le-Comte Abbey, of which the abbey church remains. Founded in the 12th century by Guillaume VIII, Count of Poitiers, it sheltered a community of regular canons. Continuing their route through Coulombiers, the pilgrims crossed the Vonne R. opposite the town whose foundation legend attributed to the fairy Melusine, and which was the seat of the powerful Lusignan family. Its members had participated in Crusades starting in 1096, had become kings of Cyprus and Jerusalem. Powerfully fortified, Lusignan contained a Benedictine priory depending on the abbey of Nouaillé, of which the church, named for both Our Lady and Saint Junien, remains. Via Chenay and Chey, the pilgrims reached the abbey at Celles-sur-Belle, where the Virgin was particularly worshipped after the 12th century. Founded in the 11th century, destroyed during the Wars of Religion, the abbey was entirely rebuilt in the 17th century, in Late Gothic style. Melle was the next stage for the pilgrims. Starting in the Merovingian period, the town had produced money in the workshops supplied by the silver-bearing lead mines in the valley of the Béronne, the river running through the town. Melle contains three churches – the ancient Saint Savinien, Saint Peter's, and the most important, Saint Hilaire. This is the only remnant of a Benedictine priory that depended on the abbey at Saint-Jean d'Angély. Built in the 12th century, it contains a nave encircled with side aisles, a transept opening onto two chapels, and a chancel with an ambulatory with three radiating chapels. It contains many sculpted capitals. Its northern doorway, decorated with triple voussoirs, is surmounted by an equestrian statue, a common portrayal in Poitou. Raised to the glory of Emperor Constantine, who had granted freedom of worship to Christians by the Edict of Milan in 313, it symbolized the triumph of Christianity over paganism, represented by the small figure placed under the horse.

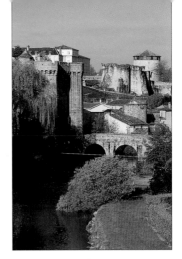

Parthenay

Equestrian statue at north door of Saint-Hilaire Church in Melle

AIMERY PICAUD, FROM POITOU

According to the apocryphal letter of Innocent II (1130-1143) recommending and authenticating the *Liber Sancti Jacobi* kept in Santiago de Compostela, the author of *The Pilgrims's Guide* was a monk from Parthenay-le-Vieux in Poitou, called Aimery Picaud. If verifying the statement is difficult, it is in any case sure that the *Guide*'s author does not stop praising the Poitou region, "fertile, excellent and full of all bliss", nor its inhabitants, "vigorous people, [...] good warriors, clever at using bows, arrows and lances in war, brave on the battlefront, very fast in running, elegant in their way of dressing, handsome faces, witty, very generous, generous in hospitality."

Aulnay

Leaving Melle, the pilgrims crossed the Boutonne River, and through La Villedieu, reached Aulnay in Saintonge. Outside the village, St. Peter's Church watches over a cemetery planted with yew trees. In 1119, this church depended on Saint Cyprien de Poitiers Abbey, before passing under the control of the city's cathedral chapter in 1122. Construction of the current church, whose sculptures are included among the masterpieces of Romanesque art in Saintonge, began in 1130. Vaulted with slightly Gothic barrel vaults, it contains a nave with five bays, flanked with side aisles, a protruding transept and a chancel ending with an apse framed by two apsidal chapels. The harmony of the design and the wreathed columns used instead of buttresses as supports for exterior wall arcading, or for inside pillars, provide it with rare elegance. Pierced by a single doorway framed by two blind arcades with sculpted tympana, the western façade had four buttresses added in the 15th century. Troubles during the Revolution deprived the church of its equestrian statue, formerly placed on the cornice of the upper level. The iconographic riches and the quality of the sculptures are of very high level, particularly on the voussoirs of the central doorway. The first, on the outside, represents the glorification of the Lamb, adored by angels; the second, the victorious combat of Virtue against Vice; the third illustrates the parable of the wise and foolish Virgins; finally, the last one shows the work of the months and the signs of the zodiac. The southern doorway and the interior capitals are also sculpted with ornamental designs, chimera, biblical scenes, such as that of Samson and Delilah on the north-western pillar of the transept crossing. The transept crossing is topped by a square steeple, a visible reference point for pilgrims. The door of the right transept has, like that on the western façade, a set of four sculpted buttresses. On the third, there are thirty-one old men of the Apocalypse, or seven more than in the texts.

Fantastic animals, south doorway of Aulnay church

Nave in Aulnay church

St Peter Church in Aulnay

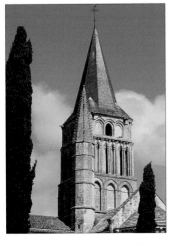

Steeple of Aulnay church

THE HOSANNA CROSS OF AULNAY

Scattered with tomb stones and sarcophagi on stilts, the old cemetery in Aulnay has kept its fine Hosanna cross from the 15th century. On the Sunday before Easter, the priest read the Gospels celebrating the entrance of Jesus into Jerusalem there. Then the worshippers came past, chanting Hosannas, and laid their palm branches down.

The Hosanna Cross in Aulnay

St John the Baptist

Saint-Jean-d'Angély

From Aulnay, the pilgrims reached Saint-Jean d'Angély. It was in 817 that the monk Felix, returning from a pilgrimage to the Holy Land, brought back the relic of John the Baptist's head from Alexandria to the king of Aquitaine, Pepin 1st (817-838). A monastery was founded to receive it, on the right bank of the Boutonne River. But it was a victim of Viking raids and during one of them, the relic disappeared. It was found only in 1010, when Guillaume the Great, Duke of Aquitaine, undertook the construction of the abbey whose reform he entrusted to the abbot of Cluny. Contained in a silver reliquary placed in the chancel of the new abbey church consecrated in 1050, the relic attracted many pilgrims, bringing prosperity to the abbey and the town born beside it. The abbey, devastated during the Hundred Years War, was rebuilt before being destroyed once again in 1568, during the Wars of Religion. The relic then disappeared. Rebuilt in the 17th century, a century later the monks decided to give it a Baroque church that the Revolution left unfinished and of which the two high towers of the façade remain.

TRANSLATIO SANCTI PRAECURSORIS

....

A famous pilgrimage shrine during the Medieval period, Saint-Jean-d-Angély is mentioned in chapter VIII of *The Pilgrim's Guide.* "One must go and see [...] the venerable head of Saint John the Baptist which was brought by monks from Jerusalem to a place named Angély in Poitou. The very sacred head is worshipped there night and day by a choir of a hundred monks and is famed for numberless miracles. While it was being transported by land and by sea, this head distinguished itself by its many marvels. At sea, it chased away many storms, and on land, if one believes the book of its translation, it gave back life to several dead. Thus, it is believed that it is indeed the veritable head of the venerated Precursor."

Towers of abbey church of Saint-Jean-d'Angély

Saintes

Leaving Saint-Jean-d'Angély, after passing close to Fenioux, the pilgrims reached the shores of the Charente River and the town of Saintes. The antique *Mediolanum Santonum* had been founded in 20 BC by Agrippa, the governor of Gaul, at the end of a strategic axis that left from Lyons and crossed the Massif Central range. Remnants of the old city include the Germanicus arch and the green ruins of the ampitheatre outside the town. On the river's right bank, pilgrims always stopped in the splendid Romanesque abbey church run by Benedictine nuns from the Abbaye-aux-Dames, founded in the 11th century by the Count of Anjou, Geoffroy Martel and his wife, Agnes of Burgundy, the widow of Guillaume the Great, Count of Poitou, who was later to take the veil there. Powerful and influential, the abbey possessed much land in Poitou, Anjou, Aunis and Saintonge, and contained a large community, run by abbesses from the kingdom's greatest families. Although the Hundred Years War, the troubles of the Wars of Religion and the terrible fire of 1648 left lasting scars on the abbey's architecture, its abbey church still contains treasures of Romanesque sculpture and architecture. Consecrated in 1047, it has a nave, a large transept, and a semicircular chancel of great sobriety. In the 12th century, it was given a fine sculpted façade and a powerful steeple, topped with a cone-shaped spire with scales, raised at the transept crossing. On the other side of the Charente, the pilgrims were welcomed in the many hospices of the town. They made a detour by Saint Peter's Cathedral, built in the 15th century on the site of a Romanesque church. They then went to worship the relics of the evangelist of the Santons, Saint Eutrope, to whom the *Guide* dedicated a long section. At his death at the end of the 4th century, the apostle-martyr of Saintonge, a contemporary of Christ and Peter according to legend, was buried outside the walls by ancient custom. Several buildings followed each other until the end of the 11th century,

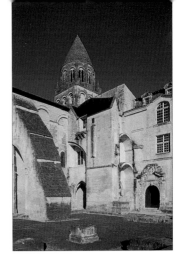

Abbaye-aux-Dames in Saintes

LANTERN FOR THE DEAD

The village of Fenioux contains a beautiful 12th century Romanesque church, which has retained, in the walls of its nave, some elements from a primitive Carolingian church. Long ago, a lantern for the dead watched over the cemetery nowadays abandoned. It was also used as a Hosanna cross. Inside its shaft, made of eleven columns joined together, a spiral staircase of thirty-seven steps leads to the tholos, formed from twelve thin columns topped with a pyramid-shaped spire.

Doorway detail of Abbaye-aux-Dames in Saintes

Lantern of the Dead in Fenioux

Capital in Saint-Eutrope church

Chevet of Saint-Eutrope

Tomb in Saint-Eutrope

when Cluniac monks settled near the tomb, building a monastery and a church worthy of the pilgrim crowds' fervour. With its clever design, it had a low church, or crypt, formed by a transept opening onto two apses, and an elongated chancel consisting of a nave with four bays, its side aisles opening onto an apse with an ambulatory and three apsidal chapels. The same plan was reproduced above in the high church. A common nave, on the intermediate level, permitted access by staircases either to the vast upper chancel, consecrated by Pope Urban II on April 20, 1096, or else to the semi-subterranean crypt, barely lit by bay windows made in the side aisles. During the 15th century, Louis XI, who believed the cure for his dropsy was the work of Saint Eutrope, had work carried out, in particular the building, above the north transept, of the steeple, which rises to a height of sixty-five metres. Even though the large Romanesque building survived the fires lit by Huguenots in 1568, then the Revolution, its nave was stupidly amputated in 1803 by a First Empire prefect of Saintonge, who preferred to replace it with the actual Place Saint Eutrope, rather than having it restored. Saint Eutrope church did however retain its Romanesque chevet and its crypt, whose chancel contains the saint's sarcophagus from the 4th century. In the chancel of the upper church, the capitals are decorated with biblical scenes, including Daniel in the lion's den and the weighing of souls, or else floral motifs characteristic of Romanesque art in Saintonge.

THE LEGEND OF SAINT EUTROPE

According to the *Guide*, Eutrope was the son of the Emir of Babylon, Xerxes, and Queen Guiva. As a child, he went to Galilee, to see Christ whose miracles he had heard about, and was there for the miracle of the loaves and fishes. Back at the emir's court, Eutrope told him what he had seen, then left again for Jerusalem because he secretly believed in the new religion. After the crucifixion and Pentecost, he helped Simon and Thaddeus to found a church in Babylon, then went to Rome to the apostle Peter, who sent him on a mission. Arriving in Saintes, as he saw the town "very well encircled in antique walls, decorated with high towers, located on a marvellous site, of perfect length and width, rich in every-

thing and abounding in victuals, well supplied with fine fields and clear fountains, crossed by a great river, fertile with gardens, orchards and vineyards all around, supplied with pleasant streets and squares", he decided to convert it from paganism. Some time later, back in Rome with Pope Clement, Peter's successor, he received the order to complete his mission with martyrdom, and left in the company of Denis, who went to Paris. In Saintes, Eutrope attracted many followers, including the daughter of the local prince, Eustelle. But furious upon learning this, the prince had Eutrope killed. Buried by Eustelle and the Christians in Saintes, he has been ever since worshipped as a holy martyr.

Arena and Saint-Eutrope Church in Saintes

From Pons to Blaye

Going directly south upon leaving Saintes, the pilgrims reached the valley of the Seugne River and the town of Pons. An imposing keep remains from the powerful fortress that protected the town during the medieval period. After praying in Saint Gilles' Chapel or in Saint Vivien's Church, the pilgrims went under an arched passageway linking Saint Martin's Church to the New Hospital, where they found refuge before continuing on their way. Going beyond Belluire and the tower of Plassac, via the Benedictine Abbey of La Tenaille and the village of Mirambeau, the pilgrims soon arrived at the shores of the Gironde River and the abbey of Saint-Romain in Blaye. One of the most impressive stages of the pilgrimage, linked to legendary episodes of Charlemagne's struggle against the Moors of al-Andalus as sung by Pseudo-Turpin, it was totally destroyed in the 17th century, to be replaced by the fortifications of Vauban's citadel. On the rocky slopes of the antique Blavia, lived the hermit Romain, the evangelist of the area in the 4th century. After his death in 385, a basilica was raised in his name. The patron saint of travellers, Saint Romain saved from shipwreck all those who called on him in danger on the waves, and by the 7th century, a famous cemetery surrounded the basilica. This was the burial place of Caribert, son of Clotaire II (584-629), and it was here that Charlemagne, back from the disastrous ambush at Roncesvalles in 778, decided to bury his nephew, valiant Roland. An important abbey, served by a community of regular canons of Saint Augustine, watched over the sepulchres of Saint Romain and Roland even before the 12th century, welcoming the fervour of the pilgrims on the *via Turonensis*, before their dangerous crossing of the estuary. It was in Blaye that pilgrims embarked for their voyage up the Gironde, and then the Garonne River, as far as Bordeaux. However, some preferred to sail, by way of Saint-Christoly-Médoc and Port-de-By to Saint Veronica's shrine in Soulac, where they rejoined other pilgrims coming from Saintes by Talmont.

Blaye Citadel

Portico of Pons Hospital

OUR LADY OF LAND'S END

The "daughter of Jerusalem" who, with her veil, wiped Jesus's face when he collapsed under the weight of the cross during the ascension of Calvary, is allegedly buried in Soulac. The image of the Saviour, the *vera icon*, which was imprinted on the veil she used as a divine sign, is the origin of her name. Leaving Jerusalem with her husband, the future Saint Amadour, on a boat guided by the wind of Providence, they landed on the shores of Médoc, and Veronica retired to Soulac, where she built a small oratory dedicated to the Virgin, while Amadour went to the rocky solitudes of the valley of Alzou. Such is the origin of the Benedictine priory of Our Lady of Land's End in Soulac, attached to Holy Cross in Bordeaux, and whose existence was mentioned for the first time in a charter in 980. In 1079, monks began the reconstruction of their church, to better welcome the many Santiago pilgrims who were arriving by sea from Talmont, and from the lands of Vendée, Brittany or Great Britain to worship at the tomb of Saint Veronica. They could then rejoin the *via Turonensis* in Bordeaux through Hourtin and Sainte-Hélène, or at Barp, via Lacanau, Le Porge or Mios. Others preferred to continue along the Atlantic coast through Mimizan, Bayonne and Saint-Jean-de-Luz, to arrive in Irún and join the *Camino francés* at Burgos, or to take the coast road through Bilbao, Santander and Oviedo. Buried in the sand during the 18th century, the church dedicated to Our Lady of Land's End in Soulac, dug out and restored starting in 1859, has once again become a religious centre, the object of worship and pilgrimage.

Church in Talmont

Saint-Jean-de-Luz

The Virgin of Soulac

Saint Andrew's Cathedral, Bordeaux

THE BORDELAIS, BY THE GUIDE

....

T he *Pilgrim's Guide* is full of juicy remarks about the lands crossed by the pilgrimage routes to Santiago. Thus, "after crossing an arm of the sea and the Garonne, one arrives in the Bordelais where the wine is excellent, fish abundant, but the language is rough", considered Aimery Picaud.

St James, Museum of Aquitaine

Bordeaux

Founded in the 3rd century BC by the Celtic tribe of Bituriges Vivisques, the port of *Burdigala* developed with the trade in tin. Conquered by Crassus in 56 BC, it also began to import Italian wine, before exporting its own wines in the first century AD, thanks to the planting of a vine originating in Albania on the shores of the Garonne River. Becoming the capital of Aquitaine, to the detriment of Saintes, under Vespasian (69-79) the city of *Burdigala* prospered. Its cultural influence was mentioned in the work of the poet Ausone (310-380), rhetorician and grammarian at the city's university, before becoming the tutor of the future emperor Gratian (375-383). After undergoing the tribulations of the Barbarian and then the Norse invasions, under English domination until 1453 after the accession to the English throne in 1154 of Henry II Plantagenet, second husband of Eleanor of Aquitaine, Bordeaux became wealthy because of its wine trade, much appreciated by English kings who granted Bordeaux merchants commercial privileges. Disembarking in Bordeaux at the port of *Peregris*, following the *Guide*'s advice the pilgrims went to worship at the tomb of Saint Seurin, a bishop of the city during the first third of the 5th century. An abbey, served by Benedictine monks, then by regular canons, was built on the site of the sepulchre, and it was in this abbey church that Charlemagne placed Roland's ivory horn, split by the power of his breath when he vainly called for his uncle's aid at Roncesvalles. After a detour at Saint Andrew's Cathedral, pilgrims in the 13th century left the town by the rue Saint-James and the present Saint-Eloi gate, to find a welcome at Saint-James hospital, of which the chapel remains at the beginning of today's rue du Mirail. An important illuminated register testifies to the activity of the Saint James Confraternity of Bordeaux, whose seat was in Saint James Chapel of Saint Michael's Church, dominated by a fine Gothic spire built between 1472 and 1492.

Sarcophagus in crypt of Saint-Seurin Church in Bordeaux

SAUVE-MAJEURE

In the second half of the 11th century, Gerard, a former monk of the Benedictine monastery at Corbie, in Picardy, who had become abbot of Saint-Vincent-De-Laon, left his abbey looking for greater perfection. Inspired by the reforming ideas of Pope Gregory VII (1073-1085), and won over, like so many of his contemporaries, by the return to eremitic life characterizing the end of the century, he travelled until he reached a place six leagues east of Bordeaux, between the Garonne and Dordogne Rivers, in the loneliness of the great forest, the *Sylva Major*, that then covered the region. There, on the ruins of the castle of Hauteville, on the site he received from Augier de Rioms, a vassal of Guillaume VIII of Aquitaine, he installed his holy retreat, building a small oratory, in the year of grace 1079. Encouraged by the many disciples attracted by the holiness of his existence, and the material support of powerful protectors, especially the Duke of Aquitaine, Guillaume VIII, Gerard soon became the abbot of a new monastery, to which he gave the rule of Saint Benedict. He managed to convince the duke of Aquitaine to abandon his power of justice over the abbey's lands, thus founding a safe area that was rapidly inhabited and a new large town sprang up. It became a favoured stage for Santiago pilgrims arriving by the variation of the *via Turonensis*, who from Poitiers, came to Belin via Charroux and Angoulême. Placed under the pope's protection, and granted innumerable donations, Sauve-Majeure Abbey quickly prospered. In 1095, at the death of its founder, it held a community of three hun-dred monks and possessed many priories, spread over Guyenne and Champagne, but also in Spain and England. Restored after the Hundred Years War of the 15th century, it once again suffered during the Wars of Religion in the 16th. Although the Congregation of Saint Maur took community life in hand starting in 1621, carrying out many improvements in the convent buildings, the badly damaged abbey church col-lapsed shortly after the Revolution. Nowadays, from the ruins of the abbey church, we can imagine the delicacy of the voussoirs on the arches, the sculpted decorations of the capitals with their vegetal motifs, monsters from the Romanesque bestiary, or biblical scenes. We must imagine too the beauty of the nave, with the consecrating medallion showing James the Greater, and the chevet with its parallel apsidal chapels.

Sauve-Majeure

Crossing the Landes

Leaving Bordeaux in the direction of the priory-hospital of Cayac de Gradignan, founded in the 12th century by the Hospitallers of Saint John of Jerusalem, the pilgrims began the feared crossing of the Landes. Passing le Barp and l'Hospitalet, they crossed the Eyre River by the old Belin bridge, stopping to pray in the cemetery of the little Romanesque church at Mons before the bodies of the valiant knights fallen at Roncesvalles – Olivier, Gondebaud, King of Frisia, Ogier, King of Dacia, Arastain, King of Brittany, Garin, Duke of Lorraine, and many others buried there by Charlemagne in 778. After Saugnacq-et-Muret, though some went off to Moustey, the seat of two churches, and to Vieux-Richet, the route continued through Liposthey to reach the village of Herbe-fanée (wilted grass), today Labouheyre, where Carmelites had founded a hospi-taller convent in 1150. Labouheyre still contains its Saint James Church with its portal gate decorated with scallop shells, and its fountain also dedicated to the apostle of Galicia. After Escource and Onesse-et-Laharie, the pilgrims passed the village of Lesperon to reach, at Taller, where Guillaume Sanche of Aquitaine allegedly defeated the Norsemen in 982, the hospital founded by Saint Louis (1226-1270). Continuing on their way, they arrived on the shores of the Adour River and the Romanesque church of Saint Paul, the final stage before Dax, where the hospitals of the Holy Spirit, founded in Sablar in 1217 and Bout-du-Pont (end of the bridge), both located outside the ramparts, welcomed them at any hour. Coming out of the town, at the Torte Commandery, some went in the direction of Cagnotte and crossed the Gaves Réunis at the level of Peyrehorade, before reaching Arthous Abbey, founded by the Premonstrants in 1167. The others headed by Pouillon to cross the gave or stream of Pau, then that of Oloron. On the latter's right bank, they found refuge, sometimes for the winter before starting over the Pyrenees, at the hospital of the Benedictine abbey of Saint-Jean de Sorde that ran a prosperous fish farm.

Bas-relief on chevet of Saint-Paul-lès-Dax Church

Chevet of Saint-Jean de Sorde

Church in Saugnacq-et-Muret

ANNOYING BOATMEN

The museum at Arthous Abbey contains a copy of one of the boats used by pilgrims to cross the mountain streams, called *gaves*, of Pau and Oloron. On these makeshift craft, risks were high, especially since the boatmen, cruel and thieving according to the *Guide*, did not hesitate to tip them over in order to better rob their passengers. "[...] The route to Santiago crosses two rivers that run near the village of Saint-Jean de Sorde [...]; it is impossible to cross them otherwise than in boats. May their boatmen be damned! Indeed, although these rivers are perfectly narrow, these people nonetheless are used to demanding from every man that they take across to the other side, from poor as well as from rich, a coin, and for a horse, they shamefully extort by force, four. And their boats are small, made of a single tree trunk, barely able to carry a horse. Thus, when one boards, one has to be careful not to fall in the water [...]. Many times too, after having received the money, the passers make such a large number of pilgrims get on board that the boat tips over and the pilgrims drown; and then the boatmen rejoice nastily after grabbing the spoils of the dead."

Chevet of Arthous Abbey Church

Modillion on the chevet, Arthous

Bridge of legend, Sauveterre-de-Béarn

FROM THE TOP OF THE BRIDGE

T he wife of Gaston of Béarn and daughter of the king of Navarre, Sancha, also called Léofas, ended up a childless widow. But she was pregnant, filling the Bearn people with hope. Alas, when she had a miscarriage and was suspected of provoking an abortion, the population bound her hands and feet and threw her from the top of Sauveterre bridge, leaving the river's current to provide God's judgement. But Léofas implored the help of Our Lady of Rocamadour, and was soon gently carried by the water to a sandbank on the shore. Rushing up, the inhabitants carried her triumphantly to the castle. And in thanksgiving, in 1170 Sancha offered the abbot of Rocamadour a tapestry to decorate Our Lady's Chapel.

Tympanum on Sauveterre church

Harambels Chapel

Church of Sauveterre-de-Béarn

From the Gave of Oloron to the Nive

Leaving Sorde-l'Abbaye and passing by the high walled town of Villefranche, the pilgrims on the *via Turonensis* followed the gave (mountain stream) of Oloron as far as Sauveterre-de-Béarn, where they were joined by pilgrims from the *via Lemovicensis* coming from Arué. Crossing the gave by the fortified bridge in Sauveterre, the famous legendary bridge, by way of Osserain and Camou-Mixe the faithful walkers soon arrived in Saint-Palais, at the confluence of the Bidouze and Joyeuse rivers. Here they found other *via Turonensis* pilgrims who were coming by the path linking Arthous Abbey to Garris. A new town founded at the beginning of the 13th century around the priory-hospital of Saint Magdelene of Lagarrague, Saint-Palais – from San Pelay, in memory of Pelayo, an adolescent martyr in Cordoba around 850 – was the capital of Lower Navarre in the early 16th century. It contained at least six hostels, as well as the main hospital of Lagarrague. South of the town, on Saint Saviour's Hill, pilgrims from the *via Podiensis* rejoined those on the other two routes at the crossroads called Gibraltar, indicated since 1964 by a disc-shaped Basque stele. Continuing on their way in the direction of Ostabat via Uhart-Mixe, the pilgrims could stop at Saint Nicholas d'Harambels priory-hospital, of which the chapel and the four houses of the last brothers remain. These lay brothers had made vows of poverty, obedience to the prior, of chastity in the event of becoming widowers, and were responsible for organizing the hospital. At the foot of Ipharlatcé Pass, on the Roman road from Bordeaux to Astorga, Ostabat, whose ramparts were removed in 1228 by Sancho the Strong demanding homage from the town's lord, possessed not only many hostels, but also two hospitals – Saint Anthony and Saint Catherine – that provided pilgrims with care. Then through the village of Gamarthe, passing the commandery of the Knights of Saint John of Jerusalem in Aphat-Ospital and its Saint Blaise chapel, the road reached Saint-Jean-le-Vieux, then Saint-Jean-Pied-de-Port, the final stage before crossing the *Summus Pyreneus.*

Gibraltar Stele

A MUSEUM ON THE ROAD

The Museum of Lower Navarre in Saint-Palais is dedicated to the history and popular arts and traditions of the region. The route to Santiago is not forgotten, with pilgrims' attributes and a metal scallop shell brought back from the *Paradisus* in Compostela by a pilgrim. A painting by Bordes, a disciple of Bonnat, shows a cleric passing the Pyrenees. Might it be Godescalc? And the copies of bas-reliefs from the church in Arué present the visitor with sculptures at eye-level, that require some contorsions to be seen in their usual location.

Aphat-Ospital Chapel

Staff and gourds

Church and Notre-Dame Bridge over the Nive in Saint-Jean-Pied-de-Port

Saint-Jean-Pied-de-Port

Founded during the 12th century after the destruction of the fortress of Saint-Jean-le-Vieux, Saint-Jean-Pied-de-Port, the capital of Navarre Beyond the Mountains in the medieval period, owed its name to its location at the foot of the passes – *ports* – of Cize and Ibañeta. Arriving in the north by the Chapel of Magdalene, the pilgrims entered the upper town through Saint James Gate, then followed the rue d'Espagne as far as the bridge over the Nive River. There, two possible itineraries led to Roncesvalles: one through Cize Pass, following the path of the antique *via Traiana* linking Bordeaux and Astorga, or the easier route that gets to Ibañeta via *Valcarlos*, the valley where Charlemagne established his camp before hurrying to help Roland in Roncesvalles. The route through Cize was used more often during the Middle Ages, even though climbing this "remarkable mountain", according to Aimery Picaud, was rather difficult. "To cross it, there are eight thousand to climb and as many to descend. [...] He who makes the ascent believes that, with his own hand, he can touch the sky." Furthermore, one had to be wary because, still in the *Guide*, "the Navarrese and the irreligious Basques", not content to simply rob pilgrims, used to "ride them like donkeys and make them perish". Leaving Saint-Jean, the pilgrims set off in the direction of Saint Michel village, the seat of Saint Vincent's hospitals, entrusted in 1072 to the Benedictine monks of Leyre and to Saint Michael the Archangel, both attached to Roncesvalles in 1246. After climbing Orisson Peak, where there was a priory, they left the road towards the Roman *trophy* in Urkulu, and passed Mount Lethar-Atheka to cross Cize Pass, overlooked by the Mendi Chipy. They rejoined Holy Saviour of Ibañeta where the *Guide* said, "it is in this place [...] that Charlemagne going to Spain with his armies [...] first symbolically raised the Cross of the Lord, and then bending his knee, turned towards Galicia, addressed a prayer to God and Saint James", a act copied by generations of pilgrims.

Saint James Gate

THE MIRACLE OF CIZE PASS

In the year 1080, thirty knights from Lorraine decided to make a pilgrimage to Santiago, all except one of them promising each other mutual help on the way. They had arrived in Gascony when one fell ill in the village of *Porta Clausa* and was unable to walk. Supporting him with great difficulty, his companions took two weeks instead of five days to reach the village of Saint Michel, at the foot of Cize Pass, where they abandoned him, betraying their oath. Only he who had not promised stayed at his bedside. The next day, with great effort, they both climbed up to the crest of the hill, where at nightfall, the sick man's soul left this world, to be carried to the next by Saint James. Frozen with fear, wishing to offer the dead man a burial, the knight begged the saint for help. Saint James loomed out of the darkness on his horse, took the dead man in his arms and invited the knight to mount behind him. Before sunrise, they had arrived at *Monte del Gozo* overlooking Santiago de Compostela, where the dead man was buried by canons from the basilica. By order of Saint James, the knight joined his compatriots in Leon, described the miracle to them, and all completed their pilgrimage in repentance.

The Urkulu trophy

149

The Puerto de Ibañeta

Saint James Chapel and Holy Spirit Chapel

Roncesvalles

The Puerto de Ibañeta, at an altitude of 1057 metres, had always been a frequent crossing point between the two sides of the Pyrenees. The Celts had used it to invest the Iberian peninsula during the 8th and 7th centuries BC. To link Bordeaux and Astorga, the Romans laid a road through it, which was used by Suevi, Alans and Vandals in the 5th century AD, and in 732, in the other direction, by Muslim troops heading for their unfortunate encounter with Charles Martel. On August 15, 778 a tragic episode that supplied the legendary theme of the *Song of Roland* and part of the *Chronicle by Pseudo-Turpin* took place in these mountainous surroundings. The rearguard of Charlemagne's army came to lend a hand to the Muslim governor of Barcelona, who had revolted against the emir of Cordoba. On their way back, they were ambushed by Basques and, during the battle, Roland perished. In 1071, the King of Navarre, Sancho IV Garcés (1054-1076), gave the Abbey of Leyre San Salvador of Ibañeta monastery, which welcomed and cared for pilgrims at the top of the pass. In 1271, it was annexed to Our Lady of Roncesvalles. At Puerto de Ibañeta, a monolith carved with a Virgin and Child has replaced the cross that, according to legend, Charlemagne had raised there before praying in the direction of Santiago. And a chapel dating from 1965 stands near the site once occupied by San Salvador de Ibañeta.

In 1132, at the demand of Alfonso the Warrior (1126-1157), the bishop of Pamplona, Sancho de Larrosa, founded the hospital of Our Lady of Roncesvalles that, thanks to donations and devotion of a community of Augustinian canons, took on great importance. The hospital provided a charitable welcome for many passing pilgrims, attracted by the legendary aura of the location. In Roland's chapel, today called Holy Spirit where, according to tradition, the companions of Charlemagne's nephew were buried, they could see the rock on which the hero had tried to break his sword,

Stele of Roncesvalles

SAINTE-ENGRÂCE

The Navarrese abbey in Leyre, attached to the Cistercian Order in 1269, was not itself located on one of the routes to Santiago, but it possessed chapels, hospitals and priories, especially on the secondary roads that came from the northern side of the Pyrenees and followed the valleys of Salazar and Roncal on the southern side. Hence in Soule, Sainte-Engrâce Collegiate Church, built in 1085, was one of these possessions. The pilgrims were welcomed in a hospital when they came to worship the relic, one of the arms of Saint Engrâce, who had been martyred in Zaragoza about 300. The relic, allegedly discovered at the foot of an oak tree by a bull, disappeared in 1569 during the Wars of Religion. After that, pilgrims avoided crossing the Pyrenees at an altitude of 1,600 metres, and instead passed through Mauléon, Ostabat and Cize Pass towards Roncesvalles.

Our Lady of Roncesvalles Hospital

Capital in Sainte-Engrâce

BEHIND THE GATES OF LEGEND

In 777, Soliman ben Alarabi, the governor of Barcelona, promised Charlemagne that he would give him three strongholds held by the Saracens south of the Pyrenees. In the spring of 778, the Frankish army, divided into two corps, crossed the Pyrenees; one corps in the east, through Septimania, the other in the west through Navarre. The first operations were successful, since Pamplona surrendered without a fight. But at Zaragoza, where the two corps met, Charlemagne's troops were driven back. On their way back, they destroyed Pamplona's city walls before crossing the Pyrenees through Roncesvalles, where the Basques were waiting for them. At nightfall Basques ambushed the rearguard. All the Frankish soldiers in it were massacred and their convoy was looted. Among the dead were Roland, prefect of the Brittany March, and the cup-bearer Eggihard, whose epitaph permitted precise dating of the battle – August 15, 778. The Song of Roland was written in about 1100, in assonant decasyllabic couplets, providing an epic version of the tragic episode that was a real setback for the future Emperor of the West. It was a panegyric of the champion of Christianity, the conqueror of paganism. In this masterpiece of the chanson de geste, within seven years Charlemagne had conquered the entire peninsula, except for Zaragoza where the Moorish king Marsile resisted. Two knights in his entourage differed over the strategy to be followed: Roland, his nephew, advised war; Ganelon wanted peace. Ganelon was sent as an emissary to Marsile and made a pact with the latter to attack Roland. Back in the Frankish camp, he convinced Charlemagne to return to his lands

and to entrust Roland with leading his army's rearguard. In Roncesvalles, the Saracens were waiting for Roland and his knights. Olivier, Roland's companion-in-arms, begged Roland to sound his horn to inform Charlemagne. But Roland refused to ask for help before starting to fight. A hundred and twenty thousand Saracens wiped out twenty thousand Franks, of which a group of sixty held out. Roland finally decided to sound his hunting horn. Olivier, annoyed, this time opposed the action and Archbishop Turpin settled the quarrel between the two friends. Roland blew the horn so hard that his veins burst. Charlemagne heard it and turned back. Struck in the back, Olivier died, as did Turpin, wounded and at the end of his strength. Although he was unvanquished, Roland's destiny was the same. Charlemagne arrived then, pursued the Saracens and routed them. The Christians were burying their dead when Baligant, the Emir of Babylon, arrived with his army. A new battle took place. At the heart of the bloody fight, Charlemagne and Baligant recognized each other and faced off in single

combat in which Charlemagne was the winner. Christianity triumphed. The Frankish heroes were buried in Roncesvalles and Blaye, on the shores of the Gironde. In Aachen, a judicial duel found against Ganelon, who was drawn apart by horses. Divine justice was thus rendered. To narrate the event, the author of the *Chronicle of Pseudo-Turpin* generally used the same plot as that of two other epic poems written in the Occitanian language, *Rollan a Saragossa* and *Ronsavals*, written in the first quarter of the 12th century and whose 14th century manuscripts were found in 1912. The *Kaiserchronik*, written in about 1150, started off from historical facts. After his defeat, Charlemagne was completely despondent. An angel appeared to him and advised him to put together a battalion of young girls. And so fifty-three thousand and sixty-six, not one more, not one less, gathered around Charlemagne. They dressed as soldiers and took up arms. The Moorish sentinels alerted their king who, afraid, preferred to surrender and convert to Christianity. The young girls returned home and, stopping to rest on their way, planted their lances in a field. A miracle happened! The next morning leaves and branches had grown on the lances! Popular imagination filled in the rest. Roland, after vainly trying to break his sword, Durandal, on a rock, did he not throw it away in a last, despairing act? And did the weapon not plant itself into the rock face of the cliff at Roc Amadour? Or, did it not, upon falling, cut the famous breach into the rock above the Cirque de Gavarnie, through which some adventurous pilgrims crossed over the Pyrenees before rejoining Torla, Biescas and then Jaca…

Roland's Breach

Durandal, so that it would not fall into the hands of the Saracens. In the 17th century, the hospital was still serving over twenty thousand meals to pilgrims annually, or more than fifty a day.

It was Sancho the Strong (1194-1234) who undertook the construction of Roncesvalles collegiate church in 1207. Under a dais, behind the high altar of this Gothic church, shines the statue of Our Lady of Roncesvalles. Made of cedar wood covered with silver plate, it is a French work from the beginning of the 14th century. The cloister was rebuilt in the 17th century, after the galleries of the primitive cloister collapsed because of a heavy snowfall. The former chapter house, from the 14th century, contains the recumbent statue of Sancho the Strong. This room also presents the chains, shown on the Navarre coat of arms, that encircled the head of Miramamolin, the Almohad chief defeated at the battle of Las Navas de Tolosa in 1212. The museum's collections include fine pieces such as a 12th century pyxidium of silver and gold, a reliquary, called Charlemagne's chessboard, from the 14th century, the emerald that was supposed to have decorated Miramamolin's turban, a Romanesque book of the Gospels from the early 13th century, sculpted panels from an ancient reredos of the collegiate church, including one showing pilgrims attacked by wolves. South of the collegiate church, Saint James's Chapel dates from the 13th century, and the Holy Spirit Chapel, also called Charlemagne's Silo, from the 12th. On the left side of the road between Roncesvalles and Burgette stands a pilgrims cross.

Our Lady of Roncesvalles

LAS NAVAS DE TOLOSA

At the beginning of the year 1212, the Almohads under the authority of caliph al Nasr, known by the name of Miramamolin, prepared an offensive and concentrated an army of 300,000 men in Sevilla. Alfonso VIII had Pope Innocent III decree a crusade against the Almohads, with the same indulgences for the crusaders as those granted to warriors in the Holy Land. The crusaders gathered in Toledo at the end of May. There were 60,000 Castilians led by Alfonso VIII, 50,000 Aragonese under Pedro II, and over 60,000 *Francos* with prelates from Narbonne, Bordeaux and Nantes. After capturing Calatrava, Sancho VII the Strong, the king of Navarre, rejoined the army that most of the Frankish troops had abandoned, with the exception of those following Arnaud-Amaury, the spiritual leader of another crusade, that against the Albigensian heresy in Languedoc. The battle took place at Las Navas de Tolosa on July 16, 1212. While the first fighting was beginning, Miramamolin was reading the Koran in his tent, surrounded by thousands of chained slaves armed with lances. Learning of his troops' defeat, he fled to Sevilla. The crusaders then captured other places like Ubeda and Baeza. According to legend this victory of the Christians was helped by the intervention of Our Lady of Rocamadour and was the beginning of the decline of the Almohad kingdom.

Charlemagne's checkerboard, Roncesvalles Museum

The Puerta Preciosa in Pamplona Cathedral

Pamplona

Between Burguete and Pamplona, pilgrims had to cross the Arga River several times, once at the entrance to the town by the Magdalena Bridge. The antique town of *Pompaelo* was allegedly founded by Pompey in about 75 BC. In the 8th century, it was occupied by the Moors, chased out by Charlemagne in 778. In 905, it became the capital of Navarre. Under Alfonso VII (1126-1157), *Francos* settled in the village of San Cernin. Another Frankish town, San Nicolás, was created at the end of the 12th century. Jealousy between the two villages and the primitive site of Navarreria, each protected by walls, caused conflicts but did not slow the development created by the passage of pilgrims. During the 16th century, walls surrounded the town and pilgrims entered through the France Gate, near Saint Mary's Cathedral. This church had been rebuilt on the initiative of Charles III the Noble (1387-1425) during the 14th and 15th centuries on the site of the primitive Romanesque church, whose capitals can been seen at the Museum of Navarre. In the 18th century, it received its Neo-Classical façade. It contains the alabaster tomb, made in 1426, of Charles III the Noble and his wife Eleonore. A splendid flamboyant cloister flanks the south side of the cathedral. It has large, elegant bays and finely sculpted doors, like the *Puerta preciosa*. The sacristy, in exuberant Baroque style, supposedly made Victor Hugo say, "It's the sacristy of Madame de Pompadour!". The diocesan museum, occupying the former refectory of the cathedral's canons, built in 1330, presents fine pieces, including two reliquaries – one of the Holy Sepulchre, offered in 1258 by Saint Louis to King Thibaud of Navarre (1253-1270), and one of *Lignum Crucis*, offered by Byzantine Emperor Manuel II Paleologus to Charles III the Noble in 1401. At the exit of Pamplona, pilgrims crossed Cizur, then climbed the Sierra del Perdón, whose crest today is covered with a group of modern white windmills, before reaching Obanos near the entrance into Puente la Reina.

Cloister, Pamplona Cathedral

THE ROMANESQUE CATHEDRAL

The construction of the cathedral of Pamplona was started in the early 12th century during the bishopric of don Pedro de Roda, a former monk in Conques. This large church was completely destroyed in 1277, when the towns of San Cernin and San Nicolás, supported by the French troops of the Count of Arras, confronted each other at Navarreria. The architect had been Master Esteban, who had also made the sculptures on the doorway. A genial anonymous master carved the cloister's capitals, some of which are presented at the Museum of Navarre.

Calvary Triptych, Diocesan Museum, Pamplona

Capital, Museum of Navarre

Nave in St Mary Magdalene Basilica, Vézelay

Via Lemovicensis

Coming from Belgium, the Ardennes, Lorraine or Champagne, the pilgrims of the *via Lemovicensis* gathered in Burgundy, around the Romanesque splendour of Saint Mary Magdalene of Vezelay. Through Nevers or the cathedral in Bourges, filled with the brilliance of its stained glass windows, the *via Lemovicensis* entered the Limousin, taking its name, to reach Saint Leonard's famous shrine, dear to Aimery Picaud. After Périgueux, once the Dordogne and Garonne Rivers had been crossed, the feared crossing of the Landes was quite short by this route that joined the *via Turonensis* at Sauveterre-en-Béarn. Then at the Gibraltar crossroads, near Saint-Palais, came the junction with the *via Podiensis*.

Vézelay

It was between 855 and 859 that Girart de Roussillon, Count of Vienne, Regent of Provence and posthumous hero of the lovely chanson de geste bearing his name, founded a monastery for women on his lands in Vézelay, in the valley of the Cure River, on the site of the present village of Saint-Père. By the end of the 9th century, monks had replaced nuns when Norsemen sacked the abbey in 887, leading the abbot Eudes to install his community on a neighbouring hill, the "inspired hill" of Vézelay, where a new

Girart de Roussillon

The husband of Berthe, daughter of Count Hugues of Tours, Girart became Count of Paris around 829. However, he had to abandon his title around 840 after supporting Lothaire against his brothers Charles the Bald (843-877) and Louis the German. Remaining faithful to the vanquished, and after the latter's death in 855, to his son Charles, an epileptic child, Girart became the regent of the kingdom of Provence. Before 860, with his wife he founded two Burgundy monasteries in Pothières and Vézelay. But after the death of Lothaire 1st's two sons, Charles of Provence and Lothaire II of Lorraine (825-869), Girart was forced to deliver besieged Vienne to Charles the Bald. He retired to Avignon where he died four years

after Berthe, in 877. According to their last wishes, the husband and wife were buried in the abbey of Pothières. Composed between 1136 and 1180, the *Song of Girart of Roussillon* provided its eponymous hero some of the characteristics of the historical Girart. It tells how, after years of struggling against Charles, his sovereign, a vanquished and dispossessed Girart found refuge with his wife Berthe, daughter of the Emperor of Constantinople, in the Ardennes forest. There, following the advice of an old hermit, he did penance for his sins and became a humble charcoal-burner. After twenty-two years, he was finally reconciled with his king and founded many monasteries before becoming a monk himself.

Stages	Kms
Vézelay *	925
Bazoches	915
Nevers	839
Saint-Pierre-le-Moûtier	817
Saint-Amand-Montrond	753
Neuvy-Saint-Sépulcre	685
Éguzon	654
La Souterraine	621
Bénévent-l'Abbaye	599
Saint-Léonard-de-Noblat *	551
Limoges	530
Châlus	492
Thiviers	463
Périgueux *	425
Bergerac	377
Duras	334
Monségur	324
La Réole	315
Bazas	286
Roquefort	240
Saint-Pierre-du-Mont	215
Saint-Sever	203
Hagetmau	191
Orthez	166
Sauveterre-de-Béarn	145
Puente la Reina	0

Berry variation:
Vézelay, La Charité-sur-Loire, Bourges, Châteauroux, Éguzon

References to Aimery Picaud's *Guide*.
*: presence of "holy bodies"

Vézelay Hill

PENTECOST

O n the central tympanum of the narthex in the basilica of Vézelay, Christ in majesty, radiant and surrounded by a mandorla, sends the Holy Spirit, shown as rays from His hands, onto the heads of the apostles.

Benedictine monastery was established. Starting in the 11th century, Vézelay Abbey, that joined the Cluniac order about 1055, lived its hours of glory with the arrival of the relics of Mary Magdalene, brought by the monk Badilon, and solemnly authenticated by the papacy in 1058, to the detriment of the Provencal shrine of Saint Maximin. From then on, crowds of pilgrims arrived to pray at the holy remains of the first person to have seen Christ resuscitated. Vézelay was where Bernard de Clairvaux preached the Second Crusade in a fiery speech on March 31, 1146. Here too Richard the Lionheart and Philippe Auguste of France met to leave on the Third Crusade in 1190. Saint Mary Magdalene of Vézelay was also the gathering point of Santiago pilgrims taking the *via Lemovicensis*. Begun after the violent fire that destroyed a first building in 1120, the long Romanesque nave of the abbey church, harmonious and light, two storeys high, with groined arches also over the aisles, was completed around 1140. The surprising ochre and white double-colouring of its beam arches are a reminder of distant Moorish Spain, probably arrived here with the passage of pilgrims along the route from Santiago de Compostela. Between 1140 and 1160, the building received a large narthex that increased its capacity to contain the faithful. Tympana and capitals, decorated with rich sculptures, completed the basilica and placed it among the masterpieces of Romanesque architecture. Encircled by an ambulatory with radiating chapels, the chancel, covered by an ogival arch, announcing the begin-

Central tympanum of narthex of St Mary Magdalene Basilica, Vézelay

MARY MAGDALENE

"Healed of seven demons" by the great power of the Son of Man, Mary Magdalene, sometimes called Mary of Magdala in the Gospels, from the town on the Sea of Galilee, was one of the women from Galilee who followed Christ and his apostles in their wanderings. She attended the crucifixion and the laying in the tomb, and was among those who, in the morning, found the empty sepulchre. Christ resuscitated appeared first of all to Mary Magdalene. The first to believe, she carried to news to the apostles. The Latin church identified Mary Magdalene with Mary of Bethany, the sister of Martha and Lazarus, as well as an anonymous sinner who, interrupting a meal in the Pharisee's house, threw herself at Jesus's feet, covered them with tears, kisses and perfume and dried them with her hair. Worshipped in Ephesus by the 6th century, according to Byzantine tradition her tomb was allegedly carried to Constantinople in 899.

However, in 1050, a papal bull of the Roman Leon XI recognized the presence of the saint's remains in Vézelay where, if one believed the *Gesta episcoporum Cameracensium* written in 1024-1025, they had been brought by the monk Badilon returning from a pilgrimage to Jerusalem. But by the 12th century, the monk's action had been somewhat modified. At that time, the *Vita apostolica Beatae Mariae Magdalenae*, probably written in Vézelay, claimed that, fleeing persecution by Herod Agrippa, Mary Magdalene had long ago landed in Provence, accompanied by her sister Martha, her brother Lazarus, their servant Sara, Mary Salome and Mary Jacobe, at the location now known as Saintes-Maries-de-la-Mer. Preferring solitude, Mary Magdalene then retired to live as a penitent east of Marseilles, in the cave known as "Sainte Baume", before being buried in Saint Maximin. Based on this tale, the *Chronicle* of Sigebert de

Mary Magdalene arrives in Provence

Gembloux thus explained how, during the 9th century, while Saracens were devastating Provence, at the risk of profaning the tomb of Mary Magdalene, Count Girart and the abbot Eudes had charged the monk Badilon with obtaining the relics from Saint Maximin and bringing them to safety in Vézelay. If this modification helped to increase the fame of Mary Magdalene, making her at least the equal of Saint Foy of Conques, by a strange irony of fate, she was also to be the cause of the ruin of the abbey in Vézelay. Because a conflict broke out between the abbey in Burgundy and the Provencal shrine in Saint Maximin, who claimed that, at the approach of the Saracens, the saint's tomb had in fact been hidden in a place unknown to all. And when in 1279, they rediscovered the sarcophagus, devoutly buried such a long time before, Pope Boniface VIII decided in their favour and charged the brothers of Saint Dominic to watch over the coveted remains of Mary Magdalene, ever since worshipped at Saint Maximin.

Mary Magdalene announces the resuscitated Christ to the apostles

Saint Mary Magdalene Basilica in Vézelay

nings of Gothic architecture, was constructed during the abbacy of Girart d'Arcy (1171-1198). To house pilgrims, the abbey counted on its hostelry, on the generosity of the town's inhabitants, but also on its neighbouring dependencies. Hence, the priory it possessed at Asquins, two kilometres to the north, was especially destined for Santiago pilgrims, who could worship in the *ecclesia peregrinorum* – the pilgrims' church – dedicated to Saint James and consecrated in 1132 by the bishop of Autun. It was in Asquins that Olivier d'Iscans, alias Aimery Picaud, supposedly retired in about 1135 to write his *Guide* and to complete the collection of the different books of the *Codex Calixtinus*, that he allegedly took to Santiago in about 1150, in company of a Flemish woman name Gerberge. The chapel of Saint Vincent in Saint James's church in Asquins still contains the reliquary bust of its patron saint, made of polychrome wood at the end of the 16th century. Nobody knows the origin nor the nature of the relics it contained and they no longer exist. Although Pope Boniface VIII rang the death knell of the pilgrimage to Vézelay and ended the prosperity of its abbey by recognizing the authenticity of the relics kept at Saint-Maximin in 1279, the Burgundian shrine of the great penitent was still popular among Santiago pilgrims. Gathering in Saint-Père or Asquins, they had the choice of two itineraries – through La Charité-sur-Loire, Bourges and Châteauroux, or via Nevers, Saint-Pierre-le-Moûtier and Neuvy-Saint-Sépulcre.

Angel with horn, Vézelay basilica

Burgundy Roads

C oming from the north, from Châlons-en-Champagne or Troyes, the Santiago pilgrims arrived in Vézelay through Saint Florentin and Auxerre, where they were welcomed by the Benedictine monks of the powerful abbey of Saint Germain. In the crypt of the abbey church, decorated with magnificent pre-Romanesque frescoes illustrating the martyrdom of Saint Stephen, the pilgrims came to worship at the tomb of the great bishop of Auxerre. They did not leave the town without going to Saint Stephen's Cathedral, rebuilt in Gothic style starting in 1215 by the bishop Guillaume de Seignelay. The only reminder of the Romanesque cathedral is the crypt, located under the chancel, containing a unique kind of fresco, painted around 1100, showing Christ riding on a white donkey. Another important itinerary led to Vézelay through Autun, where pilgrims never failed to go and worship the relics of Saint Lazarus, protected within the admirable cathedral, a jewel of Romanesque sculptural art, that was built by bishop Étienne de Bagé at the beginning of the 12th century. From Autun, the pilgrims reached Vézelay via Saulieu and its Saint Andoche Collegiate Church, but they could also rejoin the *via Lemovicensis* in Nevers.

Christ riding a white horse, fresco in Auxerre Cathedral

Stoning of Saint Stephen, crypt of Saint-Germain in Auxerre

Capital in Saint-Andoche, Saulieu

La Charité-sur-Loire

Saint Stephen's Cathedral in Bourges

162

Saint James preaching

JACQUES CŒUR

....

T he son of a furrier from
   Bourges, in 1432 Jacques
Cœur left for Syria and Egypt
in order to establish trade with
merchants in Damascus and
Alexandria, the main locations
of eastern commerce. During his
return, his ship was wrecked near
Corsica and its cargo was lost.
Ruined, but faithful to his motto,
"To brave hearts, nothing is
impossible", Jacques did not get
discouraged but established a
business in Montpellier, then in
Marseilles, from where his seven
ships carried cloth and weapons,
as well as pilgrims, eastwards,
and returned loaded with silks,
carpets, velvet, spices and
perfumes. Jacques acquired
trading posts and branches in
various cities in France and the
Mediterranean basin, created a
silk manufacture in Florence,
a dye works in Montpellier, mines
and a paper factory. A supplier to
Charles VII's court established in
Bourges, Jacques Cœur obtained
the king's trust. But he was
disgraced in 1451 and thrown into
prison. Escaping, he fled to Rome
where he entered the pope's
service, before his death in 1456.

The Route through Berry

Pilgrims leaving Vézelay in the direction of La Charité-sur-Loire,
where they received charity from the "good fathers" of its abbey
founded in 1052 by a lord of La Marche and a Cluniac monk named
Gérart. A "daughter" of Cluny, it contained a community of about
two hundred monks and controlled over forty-five priories spread all
over France, but also in England, Italy, Portugal and even in
Constantinople. Between the Loire and Cher Rivers, Bourges was the
next stage on the pilgrims' route. First of all ruled by Charlemagne's
descendants, then by the Counts of Bourges, the city was annexed to
the kingdom of France by Philippe 1st (1060-1108). Bourges had
become the capital and it was from there that Charles VII (1422-
1461), crowned in Reims in 1429 thanks to Joan of Arc, managed to
regain the kingdom of France from the English starting in 1449, thus
putting an end to the Hundred Years War in 1453. He had been
helped in this by the financial aid of his great treasurer and principal
advisor, Jacques Cœur. Saint Stephen's Cathedral was built at the initiative of archbishop Henry de Sully in 1195. Without a transept, with
its five long, high Gothic naves opening onto the façade by five
sculpted doorways, it lets light burst into a unified space that nothing
impedes. Pilgrims used to worship in the chapel of Saint François de
Sales in the apse, whose left stained glass window, dating from the
13th century like most of the exceptional stained glass windows in the
cathedral, is entirely devoted to the story of James the Greater.
Leaving the episcopal city, the road crossed the Cher River by the fortified bridge of Villeneuve, passed the Benedictine priory of Chârost
on the Arnon River, and arrived at the fortified town of Issoudun, at
the confluence of the Théols and Vignole rivers. Depending on the
Duchy of Aquitaine, Issoudun was placed under the authority of the
Kingdom of France in 1137, when Louis VII (1137-1180) married
Eleanor of Aquitaine, then under that of the Kingdom of England
after the accession of Henry II Plantagenet, Eleanor's second husband, as king of England in 1154. An important stake, it was besieged

The Last Judgement, tympanum of central doorway in Bourges Cathedral

Opus Francigenum

"Shines in splendour that which one unites splendidly, and the magnificent work, flooded with a new light, is resplendent."
Inscription at Saint Denis

The first Gothic art was born in the middle of the 12th century, in Île de France, and more specifically, at Saint Denis, under the impetus of Abbot Suger. To decorate the triple doorway of the western façade of his abbey church, competed in 1140, Suger invented statue-columns, set into piedroits and carved out of the same block of stone. They thus participated in the monument's vertical tension. The chevet, consecrated in 1144, was of ambitious design, with a double ambulatory and radiating chapels. Using an ogival crossing and directing the thrust of the arches into several discrete points – the pillars, and not over the entire supporting walls, allowed an opening up of the radiating chapels by piercing the walls with large arched openings, hence emphasizing the emptiness rather than the solid. The appearance of flying buttresses, that could move the buttresses away from their former place right against the walls, freed enormous spaces for windows and let a stream of coloured light flood into the chancel. Bringing their reflections to bear on the elevation and unification of interior volume, the architects of the cathedrals in Sens (1140), Senlis and Paris (1160) or Bourges (1170) chose plans without a transept. Using all together arches on ogival crossings, flying buttresses and Gothic arches, enabling arches to be raised higher by getting rid of the keystone, their

buildings reached heights never before seen. Gothic art reached its full flowering and its style was completely mastered between 1190 and 1240. A perfect example of the style was the cathedral in Chartres, built between 1190 and 1220. It restored the transept and renewed the relationship between solids and emptiness. Its master builder abandoned galleries, a buttressing element that had become useless thanks to the development of flying buttress techniques. The nave was raised to three storeys, and large arches and high windows, separated by a triforium, were of equal height. He also replaced the six-sectioned vault by a four-sectioned one, hence eliminating alternate supports and establishing a correspondence between the nave and the side aisles. The bays thus became repetitive modules, creating interior volume and contributing to the vertical dynamics of the building. Reims, the cathedral where kings were crowned, started in 1211, and Amiens about 1220, adopted the Chartres model. On the facades of Gothic cathedrals, sculptures looked more human, more realistic and the themes used were closer to the faithful. Beside scenes with Christ – Ascension, Last Judgement – there appeared the Coronation, the Dormition, or the Assumption of the Virgin, as well as

Detail of column-statues, Laon

the story of the town's patron saint. The end of the first half of the 13th century marked the beginning of Rayonnant Gothic style, where light played an essential role. Architects emphasized opening up the walls, enlarging arcades, and provided the facades of their cathedrals with enormous rose windows of stained glass, the tracery imitating the spokes of a wheel (*rayon* in French). This was the high point of stained glass work, a distinctive element of cathedral decoration. A fourth period, called Flamboyant Gothic, appeared during the second half of the 14th century. The curving lines, reminiscent of flames, were used as tracery in the windows. On facades, portals' Gothic arches were raised with brackets. Using vaults with liernes and tiercerons became general, the keystone often hanging and lavishly decorated. Born in Île de France, and hence named *opus francigenum*, Gothic style spread throughout Christian Europe during the 13th and 14th centuries, even reaching the Holy Land, before dying in the early 16th century at the end of the Middle Ages. The term "Gothic" was coined during the Renaissance, its writers judging medieval art with contempt, attributing it to the barbarian Gothic tribes that had destroyed classical Roman culture. However, these cathedrals, the "homes of God with man", reaching for the sky with their forests of flying buttresses, the walls of shining glass resplendent "as much as the most precious stone, like jasper", and the faces, lively and familiar as well as enigmatic, on the statues and angels, still stand like an invitation to "make use of the tree of life, and enter into the City, through the doors".

St James, Issoudun Museum

Our Lady of the Rosary Chapel, Saint-Cyr Collegiate Church in Issoudun

several times by Philippe Auguste (1180-1223) between 1187 and 1199, then fortified by the king of England, Richard the Lionheart, starting in 1195, before being definitely integrated into the French kingdom in 1240. During the medieval period, the city possessed several shrines, the only one surviving today is the former collegiate church of Saint Cyr. The canons of the Saint Cyr chapter served Saint Roch Hospital, where pilgrims received a warm welcome. They could also find shelter at the hostelry of the important Benedictine monastery dedicated to Our Lady, which contained the relics of Saint Patrice, Saint Brigide and Saint Paterne, the bishop of Vanne. Continuing on their way, the pilgrims reached the Cluniac abbey of Notre-Dame in Déols, founded in 917 by Ebbes le Noble. Unfortunately, only vestiges are still visible, including the abbey church's steeple. The crypt in the church of Saint Stephen in Déols has retained the sepulchres of two local saints – Saint Ludre and his father Léocade. Once the Indre River crossed and the town of Châteauroux passed, with its Saint Gildas Abbey and Saint James Hospital, the road reached the priory of Argenton, then followed the Creuse River in the direction of Gargilesse. There, pilgrims worshipped in the Romanesque church of Our Lady, endowed with historiated capitals and whose crypt is decorated with frescoes. They found lodging at the "Pilgrims' Shelter", a priory depending on Déols Abbey, of which only a tower remains. Past Cuzion, the road crossed the Creuse at the Pont-des-Piles, at the foot of Châteaubrun castle, and continued in the direction of Eguzon, where it joined the road from Nevers.

Notre-Dame steeple in Déols

Fresco in Notre-Dame, Gargilesse

THE KING'S CUSTOMARY ENGINEER

S ébastien Le Prestre, Marquis of Vauban, began his career in 1651 in the regiment of the Duke of Condé, rebelling against royal power. As a prisoner in 1653, he was noticed by Mazarin and entered the service of the general commissioner for fortifications. In 1655 he obtained his military engineer's certificate. Vauban took part in most of the military constructions during Louis XIV's reign (1661-1715). The governor of Lille in 1668, then general commissioner of fortifications in 1678, he was named lieutenant of the king's armies in 1688, and marshal in 1703. Not only an engineer who organized more than a hundred fortresses and about thirty walls and citadels, Vauban was also a thinker and reformer. After the revocation of the Edict of Nantes, in 1686 he published *Mémoire pour un rappel des huguenots*, then in 1698 wrote his *Projet d'une dixme royale*, for the elimination of the privileges of nobles and clergy and the adoption of tax proportional to income. After its unauthorized publication in 1706, it was condemned by the king in 1707. Sick and bruised, Vauban died shortly afterwards. He lies in the church at Bazoches, a town where he liked to stay, near his family, in a castle formerly belonging to Louis de la Perrière, his great-grandfather, that Vauban had acquired in 1675.

Portrait of Vauban, Bazoches

The Nevers Route

Leaving from Vézelay, the route to Nevers took the direction of Pierre-Perthuis, where pilgrims could hear Mass in the former chapel of the town's castle. Once the Cure River was crossed, and the lord's domain at Bazoches, with its Saint Roch chapel, passed, they reached the village of Corbigny, born in the 9th century around the Benedictine abbey of Saint Leonard, destroyed in 1420 during the struggle between Armagnacs and Burgundians. Moving westwards, the road crossed the Nivernais canal and passed by the Cluniac priory of Saint Riverien. Here the prior's house and a church of Romanesque origin remain, modified although still conserving its remarkable sculpted capitals. From Prémery, the summer residence of the bishops of Nevers, who held the title of Count of Prémery, the route followed the picturesque valley of the Nièvre River, passing through Sichamps, Poiseux, Guerigny and Urzy, before arriving in Nevers. A bishopric occupied by the Bishop Eulade by the 6th century, the first cathedral of Nevers was located on the site of the present cathedral of Saint-Cyr-et- Sainte-Julitte, as attested in the 6th century baptistery, discovered under the Gothic chancel. The entire western section including the apse, the crypt and the large transept remain from the 11th century Romanesque cathedral that faced west and was burned in 1221. A Gothic nave, built during the reconstruction in the 13th century, leads to a new chancel, facing east, dating from the 14th century. The present

Baptistery in Nevers Cathedral

AN AUVERGNE ROAD

An alternative to the *via Lemovicensis* left from Nevers in the direction of Clermont. Following the course of the Allier River, pilgrims were welcomed by the Benedictine monks at the abbey of Souvigny which, like Sauxillanges, was one of the "daughters" of Cluny. Arriving in the valley of the Sioule, between Dôme and Dore, they went to worship the Virgin at the abbey in Orcival, before once again meeting the Allier River at Issoire Abbey, founded according to tradition by an apostle of Auvergne, the devout Austremoine, towards the middle of the 3rd century. Then, past Sauxillanges Abbey, the road took the direction of Brioude where the holy martyr Julian was buried. It was in Brioude that Pope Urban II, on his way from Le Puy to Clermont in December 1095, signed the decree making Santiago de Compostela a bishopric. Brioude at the time had a church dedicated to James the Greater. From Brioude, the pilgrims could join the *via Podiensis* at Le Puy, or get to the shores of the Jordanne River and Aurillac Abbey, founded in 894 by Count Géraud. Reformed by Cluny, the abbey included Saint Odon (879-942), the second abbot of Cluny, among its own abbots. His school shaped eminent personalities, such as the monk Gerbert, who went to study mathematics in Catalonia, directed the school of Reims in 972, then became abbot of Bobbio at the request of Emperor Otto II in 982. He helped Hugues Capet triumph in 987, and ran the archbishopric of Ravenna in 998. After being an advisor to Otto III, he became pope taking the name Sylvester II (999-1003). During the 11th century, monks from Aurillac also served the mountain church of Cebreiro on the *Camino francés*. From Aurillac, pilgrims rejoined the *via Podiensis* through Souillac and Agen, or else by Rocamadour.

Detail of Last Judgement, wall painting in Brioude basilica

St Michael, Issoire Abbey Church

St Géraud, Aurillac church

Capital in Bénévent-l'Abbaye

St James, La Souterraine

La Souterraine and Bénévent-l'Abbaye

Coming from Eguzon, the pilgrims discovered La Souterraine, a fortified city that owed its name (meaning underground) to the underground shrine of Gallo-Roman origin that it contained. Around 1015, Gérald de Crozant, Lord of Bridiers, offered his fief of La Souterraine to Saint Martial's Abbey in Limoges. Under the direction of the prior Rodolphe, the monks restored and enlarged the Gallo-Roman crypt where the donor had been buried in 1022. Construction of the upper church, dedicated to Our Lady, began in 1070, not without arousing hostility from the inhabitants, not wanting to pay tallage and tax to fund the work. In the shape of a Latin cross, Notre-Dame Church was finally completed at the beginning of the 13th century. It possesses a fine Romanesque polyfoiled portal, decorated with three voussoirs scalloped from the base, betraying the influence of Mozarab architecture that most likely arrived here with pilgrims coming from Santiago de Compostela. Guiding them on their way, the steeple's white stone indicated the direction of Bénévent Abbey, the next stage on their journey. At the dawn of the 11th century, the monastic community that had been founded by the cathedral chapter of Limoges on the lands of Segondelas – nowadays, Cigoulet – was transferred to its present location under the impetus of its prior, Dom Humbert, and bishop Jourdain de Laron (1023-1051). In 1028, on the day of its consecration, the new abbey church received the relics of Saint Bartholomew. They came from the town of Benevento in Italy, providing the monastery with its name. Given the flood of pilgrims, construction of the much larger present church was begun during the second half of the 11th century. Opening with a polyfoiled portal of Mozarab style, decorated with five voussoirs, it comprises a nave, a protruding transept flanked with two apsidal chapels, and ends with a choir with a semi-dome vault, encircled by a narrow ambulatory with three radiating chapels. Its capitals were decorated with palms and stylized motifs, but also with lions, serpents, griffons and man-eating monsters.

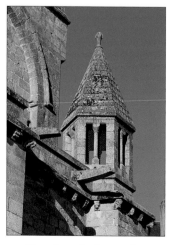

Pinnacle on La Souterraine

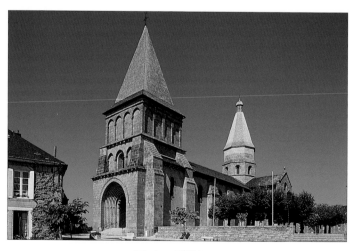

Bénévent-l'Abbaye

CROSS ROADS

From Bénévent abbey, a secondary road passed through Bourganeuf, seat of a commandery belonging to the Hospitallers of Saint John of Jerusalem, continued through Eymoutiers and its Saint Stephen's Collegiate Church. Via Treignac, it reached the shores of the Corrèze River and the city of Tulle, born around a former Benedictine monastery dedicated to Saint Martin. In 1317, Pope John XXII raised the city to a bishopric and Saint Martin's Abbey Church, with its Gothic cloister at its south, became a cathedral. After the abbey at Obazine, part of the Cistercian order since 1147, the path ran directly south via Lanteuil and crossed Collonges-la-Rouge, a fortified town that developed around a former priory depending on the powerful Poitou abbey of Charroux. Its church, whose doorway is decorated with a sculpted tympanum showing the Ascension, was rebuilt in the first half of the 11th century. Its square-based steeple is characteristic of Limousin art. From Collonges, the road continued in the direction of Martel and crossed the Dordogne River to reach Rocamadour. From there, the pilgrims could join the *via Podiensis* either directly by Cahors, or at Condom via Agen. From Saint-Léonard-de-Noblat, another road led to Rocamadour by the Cluniac abbey of Uzerche on the shores of the Vézère, and by Brive-la-Gaillarde, born around the monastery dedicated to Saint Martin of Spain, a martyr with the same name as the famous bishop of Tours.

Obazine Abbey Church

Collonges-la-Rouge

Fresco in chapter house, Tulle

Saint-Léonard-de-Noblat Collegiate Church

A misericord in Saint-Léonard-de-Noblat Church

Reliquary arm of St Leonard

Saint-Léonard-de-Noblat

After leaving Bénévent-l'Abbaye, past Saint-Goussaud, and having crossed the Taurion over the Dognon bridge, the *via Lemovicensis* reached the town of Saint-Léonard-de-Noblat, one of its major stages, to which Aimery Picaud's *Guide* devoted a long section. Legend had it that in the 6th century, the devout Leonard, a god-son of Clovis and a disciple of the great bishop of Reims, Rémi, left the court to live like a hermit in Pauvin forest, on the banks of the Vienne River. Thanks to his intercession while she was on the point of dying in childbirth, Wisigarde, Queen of Austrasia, gave birth, then offered Leonard a small plot of land in the Limousin forest, at *Nobiliacum*, Noble Place, where a little chapel called Our-Lady-Under-the-Trees was built. Miraculously freeing the condemned, slaves and prisoners, Leonard worked to rehabilitate them by making them work on his little domain. Having died in the odour of sanctity in 559, he was buried in his chapel, which became the object of one of the most popular pilgrimages of the Middle Ages. Rebuilt after its destruction by Norsemen in the 9th century, Saint Leonard's Church was served by Augustinian canons, when Jourdain de Laron, Lord of Noblat and bishop of Limoges in 1023, decided to build a bigger collegiate church. His successor, Itier Chabot (1051-1073) continued the work. Enlarged and progressively completed in the course of the 12th century, it has a nave with five spans, a transept and a chancel encircled by an ambulatory with seven radiating chapels. A tholos-steeple covered with a cupola rises at the transept crossing, while the bell-tower, five storeys high, a fine example of gabled Limousin bell-towers, rises to a height of fifty-two metres. No doubt it served as a reference point to devout pilgrims seeing it from a distance. In the Middle Ages, sterile couples came to rattle the bolt on the church door in order to make their union fertile. And still today, the shackles, called "*verrou*" in the collegiate church perpetuate this belief.

St Leonard

HOMAGE TO SAINT LEONARD

Rather pompously, Aimery Picaud in his *Pilgrim's Guide* emphasized the great popularity of Saint Leonard, the "breaker of chains" whose miraculous intercession was solicited by many prisoners, pilgrims coming from France, but also Germany, Austria, Italy and Britain, who left their former chains as votive offerings in his shrine. "Divine clemency has thus already spread far and wide throughout the whole world the glory of the blessed confessor Leonard of Limousin and his powerful intercession has brought thousands of captives out of their prisons; their iron chains, more barbaric than can be explained, gathered in thousands, have been hung all around his basilica, to the right and left, inside and out, as witnesses of such great miracles. One is more surprised than can be expressed upon seeing these poles loaded with so many and such huge barbaric shackles. There, indeed, hang iron handcuffs, iron collars, chains, shackles, various devices, traps, padlocks, yokes, helmets, scythes and diverse instruments from which the most powerful confessor of Christ has, by his power, delivered captives."

Shackles called *verrou*, Saint-Léonard-de-Noblat Church

Rue de la Boucherie in Limoges

LETTER FROM POPE LEON

....

I t is the scriptorium of Saint Martial's abbey, an important stage on the via Lemovicensis, that provided the oldest of the three manuscripts known in the *Apocryphal Letter from Pope Leon*, recounting the translation of Saint James in Spain.

Limoges

According to tradition, the Roman town of *Augustoritum*, that became Limoges, was evangelized in the second half of the 3rd century by Saint Martial, the town's first bishop. Starting in the 9th century, a commercial city, the domain of the Viscount of Limoges, developed around the Benedictine abbey built on the site of the saint's tomb, whose relics were exposed in the abbey church's crypt and attracted many pilgrims. Entering the Cluniac order in 1063, Saint Martial's Abbey was famous for its music school, its commentaries and liturgical poems, and the talent of its illuminators. At the end of the 12th century, the abbey specialized in manufacturing champlevé enamels, in which it became pre-eminent during the 13th century. Brought to light between 1960 and 1962, Saint Martial's crypt is the only remainder of the monastery destroyed at the Revolution. Nowadays, the saint's relics lie in Saint-Michel-des-Lions Church, where they were transferred in 1790. East of the commercial town, the medieval episcopal city gathered around Saint Stephen's Cathedral. Legend has it that the primitive cathedral was built by Martial in place of a pagan temple dedicated to Jupiter. Of the Romanesque building, consecrated in 1095 by Urban II, remain only the crypt, decorated with a fresco, and the lower storeys of the steeple. Work on the Gothic cathedral began in 1273. Crossing the Vienne River by the Saint Martial bridge, on the way out of the city, the road continued in the direction of Châlus.

Thomas à Becket's reliquary in champlevé enamel, Limoges Bishopric Municipal Museum

SAINT MARTIAL

A first legendary biography of Saint Martial appeared only in the 8th century, setting the origins of the Limoges church in apostolic times. This *Primitive Life* recounted that Martial had been sent to evangelize the Limousin by Peter. He left Rome in the company of two disciples, Alpinian and Austriclinian. When the latter died during the journey, Martial brought him back to life with Saint Peter's staff that he carried, and hence the three missionaries arrived in Limoges. They preached successfully, founding the Christian community of the Limousin, and Martial took over its leadership as bishop. However, as this tale said nothing of Martial's activities before his apostolate, in the early 11th century, Adhémar de Chabannes, a monk at Saint Martial, filled in the gap by writing a second biography, making Martial Saint Peter's cousin. Furthermore, he identified him as the little child Christ had shown to the apostles while urging them to become like children, as well as with the young boy "who had five loaves and two fishes", during the multiplication of loaves in the desert.

THE LAST SIEGE

The third son of Henry II Plantagenet (1154-1189) and Eleanor of Aquitaine (1122-1204), Richard the Lionheart received the title of Duke of Aquitaine from his mother in 1169. His reign as King of England from 1189 to 1199 was above all marked by his absence. Hardly had a few months passed after his accession to the throne when he joined Philippe Auguste (1180-1223) at Vézelay, at the start of the Third Crusade. Although the French king returned home quickly, taking advantage of the absence of his powerful vassal and English opposite number to invade the Duchy of Normandy and plot with the future king John, Richard won fame in the Holy Land, commanded the capture of Acre and defeated Saladin at Arsouf in 1191. Arrested in Vienna by Duke Leopold while he was preparing to return to England in December 1192, Richard owed his liberation in 1194 to the intervention of his mother, Eleanor. Preserving his royal title from the claims to the crown of his brother John, Eleanor raised a huge extraordinary tax in England to pay the enormous 150,000 mark ransom demanded by the emperor to free her favourite son. Returning to England, Richard took the time to receive his brother's submission and to entrust the kingdom's management to the Archbishop of Canterbury, Hubert Gautier, before leaving to defend his lands against Philippe Auguste and to consolidate his authority on the continent. Assuring his position in Normandy, Richard had Château-Gaillard built at Andelys on the Seine. But in 1199, he retaliated for his vassal Adhémar's infidelity, when the latter, Viscount of Limoges, passed into Philippe Auguste's camp, by besieging his fortress of Châlus-Chabrol. Richard was mortally wounded during the siege and died shortly afterwards. Although the church of Châlus-Haut has kept his entrails, his heart can be found in Rouen cathedral and his body lies in Fontevrault, not far from that of Eleanor.

Crypt in Saint Martial's, Limoges

Châlus Keep

Saint-Front Cathedral, Périgueux

Cloister in Saint-Front Cathedral, Périgueux

In Périgord

After Limoges and Châlus, the route entered Périgord. Through the village of La Coquille (shell), whose name is a reminder of their passage, the pilgrims reached the fortified town of Thiviers. From there, a secondary road reached the shores of the Dronne River and the Benedictine abbey of Brantôme. According to tradition, it had been founded by Emperor Charlemagne, who in 769 had donated to it the relics of Saint Sicaire, one of Herod's slaves who had converted to Christianity after seeing the massacre of the innocents. However, the direct road, passing by the Romanesque church of Saint Germain in Sorges, brought them faster to the valley of the Isle. In a meander of this river, on an escarpment, the Gallic tribe of Petrocores had installed an oppidum, at the foot of which the Romans founded the capital of a *civitas,* Vesona. After the barbarian invasions, this became the town surrounding Saint Stephen's church. On the hill – or *puy* – facing the city, was the burial place of Saint Front the legendary evangelist of this town that took the name of Perigueux in 1251, after the union of its two neighbourhoods. In the 11th century, a canonical monastery had been established at Puy-Saint-Front as guardians of the sepulchre, and many pilgrims, including those of Santiago, came to beg for the miraculous intercession of this saint capable of being in two places at once and particularly invoked against reptiles. The sculpted tomb containing his relics, made in 1077 by the monk Guinamond, who had come from La Chaise-Dieu, was destroyed in 1575 during the Wars of Religion. However, some fragments do remain, kept in the Périgord Museum, as well as laudatory descriptions, such as the one given by Aimery Picaud's *Guide.* "[…] built with care, in the shape of a rotunda like the Holy Sepulchre, […] it surpasses by the beauty of its work all the tombs of other saints." During the 12th century, a vast domed church, built to the plan of a Greek cross, and worthy of great Eastern basilicas, came to be attached to the chevet of the "old church" of Saint-Front Abbey,

Vésone Tower, Périgueux

BRANTÔME

During the High Middle Ages, hermits settled at the foot of a cliff on the shores of a meander of the Dronne River and lived in natural caves dug out of the rock face. In 769, Charlemagne had founded the abbey of Brantôme and entrusted the relics of Saint Sicaire, Herod's former slave, to it. The Benedictine monks kept the troglodytic rooms, in which they installed their heating room, washing room, a mill and a pigeon house. They even took refuge in them after the destruction of their abbey by Norsemen in the 9th century. The abbey was rebuilt in the 11th century by Abbot Guillaume. Becoming a commendatory during the 16th century, its abbot was chosen from members of the secular clergy. Among its commendatory abbots were Pierre de Mareuil, as well as his nephew Pierre de Bourdeille, born in 1540 and heir of the Bourdeille family, whose castle was located a few leagues west of the abbey. Better known under the name of Brantôme, this friend of Catherine de Medicis and a clever diplomat was able to preserve his abbey from the vicissitudes of the Wars of Religion. He took the time to write his *Mémoires*, the *Vies des hommes illustres et des grands capitaines*, and also, the lives of *Dames galantes…*

Brantôme Abbey

Saint James Church in Bergerac

consecrated in 1047 by Bishop Frotaire. The new building received a high steeple, raised over the two last spans of the former oratory's nave. In 1852 it was all in very poor condition when the architect Paul Abadie, who was to be entrusted with the construction of Sacré Cœur in Paris, undertook the "restoration", but it was finally razed and then rebuilt. Much contested, the work at least allowed the city of Périgueux to keep its Saint Front Basilica, which would otherwise today be in ruins. Leaving Périgueux, another road crossed the Dordogne River at Sainte-Foy-la-Grande, a walled town founded in 1255 on the lands of a priory depending on Conques Abbey. The main road, passing through Campsegret and Lembras, crossed the river over the Bergerac bridge. Bergerac was born in the 11th century, when the lord Elie Rudel had a castle built overlooking the Dordogne River, controlling river traffic. An important port, the city became wealthy with the trade in famous wines, such as Monbazillac, Pécharmant, Rosette or Montravel. Stocked in Bergerac, the wine was carried in flat-bottomed boats called *gabares* as far as Libourne, from where it was exported starting in the middle of the 12th century. At the time, construction of the bridge for safe and permanent crossing of the Dordogne increased the city's importance and stimulated commercial activity. After praying in Saint James Church in Bergerac, the pilgrims continued on their way south, in the direction of the Garonne River, if they had not in the meantime decided to worship the holy shroud at the abbey in Cadouin.

Covered way on a square in Libourne

St Front, Périgueux cathedral

SAINT FRONT

....

F ive *Lives* of Saint Front exist – each more edifying and fanciful than the last. According to the oldest version, dating from the 7th or 8th century, Front was born in Dordogne, in Lanquais. As an adolescent he became a monk and left for Egypt where he associated with the Fathers of the Desert, before going to Rome. There he delivered a senator's daughter from the Devil, and Saint Peter – all of this happening during apostolic times – learning of the miracle, gave him the mission of evangelizing Gaul and entrusted him with the episcopal seat of Périgueux. So Front went back to his own country in the company of a priest called George, who died three days later. In despair, Front returned to Saint Peter who gave him the pastoral staff thanks to which the dead man was to be brought back to life. The miracle happened and Front arrived in Périgueux with seventy disciples. The other *Lives* presented Front as a disciple of Christ, present during the Passion. One of them also said that he presided over the burial mass of Saint Martha in Tarascon, while celebrating the holy office in Périgueux.

THE ABBEY OF CADOUIN AND ITS SHROUD

At the end of the 11th century, Gérard de Sales, former canon of Saint-Avit-Sénieur, who had become an itinerant hermit in Périgord, founded the monastery of Cadouin for some of his disciples in the bottom of a small valley in Bessède forest. In 1119 the monastery entered the Cistercian obedience under the authority of the Abbot of Pontigny, who sent twelve of his monks to Cadouin. The construction of a new abbey began immediately. Consecrated in 1154, its abbey church was given a distinctive relic – Christ's holy shroud, brought from Antioch by a crusader for the glory and prestige of Cadouin Abbey. Locked in a silver reliquary hung by chains from the chancel's vault, Christ's shroud was presented for the worship of numerous pilgrims, either going to Santiago or anonymous walkers, or famous historical characters such as Eleanor of Aquitaine, Richard the Lionheart, Blanche of Castile or Saint Louis, who followed each other to this famous pilgrimage shrine. During the Hundred Years War that devastated the Romanesque cloister, the relic was taken to Toulouse for safekeeping. When peace returned in 1453, the shroud was returned to Cadouin, where the construction of a new cloister was undertaken. It was in Flamboyant Gothic style and was completed during the Renaissance. Affected by the commendatory system, then by the troubles of the Wars of Religion, the abbey resisted and, refusing the threatening spiritual decadence, adhered to Narrow Observance in 1643. However, the Revolution put an end to this final spurt of life and monastic fervour. In 1797, the abbey was bought by the mayor of Cadouin. Its abbey church became a parish church. Bit by bit, pilgrims started returning to Cadouin. But in 1933 a test carried out on the precious cloth, venerated by generations as being the Holy Shroud of Christ, revealed that in fact it dated from the 11th century and that in the weft there was even a Kufic inscription to the grace of Allah! Pilgrimages were immediately stopped, but still today, the lovely Fatimid cloth is exhibited in Cadouin's chapter house.

The holy shroud of Cadouin

Saint Peter's Church in La Réole

Between Dordogne and Garonne

Leaving Bergerac, the *via Lemovicensis* passed Saint-Laurent-des-Vignes and Poport to reach Sigoulès, whose 15th century church has a stained glass window showing Saint James. Through Monbas and Sainte-Innocence, crossing hills and vineyards in the valley of the Lescouroux River, the pilgrims arrived at the shores of the Drot, that they crossed opposite Eymet, a *bastide* or walled town, founded in 1271 on the lands of a Benedictine priory depending on Moissac Abbey. Continuing westwards past another bastide, La Sauvetat-du-Dropt, owned by the famous Got family to which Pope Clement V (1305-1314) belonged, before being transferred through matrimony to the just as powerful Durfort house. After crossing Monségur bastide, founded in 1265 by Queen Eléonor of Provence, the wife of the Duke of Aquitaine and the King of England Henry III (1216-1272), the pilgrims went to Roquebrune commandery, perched on a rock overlooking the Drot River valley, served by the Hospitallers of Saint John of Jerusalem. The Garonne River was crossed at La Réole. A charter dated 977 mentioned the birth of this town of passers in *gabares* (flat-bottomed boats), grown around Squir Monastery, founded by Fleury-sur-Loire Abbey. The Benedictine *Rule* there provided the name La Réole, an important port and commercial town that was the garrison for the Black Prince during the Hundred Years War.

Eymet Castle

Bastides

Mainly created between 1250 and 1350, bastides, or walled towns, were the principal urban landscape in Aquitaine, where there were about 350 of them. Originally, the creating of these new fortified towns in a rural area had a triple purpose – political, economic and strategic. Their French or English founders wished to regroup scattered populations to control them better, take advantage of growth following land clearance, and to consolidate their position in often badly marked border areas. The foundation was the result of a contract between a lord who provided the land, and county or royal agents who were in charge of populating it. The future inhabitants, obtaining a customary charter, received land to build on within the walls, the building materials, as well as a *casal*, a piece of land to cultivate beyond the town. Their safety was thus guaranteed as was the possibility of a certain material comfort, even though they had to pay certain taxes. Bastides differed from other towns by their layout, generally a checkerboard, resulting from planned urbanism. Square or rectangular blocks of houses were determined by perpendicular networks of streets and alleys, and were organized around a large square on which there often stood a market hall, surrounded by arcaded galleries or covered ways, where markets took place.

HIS ARMOUR WAS BLACK...

The son of Edward II and Philippine de Hainaut took part in the Battle of Crécy in 1346. Better known as the Black Prince, in 1355 Edward undertook a destructive military campaign in Gascony and Languedoc. His father named him Prince of Aquitaine in 1363. In 1367, he joined up with Pedro the Cruel to defeat at Nájera, in La Rioja, Henri de Trastamare whom Du Guesclin had supported. He died in 1376, before his father, and never acceded to the throne of England.

The Black Prince's helmet

CLEMENT V

The son of Béraut de Got and Ida Blanquefort, Bertrand de Got was born towards the mid-13th century in the family castle, located between Uzeste and Villandraut. A pupil at Bazas, he studied law in Orléans and Bologna, before entering the service of the king of England, whose attorney he seems to have been for the Roman Curia in 1287. The raising to a cardinal of his brother Béraut, Archbishop of Lyons, in 1294, strengthened his relations at the papal court, and Pope Boniface VIII named him bishop of Comminges in 1295, then archbishop of Bordeaux in 1299. While trying to calm the conflict between Boniface VIII and Philippe le Bel, Bertrand continued his rise and became chaplain to Cardinal Francesco Caetani in 1302. Elected to the papacy in Perugia in 1305, Bertrand received the papal tiara in Lyons, under the name Clement V. In 1307, Philippe le Bel ordered him to suppress the Order of the Temple and to begin a trial against the memory of Boniface VIII. Although Clement V managed to eliminate the grievances his late predecessor was charged with, he had to open an enquiry into the Order of the Temple. Brought before the Council of Vienna, in 1312 the affair ended with the abolition of the Order, whose goods were transferred to the Hospitallers of Saint John of Jerusalem. Starting in 1308, Clement V, who had surrounded himself with mostly French cardinals, established the papal court in the Dominican convent in Avignon, in the heart of the Comtat Venaissin, property of the Holy See. He had asked the universities of Rome, Bologna, Paris, Oxford and Salamanca to teach Hebrew, Greek, Arab and Syriac, and had gathered the *Clementine Collections*, when he died in April 1314, without having managed to prevent the execution of the last Grand Master of the Templars.

Crossing the Landes

Once the Garonne River was crossed, the pilgrims continued in the direction of Pondaurat, where there was an Antonin commandery and hospital. After crossing the Bassanne by the village's stone bridge, they passed the little Romanesque church of Savignac and the barony of Auros, with its castle overlooking the Beuve River, to arrive in Bazas, capital of the "little Landes of Bazadais". A bishopric in the 6th century, in the medieval period Bazas was also the seat of a seneschal's jurisdiction and a presidential court of justice. The Duke of Aquitaine's seneschal laid the first stone of the Gothic cathedral in 1223, to replace a Romanesque building. Dedicated to Saint John the Baptist, it was completed at the beginning of the 14th century, with the help of the Gascon pope Clement V (1305-1314). Its western façade, with its magnificent sculpted triple portal, opened onto a nave with ten spans with side aisles, a false-transept and a chancel with an ambulatory and radiating chapels. In the Saint-Antoine suburb of Bazas, the pilgrims regained their strength at the town's hospital before starting on the fearsome crossing of the Landes. Via the hospital of Beaulac and the village of Captieux, the road went past Lugaut chapel, founded by the Order of Saint James with the Red Sword, the bastide of Roquefort and the church of Sainte-Marie de Bostens, to arrive in Mont-de-Marsan at the confluence of the Midou and Douze Rivers, a city that developed around the priories of Saint-Pierre-du-Mont and la Madeleine. These two priories depended on the Benedictine Abbey in Saint-Sever, the next stage on the road, that the pilgrims reached by crossing the Adour River. According to tradition, it was on the site of the martyrdom of Saint Severus, a 5th century Scythian prince, sent to evangelize the Gauls by Pope Siricius, that Guillaume Sanche, Duke of Gascony, founded the abbey towards the year 1000. Saint-Sever acquired great fame under the abbacy of a former Cluniac monk, Grégoire de Montaner (1028-1072), who also occupied the episcopal seat of

Villandraut, the castle of Clement V

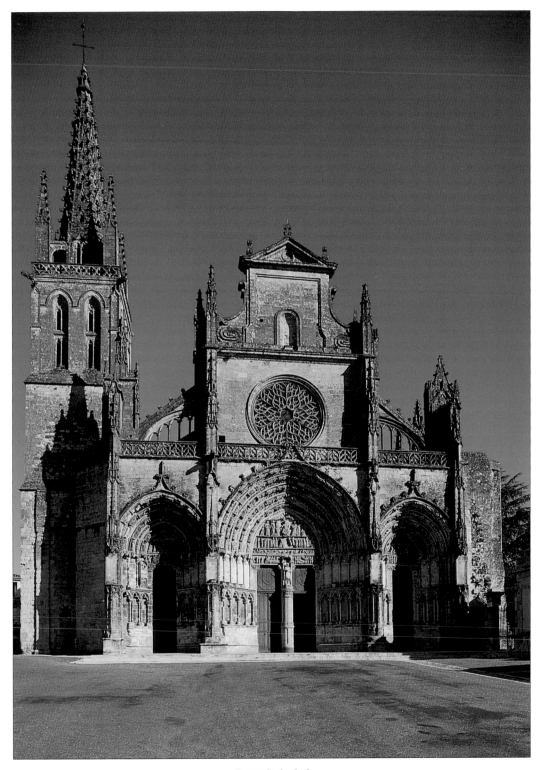

Bazas Cathedral

A capital in Saint-Sever

SEVERUS, MARTYR KING

⋯⋯⋯⋯⋯⋯⋯⋯⋯⋯⋯⋯⋯⋯⋯⋯⋯⋯

T he Christian king of Alibania,
a region of the Lower Danube,
Severus left his throne when his
subjects returned to paganism and
became a hermit. Pope Siricius
sent him on a mission to Gaul,
where Arianism was gaining
ground. He stopped in Toulouse,
prayed at the tomb of Saint
Saturnin, and shortly afterwards,
his prayers opened up the waters
of a flooding river. Informed of
the miracle, the Roman governor
of the province, Adrian, who was
ill, called Severus to his bedside.
Curing him, Severus obtained his
conversion as well as that of his
garrison. But hordes of Vandals
captured the town, and beheaded
Severus, whose blood made a
spring well forth. The martyr then
picked up his head and carried it
to the top of the hill now bearing
his name, thus indicating his burial
place. These events happened at
the beginning of the 5th century.

A capital in Saint-Sever

Lescar in 1060, and then that of Dax. Under his abbacy, a
manuscript of the *Commentaries on the Apocalypse* by Beatus of
Libana was transcribed and illuminated. It was a masterpiece of the
genre known by the name Apocalypse of Saint-Sever, and is today
kept at the National Library. Devastated by a fire in 1060, the abbey
was rebuilt by Grégoire de Montaner and his successors. With its
six parallel apsidal chapels at intervals flanking the main apse with
its chancel, Saint-Sever Abbey Church, decorated with beautiful
sculpted capitals, presents the broadest development of the plan
called benedictine. Entering Chalosse, the pilgrims continued on
their way by Audignon and Horsarrieu hospital, served by the
Order of the Hospitallers of Saint John of Jerusalem, before reaching Hagetmau and its Saint-Girons Abbey, served by a chapter of
canons and of which only a crypt with its remarkable historiated
capitals remains.

Saint-Sever Abbey Church

In Béarn

Crossing the Louts River upon leaving Hagetmau, the route took the direction of Momuy. From their hospital of the Bridge of the Haderne, the hospitallers supervised the crossing of the Luy de France, as well as that of Luy de Béarn, which took place near their commandery at Sault-de-Navailles. Leaving the Chalosse area at Sallespisse, the road to Santiago entered Béarn and ran towards Orthez. In the 13th century, Gaston VII de Moncade, Viscount of Béarn (1229-1290), fortified the town of Orthez, making it his third capital. Pilgrims found shelter at the town's Trinitarian hospital, located near Moncade Castle, but also in other establishments held by Jacobins or Franciscans. Leaving the city by the old bridge straddling the Gave de Pau, that Gaston Phébus (1343-1391) finished fortifying, the road ran past Sainte-Suzanne to reach the shores of the Saleys River and the commandery-hospital of Orion, controlled by the Hospitallers of Saint John of Jerusalem. Its Saint Mary Magdalene Church was built at the beginning of the 12th century, according to a Greek cross plan with a five-sided polygonal apse. In Sauveterre-de-Béarn, where the Gave of Oloron was crossed, the *via Lemovicensis* joined up with the *via Turonensis*. Hardly two hours walking distance away, the crowd of pilgrims who had taken these two routes reached Saint-Palais and shortly afterwards, at the Gibraltar crossroads, met up with pilgrims who had taken the *via Podiensis*.

The Moncade Tower in Orthez

GASTON PHÉBUS

A book-loving knight, the Count of Foix-Béarn Gaston III (1343-1391), nicknamed Phébus because of his golden blond hair, was the author of a book of devotion and a famous treatise on hunting, *The Book of the Hunt.*

Orthez Bridge

Le Puy

VIA PODIENSIS

Following in the footsteps of Godescalc, bishop of Le Puy and the first non-Spanish pilgrim to make the pilgrimage to Santiago de Compostela in 950, "the Burgundians and Teutons", mentioned by Aimery Picaud, and more generally, Santiago pilgrims coming from eastern Europe, began their journey from the great Marian shrine that gave its name to the *via Podiensis*. Although Godescalc's itinerary remains unknown, the pilgrims following after him have left many traces of their passage. Shrines, abbeys, hospitals and bridges, but also miracles and legends, have all left their mark on the landscape and places along the route. Starting in Le Puy, crossing the hills of Aubrac to reach Conques and the Lot River valley, crossing Quercy and stopping in Moissac, and after Gascony joining up with both the *via Lemovicensis* and the *via Turonensis* combined at the Gibraltar crossroads.

Le Puy

A gathering point for Santiago de Compostela pilgrims departing along the *via Podiensis* and location of a Marian pilgrimage centre famous since the High Middle Ages, the city of Le Puy sits on a grandiose site – a fertile basin spiked by rocky points, overlooked by the Velay volcanoes. During the Gallo-Roman period, the town of Anis was known for its miraculous spring and its dolmen, containing a pagan temple, raised on the Corneille Rock. Legend has it that the Virgin appeared to a matron from Anis on this dolmen. After miraculously healing her fever, the Virgin asked her to build a church there. This is the origin of Our Lady's Cathedral, whose first stones were laid towards 415-430 by Bishop Scutaire, and which was progressively enlarged during the 11th and 12th centuries. The importance of the town of Anicium, that became a bishopric under the name of Puy-Sainte-Marie (St Mary's Hill),

Notre-Dame Cathedral in Le Puy

Stages	Kms
Le Puy	762
Saugues	718
Nasbinals	653
Aubrac	644
Saint-Côme-d'Olt	622
Espalion	618
Estaing	608
Golinhac	591
Conques *	566
Figeac	522
Espagnac-Sainte-Eulalie	501
Marcilhac-sur-Célé	488
Cahors	442
Montcuq	416
Lauzerte	405
Moissac	382
Lectoure	328
La Romieu	313
Condom	301
Larressingle	295
Eauze	272
Nogaro	253
Aire-sur-l'Adour	233
Navarrenx	156
Gibraltar Stele	126
Puente la Reina	0

Variation via Rouergue:
Conques, Aubin, Villeneuve, Lacapelle-Livron, Caylus, Caussade, Moissac

References to Aimery Picaud's *Guide*
*: presence of "holy bodies"

continued to grow in the course of the Middle Ages. In about 951, Bishop Godescalc, the first French pilgrim to make the journey to the tomb of the apostle James in Santiago, on his return brought back specific ideas about organizing a large pilgrimage centre. While he was bishop, a first chapel dedicated to the Archangel Michael, protector of souls and emblematic figure of warrior virtues, was raised on Aiguilhe Rock. An obligatory stage for pilgrims, Saint Michael's chapel was consecrated in 962 by Godescalc's successor, Bishop Guy d'Anjou, a former monk and fervent promoter of the Peace of God, for which he convoked a council in Le Puy in about 980. On March 25, 992, the date foretold as the end of the world by the German monk Bernhard, Annunciation coincided with Good Friday. On this fateful day, pilgrims came in such numbers to beg the Virgin for help that the papacy decided to institute a jubilee at Le Puy each time the feast days of the Annunciation and Good Friday coincided. For the jubilees of 1065, 1155, 1160, and 1407, crowds were such that Le Puy's bishops begged the popes to extend the jubilee period, since some pilgrims had been crushed to death! Once fears of the millenium had passed, popes and kings came to the Marian city. One

Capital in Le Puy cloister

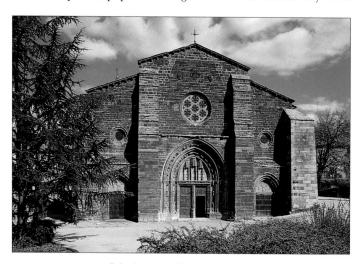

Saint-Laurent Church in Le Puy

was Pope Urban II, who named the bishop of Le Puy, Adhémar de Monteil, head of the First Crusade in 1095. Another was Saint Louis, who came three times to Le Puy on pilgrimage, and to whom chroniclers, wrongly, attribute the donation of the famous Black Virgin. During the 13th century, the preaching friars of Saint Dominic, who came to Le Puy in the last year of his life, founded a convent at the gates of the city, welcoming pilgrims arriving too late to enter the city. The Dominicans officiated in Saint Laurent's Church, whose chancel contains the funerary monument holding the entrails of Constable Bertrand du Guesclin, who died in 1380. Nowadays, the city of Le Puy, overlooked since 1850 by the statue of Our Lady of France, is the setting of an important Marian pilgrimage every year on August 15th.

THE HÔTEL-DIEU

Located at the foot of Notre-Dame cathedral, beside the cloister, the Hôtel-Dieu (general hospital) of Le Puy, founded in the first half of the 12th century, welcomed pilgrims to Santiago at the departure on the *via Podiensis*. The main building of the city's hospital network, its revenues were provided by its many properties, but also by the privilege granted by Bishop Bertrand de Chalançon in 1210 of manufacturing and selling pilgrimage medallions. The mould from which these pilgrimage medallions, decorated with shells and showing Saint James as a pilgrim, were made was found in Saint Claire's church, the seat of the Saint James of the Puy confraternity at the end of the 16th century. The great hospital establishment enjoyed yet another privilege – that of sending alms collectors all over the kingdom and even abroad. Hence the diocesan museum of Ripoll contains an alms-box, decorated with a picture of Notre-Dame du Puy and bearing the inscription *Nostra Señora del Puig de Franca*, that old inhabitants of the area of Ripoll and San Juan de las Abasedas remember seeing attached around the neck of a hermit at the beginning of the 20th century.

The Black Virgin of Le Puy

N o trace remains of the statue of the Virgin at the foot of which, according to legend, Mirat, besieged in Lourdes by Charlemagne in 778, laid down his weapons. At the end of the 10th century, it was replaced by the Black Virgin that Faujas de Saint-Fons drew in the 18th century, and is shown on the painting of *The Plague Vow* by Jean Solvain, dating from 1630 and hanging on the wall of the north aisle in Le Puy Cathedral. The statue was made of cedar wood. The Virgin, seated on a throne, held the Infant Jesus on her lap. The two faces were black, but the hands were white. Our Lady was dressed in an Eastern-style dress in red, blue-green and ochre shades, and crowned with a kind of helmet with ear-pieces of gilded copper, decorated with ancient cameos. The statue was wrapped in strips of cloth, stuck on the wood and painted. For Faujas de Saint-Fons, it was formerly a statue of Isis, transformed into a Virgin; for others, it was an Ethiopian statue, but it could also have been the work of an Arab craftsman. On June 8, 1794, on the day of Pentecost, revolutionaries burned it on the Place du Martouret. When the strips of cloth had been burned, a little door opened in the statue's back and a rolled up parchment fell out. Nobody looked to see what was written on it. The present Black Virgin on the high altar is a copy of the old one, dating from the 18th century.

Saint-Michel d'Aiguilhe

The Plague Vow

St James, Le Puy Cathedral

The Black Virgin of Le Puy

Towards the Aubrac Mountains

Leaving Le Puy by the road to Compostela, the main route went through Bains, which has kept its Romanesque church dedicated to Saint Foy of Conques since 1105. However, an alternate road that is the present itinerary, leaving behind Saint-Christophe-sur-Dolaison and the Lake of the Egg (de l'Oeuf), rejoined the main route at Villard, to cross the Allier River opposite Monistrol, a former priory depending on La Chaise-Dieu Abbey. Climbing as far as Montaure, on the edge of the Gevaudan plateau, the road meets the chapel of La Madeleine, built, according to legend, in the cave where the saint appeared long ago. Saugues, with its Saint Médard Collegiate Church and its Saint James hospital, precedes Saint Roch Pass where the Margeride is crossed at an altitude of 1309 metres. There, two hospitals welcomed pilgrims: the domain of Sauvage, today a hostel on the route, and that of l'Hospitalet, long ago built near Saint Roch fountain but fallen into ruin in the 18th century. The Sauvage was the first foundation of the Hotel-Dieu of le Puy beyond its diocese. The road then runs down to the valley of the Truyère River, and reaches Aumont-Aubrac, a former Benedictine priory. After Nasbinals, whose Romanesque church has a dome on squinches, the Santiago pilgrim wandering in the foggy solitudes of the Aubrac mountains could count on the "bell of the lost" of Notre-Dame-des-Pauvres Church to guide his steps as far as the *domerie* where he would find a welcome and comfort before arriving in the Lot River valley.

The chevet of Nasbinals Church

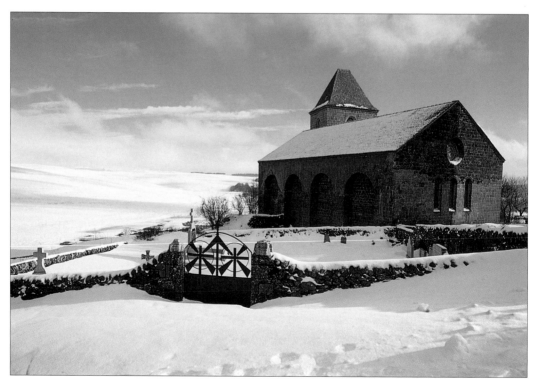

The Aubrac Domerie

SAINT ROCH

The son of Jean Roch, Consul of Montpellier in 1348, and Dame Libère, of Catalonian origin, Roch at birth bore a little cross marked on his chest – a sign of divine election. Orphaned in 1367, he gave his things away to the poor and left on a pilgrimage to Rome. But bubonic plague had arrived in Messina in 1347 on ships coming from Crimea and had then spread throughout Italy. In Acquapendente inhabitants were fleeing the town, but Roch entered to give food and drink to the sick. Three months later he went to Cesena where the plague had struck. In Rome he cared for the Great Penitentiary and received his pilgrim's bull from Urban V. However, in Piacenza, where he had gone to care for the sick, Roch himself fell ill. Feverish and with a purulent buboe above his knee, he took shelter in a forest where, every day, a dog brought him food. Once recovered, Roch took up his pilgrim's staff and went to Le Puy, before crossing la Margeride at the pass still bearing his name, in the direction of his birthplace. There, taken for a spy, this great pilgrim and plague healer was thrown into prison, where he died in a dank cell in 1379. Roch was canonized by the Council of Constance in 1414.

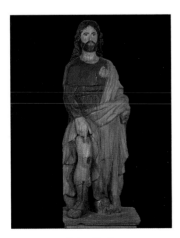

Saint Roch

THE AUBRAC DOMERIE

In 1120, upon his return from a pilgrimage to Santiago de Compostela, the noble Adalard, the Count or Viscount of Flanders according to some, the brother or butler of the Count of Flanders according to others, decided to found a hospital in the solitudes of the Aubrac mountains, after a miraculous escape from bandits there. At the side of the path, at an altitude of 1,307 metres on the south slope of the Lot pass, the foundation consisted of a church, convent buildings, a hospital and a cemetery. It was run by a community of monks following Saint Augustine's rule. Elected for life by the brothers, the community prior also had the title of Dom – an abbreviation of *Dominus* – giving the Aubrac hospital the name domerie. Established in 1162, the statutes ordering internal rules set a chapter meeting whenever a new Dom had to be elected or a new friar allowed to join. These statutes also appointed the various cloistral officers such as the chamberer, charged with buying cloth and controlling the making of clothes, the sacristan who dealt with the material organization of the cult, the cantor who taught singing and directed the chants during mass, or the infirmarer, charged with the order's sick and inspecting sick visitors to the hospital. There were five categories of personnel at the domerie. The humblest, the donats, were composed of lay brothers who had voluntarily given their person and goods to the hospital, and upon entering had pronounced vows of poverty, obedience and chastity. The brothers, whether lay or clerics, pronounced the same vows, and were admitted to the community after a year of noviciate upon favourable decision by the chapter. They were in charge of running the hospital. To help them with the hardest work, like taking care of the sick, they were helped by sisters, most often of noble background. The domerie's knights guaranteed pilgrims' security by watching the surroundings. Finally, the priests celebrated the divine offices and administered sacraments. Upon his arrival, the traveller was welcomed by the dom himself, who offered him water to wash his hands. Brothers and sisters came to serve him next with several tasks, including the unconditional washing of the feet, like cleaning his clothes, providing food and drink and preparing a bed for him. A special building lodged sick pilgrims, who could count on the monks' care and devotion. These patients received more nourishing and plentiful food, soft beds, good lighting, and holy services at their bedside. There was no limit set for their stay, and if they were travelling in a group, the companions were allowed to stay until the patient's recovery. Despite this concern, for some the hospital was the last stage of their pilgrimage. "Help to the living" but also "salvation of the dead", according to the *Guide*'s terms, and the domerie took charge of burying them, their final merciful task in favour of the walkers for God.

Bell-tower of the church in Saint-Côme-d-Olt

The castle of Calmont-d'Olt

The Old Bridge in Espalion

Conques

In the rocky emptiness of the *Vallée Pierreuse (Stony Valley)*, at the place where, opening in a kind of conch, the gorge of the Ouch River joined the Dourdon valley, Dadon installed his hermitage near the source of the Plô, during the first half of the 8th century. A noble from Rouergue, he had fought the Saracens who had tortured and killed his mother. A certain Medraldus came to share his retreat and was soon followed by other disciples. Together they built a church dedicated to the Holy Saviour. In 801, Louis the Pious extended his protection to the community, which opted for cenobitism and the Benedictine rule. It was also Louis the Pious who provided the monastery with its name of Conques, referring to the site's topography. Dadon, preferring solitude, had already retired to Grand-Vabre, and Medraldus had become the establishment's abbot. Royal favours were maintained throughout the entire 9th century, in addition to generosity from rich individuals who donated lands to the abbey but also the gold, silver, precious stones and fine cloth at the origin of its treasure. The arrival of the relics of the young Foy, martyred under Diocletian, brought to Conques in about 866 by the monk Aronisde, were to provide the abbey with its prestige and influence. First of all locally, the cult of Saint Foy, amplified by tales of her miracles, brought about the birth of a real pilgrimage that reached its apex during the 11th and 12th centuries. And since the abbey was a major stage along the *via*

Arrival of the route in Conques

PEPIN'S RELIQUARY

Offered to the abbey by Pepin II, King of Aquitaine from 817 to 838, this beautiful reliquary covered with gold and precious stones contained over twenty relics from various sources, presented to the faithful through three openings that are now closed.

Pepin's Reliquary, treasure in Conques Abbey Church

Cloister in Conques Abbey

THE CONQUES TYMPANUM

....

A t the hour of the Last Judgement, the line of the chosen advances on the right of Christ in glory. Among them, Saint Foy, prostrated before the hand of God. But on the left of the Saviour, the sinners undergo atrocious and horrible torture.

Podiensis, the cult of Saint Foy spread all along the routes to Santiago, as far as Spain and Compostela itself, where a chapel in the cathedral was dedicated to the young martyr in 1077. A monk from Conques, Pierre d'Andouque, became bishop of Pamplona before one of his brothers in religion, Pons, filled the episcopal seat of Barbastro. The abbey in Rouergue also established priories in Italy, England, and Germany. Begun during the abbacy of Odolric (1030-1065) and continued under those of Étienne II (1065-1087) and Bégon III (1087-1107), the construction of the abbey church was finally completed during the first third of the 12th century. Its cruciform plan with an ambulatory and radiating chapels around the chancel is typical of large pilgrimage churches. The dimensions of the nave, fairly short but with side aisles, and the large transept provided enough space for very many worshippers. During busier periods, the faithful could also find room in the galleries. Presented in the choir, with the abbey's treasure, Saint Foy in majesty, which contained the saint's head, was protected by beautiful gates wrought from the iron of chains brought to Conques as votive offerings by captives miraculously freed thanks to the saint's intervention. The church's sculpted capitals and, on the western façade, the splendid tympanum of the Last Judgement, still partially polychromed, is one of the masterpieces of Romanesque ornamental sculpture. South of the abbey church stand several remnants of the cloister, including six of the gemeled bays of the western gallery, razed in the 19th century.

Tympanum of Conques Abbey Church

SAINT FOY

An Occitan poem from the 12th century, the *Song of Saint Foy*, tells how the young Foy, a daughter of a rich Gallo-Roman family in Agen, was converted to Catholicism by Bishop Caprais and refused to sacrifice to the pagan gods. This was when the proconsul Dacien, governor of Aquitaine, applied Diocletian's (285-305) imperial edict, at the origin of one of the last waves of persecution against Christianity. Barely twelve years old, the young girl was condemned to be burnt alive on a grill, but a providential storm put out the flames. Foy was finally beheaded on October 6, 303. Devoutly gathered together, her mortal remains were buried in a church in Agen. Divine grace soon showed itself around the martyr's tomb and numerous miracles took place. Five centuries had gone by, according to the tale of the *Translation of Saint Foy*, when the monk Audaldus left his monastery in Conques to cross the Pyrenees in order to seek the relics of Saint Vincent. At a time when the cult of relics was increasing in importance, Conques had very few and was looking to obtain some at any price. Audaldus was denounced after he had managed to get his important loot, and had to return the relics to their owner. Obtaining the relics of a different Saint Vincent, unfortunately less well known, from the diocese of Agen, the monks from Conques finally set their hearts on Saint Foy's relics. Hiding his identity, one of the monks, Aronisde, won the confidence of the Agen monks and became the gardian of Saint Foy's tomb. He fulfilled his duty for ten years, until the Day of Epiphany 866, when he stole the relics and brought them to Conques on January 14, 866, after an eventful voyage. Saint Foy's miracles attracted many pilgrims, and towards 1015, Bernard d'Angers began writing the *Liber Miraculorum sanctae Fidis*, which was finished by a monk from Conques. Through the saint's intercession, the blind recovered their sight, and prisoners were freed. The young martyr was also very interested in her appearance. In dreams, she appeared to rich ladies of Rouergue, asking them for their finest attire – which came to enrich the treasure of her abbey.

Reliquary statue of St Foy, treasure of Conques Abbey Church

Rodez cathedral

HOLY SAVIOUR CHARTERHOUSE

....

T he Charterhouse of
Villefranche was built from
1450 to 1465, according to the
wishes of one of the city's wealthy
merchants, who died leaving his
goods to the contemplative
Carthusian Order, founded by
Saint Bruno in 1084.

From Rouergue to Lower Quercy

Crossing the Dourdou River over the "*romieus*" bridge, the route left Conques to arrive in Aubin, where pilgrims found a hospital and two churches, Notre-Dame-du-Fort and Notre-Dame-du-Pouget. During the 12th century, the bell of the Fort church rang every day for two hours straight in order to bring lost pilgrims back to the right road. Before the creation of Villefranche, once over the Riou Biou just after Aubin, the road ran towards Villeneuve, whose Holy Sepulchre church still has its 14th century frescoes showing the miracle of the *hanged-unhanged*. The road then reached Saint-Jacques d'Elbes church and the Augustinian priory of Laramière, before arriving in Lacapelle-Livron where the Templars possessed a commandery. Starting in 1252, some pilgrims preferred going through the new bastide, or walled town, of Villefranche, via Lanuéjouls, whose priory depended on Saint-Géraud of Aurillac. They were joined there by pilgrims who, from Espalion, had passed through Rodez. In the Villefranche quarter of Puech, they found shelter at Saint James's hospital, maintained after 1493 by the town's Saint James confraternity. Continuing on their way through Saint-Grat and Vaihourles Monastery, founded by Saint Géraud of Aurillac, they met up with the other pilgrims at Lacapelle-Livron. After Saint James's hospital in Caylus, the road passed through Septfonds and Caussade, before reaching the abbey in Moissac, through Albias, Cos and Lafrançaise.

Cloister in Holy Saviour Charterhouse in Villefranche-de-Rouergue

A Santiago pilgrim, fresco in Holy Sepulchre Chapel, Villeneuve-d'Aveyron

Priory in Espagnac-Sainte-Eulalie

Marcilhac-sur-Célé

Through the Lot and Célé Valleys

At their departure from Conques, some pilgrims preferred going towards the priory of Flagnac and forded the Lot River at Gerle coomb, in the direction of Figeac. The former seat of a Benedictine monastery depending on Conques, then Cluny, Figeac, located on the right bank of the Célé, was an important stage on the road to Santiago de Compostela. Pilgrims who could rejoin Rocamadour from Figeac, stopped to worship in the Holy Saviour Abbey Church or in Notre-Dame-du-Puy Church, and found shelter in one of the town's hospitals, including Saint James's. Were the stone needles at the top of Cingle Hill south of the town, or on Lissac Hill to the west, used to set the pilgrims in the right direction when they left Figeac? The mystery remains. Some continued on their way through Béduer and Gréalou, reaching the shores of the Lot River at Cajarc, then crossed Limogne causse. Others followed the course of the Célé River as far as its confluence with the Lot and, going beyond Notre-Dame-de-Val-Paradis priory in Espagnac-Sainte-Eulalie, then the Benedictine abbey of Marcilhac, reached Cahors. After worshipping in Saint Stephen's Cathedral, whose northern door is decorated with a fine sculpted tympanum presenting the Annunciation, they left the city over the Valentré Bridge, built over the Lot River at the beginning of the 14th century. Through the bastides of Montcuq and Lauzerte, in the valley of the Barguelonnette River, their route took them to the shores of the Tarn and entered Moissac.

Figeac, Cingle needle

FIGEAC ABBEY

P ursuing the policies of his grandfather Louis the Pious (814-840) in favour of Conques Abbey, Pepin II, King of Aquitaine from 838-852, granted it lands at Figeac, in Quercy, in 839. A new monastery was built there, dedicated, like Conques originally, to the Holy Saviour. Set in the heart of a fertile basin of the Célé River valley, the *New Conques* prospered so well that its abbots began to contest the supervision of the mother abbey. In the 10th century, one of the abbots, Géraud, even had himself elected abbot of Conques but, preferring to stay in Quercy, named a simple prior as the head of the abbey in Rouergue. From then on, relations between the two communities only worsened. To obtain precedence, the monks of Figeac did not hesitate to write up a false charter, dated 755, dating the foundation of their abbey to Pepin the Short and claimed that Conques was subject to them! Finally, after Figeac's request of affiliation to Cluny, in 1074, the Council of Nîmes proclaimed the complete separation of Conques and Figeac Abbeys in 1096.

Valentré Bridge in Cahors

ROCAMADOUR

In the heart of Gramat causse, the site of Rocamadour raises its rocky pinnacles between Heaven and Earth, in the narrow valley of the Alzou River. During the first years of Christianity, a man of God named Amadour retired to this arid and wild causse, where he built a little oratory dedicated to the Virgin and which was to keep his name. Around the year one thousand, served by a monk from Marcilhac-sur-Célé Abbey, Our Lady of Rocamadour chapel had already become a pilgrimage site, as is attested by the presence of *catenulae*, little chains symbolizing their sins that pilgrims wore around their necks and that were removed at the end of the pilgrimage as a sign of pardon. At the dawn of the 12th century, the pilgrimage grew in importance under the impetus of Eble, abbot of the Cluniac monastery in Tulle who, with the help of his brother, the powerful Viscount of Turenne, founded a priory and took over the organization of the pilgrimage. Monks from Tulle occupied the site by 1113-1123, not without coming into conflict with the abbey of Marcilhac, which finally had to give up its claims in 1193. Under the abbacy of Géraud d'Escorailles (1152-1188), Eble's successor, these monks built the great church of Moustier – the present Holy Saviour Basilica – supported by a lower church,

Rocamadour

A sportelle

today Saint Amadour's crypt. While an abbot's palace and many chapels were being built, the town also developed with its hostelries and shops where pilgrims could buy a *sportelle*, a medallion showing the sign of the Virgin, proving that they had completed the pilgrimage. During the 12th and 13th centuries, classed at the top of "minor pilgrimages" imposed by ecclesiastical or even civil courts, Rocamadour received many pilgrims guilty of bodily harm, robbery, threats and other wrongs. Nevertheless, during the Middle Ages, famous saints, princes, bishops or abbots also came to honour the shrine with their presence, such as Bernard de Clairvaux in 1147, the King of England Henry II Plantagenêt

St Amadour's crypt

accompanied by Thomas à Becket in 1159, or Saint Louis in 1244, who came with his mother Blanche of Castile, his brothers and their entire royal suite,

including Alphonse III of Burgundy, the future king of Portugal. In 1166, the discovery of the intact body of an unknown hermit under the church square of Our Lady's chapel further increased the pilgrimage's fame. Pilgrims began to come not only to honour Our Lady, whose miracles had been collected in 1172 in *The Book of Miracles of Our Lady of Rocamadour*, but also to pray to the relics of Saint Amadour – because it was of course his body – the holy founder of the sanctuary. Amadour was rapidly assimilated to Zacchæus, mentioned in the Gospel according to Saint Luke. This short man, a tax collector in Jericho, who, learning of the passage of Jesus in the city, climbed into a sycamore tree to be sure to see Him. Touched by grace, Zacchæus then promised to donate half his goods to the poor. Legend also had it that Zacchæus-Amadour became the Virgin's servant and married Saint Veronica. It was with her that he landed at Soulac, on the coast of Médoc, bringing the Virgin's relics with them, before retiring alone to the Alzou Valley. A destination in itself, or a stage on the great pilgrimage routes, Rocamadour welcomed pilgrims on the *via Podiensis*

Our Lady of Rocamadour

coming from Figeac, those who rejoined it via Brioude and Aurillac, and also those who had left the *via Lemovicensis* at Bénévent-l'Abbaye or Saint-Léonard-de-Noblat. This was because Our Lady of Rocamadour was particularly concerned with guaranteeing their protection on the road beyond the Pyrenees. Helping Saint James Matamoros, did she not lend a helping hand to the soldiers of the *Reconquista* when, on the point of yielding at the battle of Las Navas de Tolosa, they brandished the standard with her picture on it, causing the Muslim enemy to flee, according to the chronicle of Trois-Fontaines Abbey? Alfonso VIII (1158-1214) knew it well and counted on her divine protection in 1181, when he donated his lands of Hornillos and Orbanella near Burgos, to her. After Las Navas de Tolosa, in 1212, devotion to Our Lady of Rocamadour was permanently established in the Iberian peninsula and along the *Camino francés*, where its monks possessed important stopping points for pilgrims at Estella, Burgos, Palencia, Astorga and Salamanca.

The tomb of St Amadour

Jeremy, pier in Saint Peter of Moissac Abbey Church

Moissac

At the foot of the last Quercy hills, the abbey of Saint Peter of Moissac stands in the heart of a fertile plain, on the shores of the Tarn River. Legend attributes its foundation to Clovis in 506, but it is more likely that, between 628 and 648, Didier, the bishop of Cahors (630-655) had the idea of establishing a Benedictine abbey on this favourable site, bathed by sun and abundant water. Enriched by donations from Nizezius and Ermentrude in 680, the abbey would nonetheless undergo the vicissitudes of history, hindering its progress towards a happy destiny. Devastated by Muslim raids in 721 and 732, but rebuilt thanks to Charlemagne (768-814) and his son, Louis the Pious (814-840), it was destroyed once again during the Norsemen's passage in 850 and 864, then by the Huns in the 10th century. Its worldly goods ruined, Moissac abbey was on the point of disappearing when Odilon, the fourth abbot of Cluny (994-1049), allowed its affiliation to the Cluniac Order in 1047. It was solemnly ratified by his successor Hugues (1049-1109) in 1055. Durand de Bredon, a relative and friend of Odilon's, became the first Cluniac abbot of Moissac. At the same time named bishop of Toulouse in 1059, this great cleric raised his abbey to the ranks of the most prestigious abbeys of the kingdom. In 1063, he consecrated the new abbey church that he had raised from its ruins, and died in an odour of sanctity in Moissac in 1072. His successor, Hunaud de Gavarret (1072-1085) began important construction in

Durand de Bredon, Moissac cloister

Cloister in Saint Peter of Moissac Abbey Church

ROMANESQUE ART

Starting in 980, the end of barbarian raids and the accession of stable dynasties – Capetians, Dukes of Normandy, Counts of Poitou, Salians in the Germanic Empire – favoured a cultural renaissance and the appearance of a new kind of art. At the same time, feudal frameworks were being put in place within a hierarchical society divided into three main orders: knights, clerics and peasants. With Cluny, monasticism began to develop during the 11th century, wresting from secular supervision a large network of monasteries whose *scriptoria* were producing bibles, liturgical books and other illuminated manuscripts. The institution of the Peace of God was expressed by the development of pilgrimages, ensuring the free circulation of ideas, technology and specific architectural forms. And finally, the Gregorian reform established the authority of the Church against temporal power, which, on its side, exercised intense patronage activity that in the 12th century gave fully developed Romanesque art, beyond different regional styles. On the roads to Santiago de Compostela, large churches were built in order to receive crowds of pilgrims coming to worship local relics. They were built

as basilicas, with three or five naves, prolonged by a protruding transept flanked by side aisles at east and west, the whole ending in a shrine with an ambulatory and radiating chapels. Supporting the eastern side of the transept and the chevet's apse, these chapels, also called apsidal, allowed the presentation of relics so they would be seen from the ambulatory where the faithful gathered, but also to permit the celebration of several services at the same time. This kind of chevet, adopted at Saint Martin of Tours, Saint Foy in Conques, Saint Sernin in Toulouse or Santiago de Compostela in Spain, was in contrast to the interval chevet, called Benedictine, because it was adopted for the first time at Cluny II, where chapels of differing depths were set at intervals between the central apse of the chancel and the transept. In the principal nave of these buildings, the barrel vault replaced wooden roofs. The barrel vault was often reinforced by a second arch, a beam, itself supported by columns set in the nave's pillars. At the transept crossing, that might be covered by a dome on squinches or pendentives, sometimes a lantern tower was raised. Furthermore, in south-western France some churches were covered

Adam and Eve, Santiago

with a line of domes on pendentives, like Saint Stephen's in Périgueux or l'Abbaye-aux-Dames in Saintes. The buildings' walls, thick and reinforced with buttresses, and pillars provided support for the thrust of the vaults. Semicircular openings were narrow and quite rare so that the supporting walls would not be weakened. To shore up the entire structure, galleries were sometimes placed above the side aisles, generally as groined vaults. Crypts were often built under churches to contain the treasure. Facades were often flanked with two steeples. Starting in the 12th century, sculpted decoration – geometric or floral motifs, biblical scenes, antinomic apparitions of angels and hybrid monsters – ornamented capitals and tympana. On the latter, Christ in majesty surrounded by apostles, illustrating the theophanies of Pentecost, the Apocalypse or the Last Judgement, were the favourite themes of sculptors, who have generally remained anonymous. Inside, frescoes, tapestries, mosaics, enamelled liturgical objects all emphasized the beauty of the buildings, born of an art called Romanesque in the 19th century, by analogy with the Romance language, late vulgar Latin, spoken and written in northern Gaul in the 12th century.

The Flagellation, Las Platerías doorway, Santiago Cathedral

The old men, tympanum of Saint Peter of Moissac Abbey Church

the cloister and the monastic buildings of the abbey, which had become a major stage on the *via Podiensis*. Abbot from 1085 to 1115, Ansquitil ordered the sculptures in the cloister and the tympanum of the abbey church, that was to receive Pope Urban II in May 1097, coming to consecrate the high altar dedicated to the Holy Saviour. While the master sculptors displayed their talent carving Saint John's vision of the Revelations on the portal's tympanum, while they took their time on the lintel frieze, the marvellous monsters on the piers, on Jeremy, Paul and Peter, other artists – scribes and illuminators – worked in the silence of the *scriptorium*, making prestigious and unique manuscripts that would enrich the abbey's library. The cloister's historiated capitals, living "stone bibles" offered for the visitor's meditation, can provide an idea of the illuminated treasures of the parchments, today kept at the National Library. Under the abbacy of Roger (1115-1131), the portal and steeple-porch were completed, while distinguished relics were brought to increase the monastery's fame. Possessing numerous dependencies in Languedoc and as far away as Catalonia, Moissac's spiritual influence was greatest during the 11th and 12th centuries. If pilgrims had not found space at the hostelry, they could always count on the abbey's lazar-house, located near Saint Martin's Church, or on other hospitals in the town of Moissac, one of which was named for Saint James. Rested and enlightened, they would not have missed visiting the church of Saint James of Moissac, before setting off again on their journey.

Detail of the portico in Moissac

Fresco detail in La Romieu

LA ROMIEU

....

The name La Romieu, or rather *l'Arromieu* – pilgrim in Gascon – appeared for the first time in 1182, in a donation of land by the lords of the region, Odon de Lomagne and his wife Adélaide, to Saint Victor's Abbey in Marseilles. Twenty years later, two pilgrim monks, finding that the place was suitable for monastic life, had established a priory there, around which a village was to grow. Born in La Romieu in 1270, Arnaud d'Aux belonged to a noble family, from the lineage of the Counts of Armagnac. As a student at the university of Bologna, he developed a deep friendship with his cousin, Bertrand de Got, the future Pope Clement V. When he became archbishop of Bordeaux, Bertrand made Arnaud his great vicar, then as pope under the name Clement V, he named his cousin cardinal camerlingo, before raising him to full cardinal in 1312. As consul to Philippe le Bel, advisor to the king of England, Arnaud d'Aux presided over the trial of the Templars. In his native town, he ordered the building of Saint Peter's Collegiate Church, with a cloister and a sumptuous palace, but of which only a tower remains today.

In Gascony

Leaving Moissac through Saint James Gate, some pilgrims crossed the Garonne River in a ferry at La Pointe, in the direction of the priory of Saint Nicholas de La Grave. Although others preferred crossing the water at Malause, they all met up at Auvillar, the seat of a Benedictine priory, of the hospital called Sainte-Christine du Port, and the commandery Saint-Jean de Castens, belonging to the Hospitallers of Saint John of Jerusalem. Entering Gascony through the valley of Arrats, the pilgrims crossed the river over the bridge belonging to Saint Anthony's commandery, served by the Antonins. The local church contained relics of Saint Anthony, protected in a silver reliquary arm. Continuing through Flamerens and Saint Mary Magdalene hospital in Miradoux, some pilgrims could pause at the hospital of Saint-Jacques de la Peyronnelle before entering the town of Lectoure, an episcopal town with nine hospitals. From Lectoure, the road joined the shores of the Baïse River and the town of Condom via Abrin, the former seat of a commandery of the Hospitallers of Saint John of Jerusalem. Those who, upon leaving Lectoure, had detoured through Agen, the location of Saint Foy's martyrdom, joined the road at Abrin by using an old Roman road, la Peyrigne, passing through Saint-Médard and La Romieu. In Condom, an important Benedictine abbey received pilgrims starting in the 11th century, and after the 14th century, the town, which had become a bishopric in 1317, established several hospitals, including two hospitals dedicated to Saint James: Saint-Jacques de la

La Romieu Collegiate Church

Nave of St Peter's Cathedral in Condom

St James, Lectoure church

FLARAN ABBEY

At Condom, some pilgrims chose to rejoin the *via Tolosana* at L'Isle-de-Noé or in Montesquiou. Walking through the valley of the Baïse River, the came upon the Cistercian abbey of Flaran. Founded in 1151, at the confluence of the Auloue and the Baïse, by monks coming from L'Escale-Dieu, the abbey rapidly prospered. In the middle of the 13th century, its abbot founded the bastide of Valence with the Count of Armagnac, at the summit of a hill on the other side of the Baïse. Despite life spent in prayer and manual work, according to the rule of Saint Benedict, the abbey suffered from the trials and tribulations of history, beginnning with the troubles of the Hundred Years War, which ended only in 1481 when the county of Gascony became part of France. Burnt during the Wars of Religion, the abbey was restored by its commendatory abbots, but sold during the Revolution. In 1913, the Gers Archaeological Society managed to prevent its cloister from being sent to the Cloisters Museum in New York City. The restoration of its church with the rounded chevet and its cloister with sculpted capitals began in 1972, with the help of the Historical Monument Association.

Flaran Abbey

Capital in Larressingle church

Capital in church of Lagraulet-du-Gers

Larressingle

Tympanum in Nogaro church

Bouquerie and, at the exit from the town, Saint-Jaques de Teste, founded in 1314 by Cardinal Guillaume de Teste. Like in Roncesvalles, the patients in the latter hospital did not have to move to attend holy services but could follow them from their beds. Descending the valley of the Osse River, after Larressingle the road crossed the torrent over the Roman bridge of Artigues, near which a church belonging to the archbishopric of Santiago de Compostela had existed since 1178. In 1254, the knights of the Order of Saint James of the Sword had founded a commandery with a hospital there. In 1268, the buildings were given to the Order of Saint James of Faith and Peace, which had been created in 1226 by the archbishop of Auch, Amanieu 1st of Gresilhac. Keeping on through Lagraulet-du-Gers, the road crossed the Auzoue River, passed by the Bosc hospital at the entrance to Pardhaillan, and went through Bretagne-d'Armagnac before entering Eauze, a town built around the Benedictine monastery of Saint Gervais and Saint Protais, affiliated to Cluny in 1088. After the commandery of Manciet, the road arrived at Saint Christie hospital, a possession of the Knights of Saint John of Jerusalem. Then through Nogaro, Lanne-Soubiran and Luppé, the pilgrims reached Aire-sur-Adour and its Mas Basilica, whose crypt contained the relics of Saint Quitterie. The daughter of the governor of Galicia and Lusitania, Quitterie was allegedly martyred in Aire during the reign of Emperor Commodus (176-192). Several Spanish cities also claimed that they were the scene of the saint's martyrdom. A pilgrimage site, the Mas basilica had been acquired by La Chaise-Dieu Abbey at the end of the 12th century.

In Béarn

Coming out of Aire-sur-Adour, the road ran directly south in the direction of the commandery of Pourin, served by the Hospitallers of Saint John of Jerusalem, then turning westward, it crossed the moor of Miramont by way of the chapel Saint-Jacques de Sensac, passing the bastide of Pimbo, the seat of a Benedictine abbey, and the town of Arzacq-Arraziguet before arriving in Larreule. Through Uzan, where the pilgrims found a spring and a church dedicated to Saint Quitterie, the road ran towards Urdès whose Saint Bartholomew's Church depended on the commandery of the Hospitallers of Saint-Jean de Morlaàs. Having crossed the Gave of Pau at Lendresse, the pilgrims reached the abbey of Sauvelade, founded in 1128 by Gaston IV the Crusader, Viscount of Béarn. A stopover particularly appreciated by pilgrims, the abbey was named for Saint James, before being affiliated with the Cistercian Order in 1286, through the intermediary of the abbey of Gimont. Crossing the Gave of Oloron over the bridge in Naverrenx, the seat of an Antonin commandery, the pilgrims continued towards Charre, where they crossed the Gave of Mauléon by ford or by boat. Then, passing Arué Priory and the chapel of Lapiste, the *via Podiensis* went through the Bidouze River by a ford at Quinquil, and climbed Holy Saviour Mount. Finally, near Saint-Palais, at the Gibraltar crossroads it met up with the *via Lemovicensis* and the *via Turonensis*, which had joined at Sauveterre-de-Béarn.

Bas-relief in Arué Church

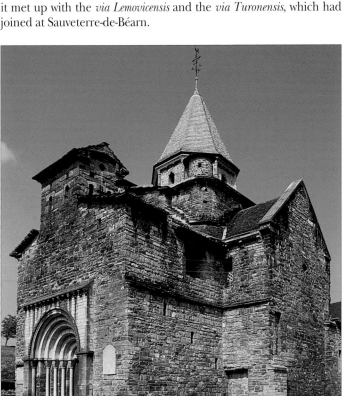

Church in L'Hôpital-Saint-Blaise

VIA L'HÔPITAL-SAINT-BLAISE

At Lacommande, instead of pursuing through the Somport Pass and Jaca, pilgrims on the *via Tolosana* could save a few kilometres by taking a secondary road that, through Lucq de Béarn and L'Hôpital-Saint-Blaise, rejoined the *viae Podiensis*, *Lemovicensis* and *Turonensis* together. The existence of the *Misericordi* commandery of Saint-Blaise, perhaps founded by the Augustinians of the great hospital of Saint Christine at Somport, is mentioned for the first time in a notary act dated 1334. Its fine church with a nervate dome at the transept crossing, and whose nave and transept are adorned with open-work lattices with geometrical motifs, were inspired by Mozarab architecture.

Cloister and steeple of Saint Trophime Cathedral

Judas' kiss, doorway in Saint-Gilles Abbey Church

Apostle, Saint-Gilles Abbey Church

Crypt in Saint-Gilles Abbey Church

Saint-Guilhem-le-Désert

Saint-Guilhem-le-Désert

Past Montpellier and Aniane Abbey, and once the Hérault River was crossed over the Devil's Bridge, the winding road of the *fenestrelles* led the Santiago pilgrims to the abbey of Saint-Guilhem-le-Désert, located at the entrance to the Verdus gorges, in the heart of the Gellone valley. It was in 804 that the valiant knight, Guillaume, or Guilhem, the cousin of Charlemagne, Count of Toulouse and Duke of Aquitaine, endowed the abbey of Gellone, with the advice of his friend Benedict, the founder of Aniane. Celebrated for his battlefield feats against the Gascons in Aquitaine and the Saracens in Septimania, in 806 Guillaume renounced his career as a warrior after a pilgrimage to Saint-Julien de Brioude. He retired to Gellone where he died in the odour of sanctity on May 28, 812, bequeathing to the abbey, from then on bearing his name, a precious *Sacramentary*, today kept at the National Library, as well as remarkable fragments of the True Cross that had been given to him by Charlemagne. Freed from Aniane's supervision in 1090 by Pope Urban II, Saint-Guilhem, famous for its relics, reached its apogee during the 12th century. Pilgrims, particularly those on their way to Santiago de Compostela, came in great numbers to its founder's tomb. Guillaume's *Life* had just been written, combining hagiography and episodes of his warrior's life in an epic poem of which he had become the hero, under the name *Guillaume d'Orange*.
A masterpiece of Languedoc Romanesque art, Saint-Guilhem Abbey Church was rebuilt in the 11th century and consecrated in 1076. Its slender nave with four bays, covered with a semicircular vault with beam arches, communicates with the aisles by large arcades. Beyond the transept, a large semicircular apse of the chevet is surrounded by two apsidal chapels. Between the north chapel and the nave, a recess contains the reliquary containing Saint Guillaume's relics, formerly presented in the pre-Romanesque crypt located under the chancel. The cloister, taken apart in the 19th century, has nonetheless kept its fine Romanesque northern gallery. As for the 12th century upper cloister, it is presently at the Cloisters Museum in New York City.

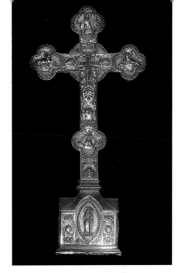

The Holy Cross, Saint-Guilhem

GUILLAUME OF ORANGE

The son of Alde and Thierry, grandson of Charles Martel, cousin of Charlemagne and tutor of the young king of Aquitaine, Guillaume received the title of Count of Toulouse from the emperor in 790. Defender of the Gothian March, he became famous against the Saracens in 793, on the shores of the Orbieu River. He also participated in several actions against Barcelona until the city's capture in 801. Following the example of his Gothic friend Witiza, better known by the name of Benedict, founder of Aniane Abbey, Guillaume put on the monk's habit in 806, before dying in 812 at Gellone Abbey that he had founded eight years earlier. He was canonized by Alexander II in 1066. During the 12th century, minstrels and troubadours used his character, rebaptized Guillaume with a short nose or Guillaume of Orange, heroic defender of Christianity against the Muslim infidels, coming to aid his nephew and adopted son Vivien, attacked at Larchamp. Inconsolable at the death of his wife, the beautiful Saracen Orable, who had become Countess of Guibourc after her marriage, Guillaume allegedly went to the desert of Gellone, before seeing her again in another world at the end of his monastic life.

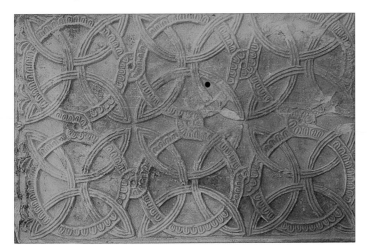

Fragment in chancel of pre-Romanesque church in Saint-Guilhem-le-Désert

Castres

In the Middle Ages, pilgrimages were among the punishments imposed on the guilty who, depending on the gravity of their crimes, had to accomplish minor, local or regional, pilgrimages, or else major ones, in other words, international ones.

Crossing Upper Languedoc

Leaving Saint-Guilhem, the *via Tolosana* went past Usclas-du-Bosc Castle where the Hospitallers of Saint John had settled in the 12th century. The scallop shell and gourd carved on the door showed pilgrims they were welcome. At the confluence of the Lergue and Soulondres rivers, the road continued towards Lodève and its fortified Saint Fulcran's Cathedral, before reaching the Benedictine abbey of Joncels. Then, crossing the northern section of the Montagne Noire, it passed Murat-sur-Vèbre and La Salvetat-sur-Agout before arriving in Castres, a town born around a monastery founded in about 810 by Benedict of Aniane. Since one of its basilicas contained the relics of Saint Vincent, Castres was one of twelve minor pilgrimages on the road to Santiago. However, at their departure from Saint-Guilhem, some pilgrims followed the *Guide's* advice and preferred to take the Hérault River valley, via Pézenas, to the Benedictine monastery of Saint-Thibéry, founded in about 770. This was the resting place of the three saints from Agde – Thibéry, Modeste and Florence – martyred under Diocletian in 304. Next came Saint James's Church and Saint Nazaire Cathedral in Béziers, the first southern Cathar city to be attacked by the crusaders of Innocent III in July 1209. Leaving the Domitian road in Narbonne, the next stage for the Santiago pilgrims was the city of Carcassonne, before Toulouse, where they met pilgrims coming from Castres, unless they had decided to take the Pyrenees Piedmont route.

Saint James Church in Béziers

Symbol of St James in Usclas-du-Bosc

BENEDICT OF ANIANE

Born in about 750, Benedict, whose real name was Witiza, son of Agulfe, Visigoth count of Maguelonne, was raised at the court of Pepin the Short. With his brother, he nearly drowned at the battle of Pavia. In thanksgiving, Witiza entered the Burgundian abbey of Saint-Seine in 774. Fascinated by monastic ideals, he practiced asceticism, studied the principal rules and collected them together into the *Concordia regularum*, and adopted that of Saint Benedict, whose name he chose for his conversion. He left Burgundy to found a Benedictine monastery on familiar ground, at Aniane. It was to become the most prestigious of the Carolingian empire. He took part in the struggle against the Adoptianist heresy, and at the request of Louis the Pious, then governor of Aquitaine, Benedict visited monasteries in Poitou, Languedoc, the Rhône valley and Burgundy. As emperor in 814, Louis the Pious placed Benedict at the head of Cornelimünster monastery and charged him with monastic reform all over the empire. Benedict gave liturgy more importance in monastic life, to the detriment of physical work. The synods of Aachen in 816, 817, 818 and 819 imposed the reforms of Benedict of Aniane, who died in Germany in 821.

SAINT THIBÉRY

Born in 293, Tiberi was the son of the Roman governor of Agde. At about the age of ten, he was converted to Christianity by his tutor, Modeste. In 303, during the last persecutions ordered by Emperor Diocletian, the child was invited to participate in a ceremony honouring Jupiter but refused to celebrate the imperial cult. Using his rights, Tiberi's father decreed his son's death. At that time, the *via Domitia*, linking Italy and Spain, ran through the town of Cassero, at the confluence of the Thongue and the Hérault, at the foot of the Ramus mountains. This was where Tiberi, Modeste and the matron Florence were executed with a sword. Piously collected inside a house, their relics became the object of a local cult. In the 5th century, the monks of Saint Sever Abbey in Agde perhaps built a first shrine near the martyrs' tombs. Having come from Burgundy, the devout Atilion retired there in 770, attracting many monks whose abbot he became. Originally from Bordeaux, Atilion, advisor and disciple of Benedict of Aniane (750-821) gave his abbey, which took the name Saint-Thibéry, the Benedictine rule reformed by his master of Aniane.

Dying in 810, he was buried at Saint-Thibéry, before being canonized by Ninfridus, Archbishop of Narbonne. The monks worked the lands of their monastery, clearing and cultivating them. The 12th century flour mill is evidence of this important operation. At the dawn of the 14th century, reconstruction of the abbey church was undertaken. The work was interrupted but began again between 1457 and 1535, although the Wars of Religion left the building unfinished. Inhabited once again during the 17th century by Benedictine monks from Saint-Maur, the abbey was rebuilt. However the church remained as it was. The three-spanned nave, with its ribbed vault and flanked with chapels, as well as the polygonal apse, lit by three geminate lancets, provide a characteristic example of Southern Gothic architecture. Acting as the building's crypt, the *gleizette*, the former abbey chapel from the 11th century, vaulted in the 15th, was long ago raised on the site of the martyrdom of Thibéry, Modeste and Florence. Isolated at the western side, the square 16th century campanile, planned in the enlargement work, was never joined to the church.

Flour Mill in Saint-Thibéry

VIA THE PYRENEES PIEDMONT

Leaving from Carcassonne, crossing Foix, Saint-Lizier, Saint-Gaudens and Lourdes, the route through the Pyrenees piedmont rejoined the *via Tolosana* at Oloron-Sainte-Marie. After Saint-Gaudens and its collegiate church dating from the 11th and 12th centuries, once the Garonne River was crossed at Labroquère, past the Romanesque church of Saint-Just in Valcabrère, the important stage of this Pyrenees route was Saint-Bertrand-de-Comminges, overlooking the antique *Lugdunum Convenarum*. Elected bishop of Comminges in 1083, Bertrand de l'Isle started construction of Saint Mary's Cathedral towards 1100, providing it with a cloister for its canons. Buried in the cathedral in 1123, tales of his miracles attracted numerous pilgrims to his tomb. A liberator of captives, Bertrand was canonized in 1218. In 1135, Bertrand de Got, the future Pope Clement V, Bishop of Comminges from 1295 to 1299, set about converting the cathedral into Gothic style, giving it a vault on intersecting ribs. Past Saint Bertrand, instead of joining the main route at Oloron via the Lannemezan plateau, some pilgrims, received at Guchen, Agos and Aragnouet by the Hospitallers of Saint John of Jerusalem, preferred crossing the Aure valley and crossing the Rioumajou in the direction of Zaragoza, where Our Lady of Pilar awaited their prayers.

Templar chapel near Aragnouet

Capital, cloister in Saint-Gaudens

Count's castle in Carcassonne

Stall showing St Bertrand

Saint-Just in Valcabrère and Saint-Bertrand-de-Comminges

Chevet of Saint Sernin Basilica in Toulouse

Toulouse

The little ford, the *badaculum*, the Bazacle, that let the Garonne River be crossed during low water, was at the origin of the creation of Toulouse by the Volques Tectosages in the 3rd century BC. But in 118 BC, they were defeated by the Romans, and *Tolosa* became a Gallo-Roman town, receiving the title of Latin Colony under Augustus. Saturnin, the city's first bishop, was martyred in about 250. In 418 the Visigoths made Toulouse the capital of their kingdom. After the defeat of the Visigoths at Vouillé in 507, Toulouse became a Frankish town. During the 11th century, having become the capital of the county dynasty of the Saint-Gilles, Toulouse became an important stage on the *via Tolosana*, to which it gave its name. A famous pilgrimage site, mentioned in Aimery Picaud's *Guide*, Saint Sernin Basilica, built starting in 1060 and consecrated by Urban II in 1096, possessed the relics of Saturnin – Sernin by popular contraction, as well as some relics of James the Greater offered, according to legend, to the basilica's canons by Charlemagne. There were also the entire bodies of six other apostles, relics of Saint George, brought from Crusades in the East by the counts of Toulouse, and fragments of the True Cross. For Santiago pilgrims, Toulouse, the site of the miracle of the *hanged-unhanged* until it was situated in Santo Domingo de la Calzada, was a foretaste of what was waiting for them at the end of the road. Except for the double side aisles of the nave, the plan of Saint Sernin Basilica, with its extended transept with apsi-

Capitole Square in Toulouse

THE CAPITOLE

In 1152, strengthened by their economic power, merchants in Toulouse formed a "communal council" as a counterweight to County power. Called *senhors del Capitol*, lords of the chapter, they called their Communal House the Capitole.

Saint James Hospital in Toulouse

St James, Saint Sernin Basilica

dal chapels and its ambulatory with radiating chapels, was approximately the same as that of Santiago de Compostela Cathedral. At the threshold of the Toulouse basilica, at the Miègeville door, walkers were welcomed by Saint James in person, trampling on women riding lions. Dominic came to Languedoc at the beginning of the 13th century to try to root out the Cathar heresy and, as soon as his order was founded in 1215, his preaching friars were established in Toulouse, where they built the monastic buildings of the Jacobins, completed in 1325. A masterpiece of Southern Gothic, its church, where Thomas Aquinas was buried in 1369, is organized around a double nave supported by eight columns, the most eastern of them holding the set of springs of the twenty-two diagonal ribs, forming a remarkable "palm tree". To the south of Saint Stephen's Cathedral, Saint James's Church, demolished in 1811, had been built, according to legend, by Charlemagne on his return from Spain. The seat of Saint James's Confraternity, it contained the head of James the Greater, formerly offered by the emperor and solemnly exhumed in 1490. Several hospitals welcomed walkers for God in Toulouse: the hostelry of the Benedictine priory of La Daurade, the hospice of Saint-Jacques-du-Bourg, the hospice of Notre-Dame-du-Puy and the Templars' hospital, established in 1408 in the Templars' former commandery by the Hospitallers of Saint John of Jerusalem. But the most important of all was certainly was the hospital called Saint-Jacques du Bout-du-Pont (Saint James at the end of the bridge), founded in the 12th century on the left bank of the Garonne.

A ROYAL PILGRIM IN TOULOUSE

I n 1157, the king of France Louis VII le Jeune, *"rediens a sancto Jacobo et per Tolosamam transiens"*, passing through Toulouse on his way back from Santiago, confirmed royal privileges on Saint Sernin Basilica.

"Palmtree" in Jacobins Church in Toulouse

THE CATHARS

During the 12th century, a heresy called Catharism spread throughout the Occitan-speaking lands. Cathars were dualistic Christians. They believed there were two creations, one of Good, the work of God, and that of Evil. At Councils, the Church excommunicated the Cathar doctrine, against which it sent preachers like Saint Bernard in 1145. But with little success since Catharism received support from many people, quite often including Occitan lords. The Count of Toulouse, Raymond VI himself, seemed open to heretical ideas and the assassination of Pierre de Castelnau, the papal legate, in Saint-Gilles in 1208, attributed to one of Raymond's aides, led Innocent III to call for a crusade against the Albigensian heresy. The crusaders led by Simon de Montfort sacked the country. The situation became political and Pedro II of Aragon allied with Raymond VI, but was killed at the Battle of Muret, near Toulouse, in 1213. Troops were sent by northern lords in 1219, others by the king of France in 1226. In 1233, the Inquisition took over to try and end the heresy. In March 1244, more than two hundred Cathars were burnt at the stake at Montségur.

"Pog" or hill of Montségur

SAINT SERNIN

The first bishop of Toulouse, Saturnin, or Sernin, was martyred in 250, during the consulate of Dece. According to the story of his *Passion*, written in the 5th century, he was the victim of a popular uprising. In fury, the pagan crowd attached the Christian preacher to a bull prepared for sacrifice. Thrown from the top of the stairs of the Capitole temple, the bishop was dragged by the animal until his head was broken. After the torture, his terrified disciples secretly buried the body and more than a century went by before Bishop Hilaire, one of Sernin's successors, started to look for the martyr's tomb. Hilaire hid the sepulchre under a brick building, and nearby he raised a little wooden oratory, the origin of the future Notre-Dame-du-Taur Church. At the end of the 4th century, the cult of Saint Sernin had become so famous that Bishop Silve had to undertake the construction of a basilica worthy of its fame, on the location of the present Romanesque basilica. The martyr's relics were solemnly transferred by Bishop Exupère at the beginning of the 5th century. Under the control of bishops of Toulouse, a community of canons was charged with celebrating the cult and watching over the tomb. In the second half of the 11th century, within the framework of the Gregorian reform, the canons of Saint Sernin adopted Saint Augustine's rule. At that time, during which the pilgrimage to Santiago developed, the Paleochristian basilica, an obligatory stage on the *via Tolosana*, became too small to hold the crowds of pilgrims. It hence had to be rebuilt, both larger and more beautiful. Under the leadership of Canon Raymond Gayrard, work on the "immense basilica", mentioned by Aimery Picaud, began towards 1060. On May 24, 1096, its transept and its chevet were completed to receive Pope Urban II, who consecrated the church and its marble altar, the work of Bernard Gilduin, in the company of fourteen archbishops and bishops, including several Spanish prelates. On the point of leaving for the First Crusade, Raymond IV of Saint-Gilles attended the ceremony. The principal work on the ambitious nave, high and narrow with double aisles, was nearly completed in 1118. In 1145, controversy here opposed Bernard of Clairvaux and Henry of Lausanne along with heretics accused of Arianism. A perfect example of Romanesque architecture, the basilica contains treasures of monumental sculpture decorating its four doorways and a great number of its interior capitals. Set in the wall of the ambulatory circling the apse since the 19th century, the seven marble bas-reliefs showing Christ in majesty, four angels and two apostles were probably sculpted by Gilduin and his master sculptors. Construction of the church ended in the 13th and 14th centuries with the creation of two crypts containing shrines and reliquaries. The steeple was raised and a Gothic reliquary containing relics of Saint Sernin under a two storey baldaquin was set in the centre of the chevet's apse. In the 18th century, the chancel was decorated with Baroque furnishings. Although the cloister and the chapter buildings disappeared during the Revolution, the church was relatively unharmed. Its restoration in the 19th century by Viollet-le-Duc was criticized, and at the end of the 20th century, the Romanesque basilica regained its original appearance.

In Gascony

After Colomiers and Léguevin, the route entered Gascony at Pujaudran, where the Antonins had a commandery with a church and a hospital, then continued through L'Isle-Jourdain, the birthplace of Saint Bertrand of Comminges. It passed Garbic and Ambon before reaching the bastide of Gimont, founded in the 13th century by Cistercians from Planselve, who owned four hospitals. Past Aubiet and its Saint James hospital, the pilgrims arrived in the episcopal city of Auch through the Betclar Gate, also called the *Couscouille*, or shell in Gascon. In Saint Mary's Cathedral, whose construction began at the end of the 14th century, Saint James is shown on one of the stained glass windows and well as in the choir stalls. The Augustinians of the cathedral chapter and the Cluniacs of Saint-Orens of Auch were dedicated to receiving pilgrims in the region, and starting in the 13th century, a Saint James hospital existed in Auch, in the Caillou quarter. Coming out of the city, the road passed Bonnefont hospital, a dependency of Saint Christine of Somport, then, after passing through Barran, L'Isle-Noé and Montesquiou, avoided Bassoues and turned to the south-west towards Saint-Christaud. Served by the Augustinians of Saint Sernin in Toulouse, the church here contained relics of Saint Christopher, protector of travellers and pilgrims, with his feast day on Saint James's day. The route then reached Maubourguet, either through Monlezun and Saint-Justin in the south, or in the north through the bastide of Marciac, founded in 1298.

Montesquiou

Church in Barran

Saint Mary's Cathedral, Officialité Palace and Armagnac Tower in Auch

Bassoues Keep

Church in Maubourguet

Doorway of Sainte-Foy Church in Morlaàs

Detail of left tympanum at Sainte-Foy in Morlaàs

Saracens at foot of pier, Sainte-Foy in Morlaàs

In Béarn

After Maubourguet, the road went past the village of Saint-Jammes – an ancient form of Saint James – to arrive in Morlaàs. After the destruction of Lescar by Norsemen in 841, Morlaàs was the capital of the Viscounty of Béarn until the end of the 12th century. In the 11th century, the viscounts of Béarn endowed its Cluniac priory with Saint Foy Church. Its Romanesque doorway was redone between 1857 and 1903 according to the original model, destroyed by a fire. Bypassing Pau in the north by Maucor and the valley of the Luy River, the route arrived in Lescar, in the plain of the Gave du Pau. Founded by the Romans after the conquest of Aquitaine, in 56 BC, the fortified town of *Beneharnum* gave its name to the province of Béarn of which it was the capital. The town became a bishopric in the 6th century. After its destruction in 841, it recovered under the name of Lescar. In 1125, under the episcopacy of Gui de Lons, work began on the cathedral, the necropolis of the kings of Navarre, princes of Béarn, during the 15th and 16th centuries. Besides the historiated capitals in its Romanesque nave with five spans, in the nave the building presents a mosaic pavement from the 12th century showing a hunting scene. Continuing southwards through Artiguelouve, the road passed by the commandery of Faget d'Aubertin, founded in the midst of a beech wood – *faget* in Old French – in the 12th century by Gaston IV the Crusader. Collapsed in 1970, this commandery gave its name to the present village of Lacommande. Its Romanesque Saint Blaise Church,

Capital in Lacommande

HE HUNTED ON ONE LEG...

The mosaic on the apse in Lescar Cathedral shows the influence of al-Andalus. The archer's artificial leg is specific to Arab surgery, and the lions bringing down gazelles was a frequent motif of Persian art.

Mosaic floor in apse of Lescar Cathedral

Chained Saracens in Oloron

THE VIRGIN OF SARRANCE

O ne day a shepherd saw an ox kneeling before a stone in the Aspe gave. The face of the Virgin appeared on this stone. The shepherd ran to the village to bring the news, confirmed by a fisherman who was a witness. The bishop had the holy image brought to his cathedral, but it returned by itself to Sarrance, which became the centre of a local pilgrimage. To put an end to the kind of abuse taking place, Henry II, father of Jeanne d'Albret, forbade entrance to "tambourine players and female sinners". In the monastery church, carved wooden panels present the miracle.

remodelled in the 14th century, still stands with its sculpted capitals ornamenting the apse of the chevet. At the confluent of the gaves (mountain streams) of Aspe and Ossau, Oloron-Sainte-Marie was the next stage for the pilgrims. Destroyed by Norsemen in the 9th century, the antique *Iluro*, a bishopric in the 6th century, produced two distinct towns in the 11th century: Sainte-Marie the bishopric, west of Aspe gave, where bishop Étienne Lavedan restored the bishopric in 1058; and Oloron the viscountcy, in the upper town. A fortified town born under the impetus of Centulle V le Jeune, Viscount of Béarn, who in 1080 decreed a charter of population, inspired by the Spanish *poblacions*. In this new town, a stage on the route to Santiago de Compostela, Holy Cross Church was built in the 12th century. Coming out of Oloron, the road followed the Aspe valley, passing through Arros, Saint-Christaud, Escot and the Premonstrant monastery in Sarrance. After Accous, Lescun and Borce, the pilgrims undertook the climb to *Summus Portus*, the Somport Pass, at an altitude of 1,632 metres.

Miracle of the Virgin, Sarrance

Sarrance Cloister

From Somport to Puente la Reina

Hardly had they crossed the pass at Somport, the pilgrims could rest at the hospital of Santa Cristina. This ancient foundation had received support from Alfonso the Warrior(1104-1134) and Gaston IV of Béarn and it became, according to Aimery Picaud, "one of the three columns needed among all for the support of the poor established by God on this earth". The two other columns were the hospital in Jerusalem and that of Mont-Joux at Great Saint Bernard Pass in the Alps. At the beginning of the 13th century, Santa Cristina controlled fourteen houses north of the Pyrenees and thirty in Aragon. From Somport, the road followed the valley of the Aragon River, crossed Campfranc, the *Campo franco*, thus named because the village's inhabitants were supposed to ensure pilgrims' free passage, and reached Jaca, at the foot of Peña de Oroel. Here they met the road that had been taken by pilgrims from Oloron preferring to take the valley of Ossau and crossing the pass of Pourtalet.

Ramiro 1st (1035-1063) made Jaca the capital of the kingdom of Aragon. Sancho Ramirez (1063-1094) granted the city many privileges that attracted numerous *Francos*. They settled in a new town on the site today occupied by the citadel built in the 16th century. The diocese of Jaca was created in about 1075. This was when the construction of Saint Peter's Cathedral began. In the early 1090's it was still being built, as attested by an act of donation made for this construction by one of Sancho Ramirez's three sisters, Doña Sancha, whose tomb is in Salvador Church at the Benedictine monastery. This cathedral was one of the very first Romanesque works in Spain where the sculptor known as the Master of Jaca intervened, particularly in carving the capitals of the western doorway. Some of the rooms that open onto the cloister contain collections from the episcopal museum, whose Romanesque and Gothic wall paintings come from churches in the region. In a silver reliquary-urn, the cathedral keeps the relics of San Indalecio, one of the seven disciples of Saint James. These relics had been

Pantocrator, Jaca Diocesan Museum

SAN JUAN DE LA PEÑA

The monastery of San Juan de la Peña, south-west of Jaca, was founded in the 9th century and became a centre of active resistance to Islam. It was connected to Cluny in 1025. The cloister was built in the 12th century under the natural overhang of the cliff. One of the sculptors who participated in work on the cloister, known as the Master of San Juan, developed, on some of the capitals, his vision of the creation of Man, Paradise Lost, the Visitation and the wedding at Cana.

Capital in cloister of San Juan de la Peña

Cloister of San Juan de la Peña

Tympanum of Jaca Cathedral

Jaca Cathedral

brought to the neighbouring monastery of San Juan de la Peña in 1084. In 1096, Huesca was recaptured from the Moors; in turn, Zaragoza was reconquered in 1116. Although Jaca lost its importance, with its hospitals and its Saint James's church whose steeple and baptismal fonts subsist, it remained a stage on the road to Santiago. Louis VII stopped there on his return from pilgrimage in 1154 and, according to tradition, Saint Francis passed through in 1213.

From Jaca the road followed the Aragon River along its left bank, as far as Puente la Reina de Jaca. Beyond, some pilgrims took the direction of Ruesta before reaching, at the confluence of the Aragon and the Irati, Sangüesa where they were joined by those who had crossed the Aragon R. at Puente la Reina de Jaca, passed through Tiermas, then Yesa at the foot of Leyre Abbey, before crossing the river once again to climb towards Javier. The route

FRANCIS XAVIER

On April 7, 1506 the son of the Royal Councillor of Navarre was born at the castle of Javier. His parents named him Francis, perhaps in memory of the passage at the castle in 1213 of a pilgrim to Santiago, Saint Francis of Assisi. In 1515, Navarre was attached to the kingdom of Castile and Francis' father died. His elder brothers, fighting for Navarre's independence, besieged, along with French troops, Pamplona defended by a captain named Ignatius de Loyola. In 1525, Francis went to study in Paris. In 1531, his roommate was Ignatius de Loyola. At the end of their studies of theology, the two men and several friends went to Rome, where they were ordained as priests. And in 1540, in the Eternal City, they founded the Company of Jesus.

Javier Castle

SAN SALVADOR DE LEYRE

Chevet in Leyre

The existence of the abbey of Leyre was attested in a letter written by Saint Eulogus in his Cordoban jail in 851. After Abd al-Rahmân had captured Pamplona in 924, the abbey was used as a refuge for religious dignitaries and the Navarrese court. From that time on until 1078, it became customary that the bishop of Pamplona was one of its abbots. Under Sancho the Great (1000-1035), Leyre reached its apogee. Although Leyre itself never joined Cluny, in 1025 it was the scene of the act by which San Juan de la Peña adopted the Cluniac reform. During this king's reign, the plans for the Romanesque chevet and the extraordinary crypt with short columns that seem to be pushed into the ground under the weight of the arches were drawn up. The first section that was built was consecrated in 1057 in the presence of Don Sancho de Peñalen (1054-1076). As construction work advanced, another consecration took place on October 24, 1098 in the presence of King Pedro 1st of Aragon (1094-1104) and of Diego Peláez, the bishop of Santiago de Compostela. The abbey's power was such that it controlled fifty-eight towns and villages, including Estella, and eleven churches and monasteries. In 1269, Leyre Abbey was attached to the Cistercian Order, becoming the daughter of another Navarrese abbey, that of La Oliva, founded in 1150 by L'Escale-Dieu.

Crypt in Leyre

La Oliva

indicated by Aimery Picaud ran directly from Yesa towards Liédena before passing the Irati south of la Hoz de Lumbier, and continuing to Monreal. A first town had occupied Rocaforte hill on the right bank of the Aragon. In 1122, Alfonso 1st the Warrior (1104-1134) granted its inhabitants a charter of privileges to persuade them to settle on the left bank at Sangüesa. In 1131, the king entrusted the new town, a bridgehead over the Aragon, to the Knights of Saint John of Jerusalem, who remained in Sangüesa until 1351. With the passage of pilgrims Sangüesa prospered and was surrounded by ramparts with six gates set in them. The town contained no less than thirteen hospices for pilgrims. Palaces of the Prince of Viana, the former residences of the kings of Navarre, or the marquises of Vallesantoro were subsequently built within the walls. Saint James's Church from the 12th and 13th centuries presents the saint being worshipped by two pilgrims on its doorway.

Column-statues on doorway of Santa María la Real in Sangüesa

Santa María la Real, Sangüesa

Eunate Chapel

Past Santa María la Real, with its fine steeple of light stone, a metal bridge, replacing the Romanesque seven-arched bridge, crosses over the Aragon. This church was built in the 12th century, and its southern doorway dates from the early 13th century. Two artists participated in the sculptures of the doorway, whose tympanum presents a scene from the Last Judgement, and one of the voussoirs illustrates different crafts. The six column-statues, whose Gothic inspiration evokes Chartres, are the work of Master Leodegarius; the two galleries topping the doorway itself, that of the Master of San Juan de la Peña.

After Monreal, the pilgrims travelled towards Puente la Reina. Before Obanos, where they met up with those coming from Roncesvalles, they stopped at the Romanesque church of Santa María de Eunate, dating from the second half of the 12th century. It was built to an octagonal plan and the church is encircled by a portico forming a circular cloister, that was perhaps a funerary chapel.

FUNERARY CHAPELS

The hypothesis according to which the churches of Santa María de Eunate and Holy Sepulchre of Torres del Rio, between Estella and Logroño, were funerary chapels is supported by the fact that both of them had stairs leading to the roof allowing maintenance of the flame in the lantern of the dead. Although such a lantern tops the mudejar dome of the Torres del Rio church, in Eumate the roof is topped with a flat steeple, but perhaps it replaced the original lantern?

2

THE CAMINO FRANCÉS

Since the 11th century, the various roads have all joined at Puente la Reina. One after the other, the stages were counted off, like beads on a rosary, or like the Stations of the Cross. After the green landscapes of Navarre and La Rioja, came the wide expanses of Castile, overheated by the summer sun or swept by the cold winter winds. After Mount Irago, the Bierzo is the antechamber of Galicia. But from the pass at Cebreiro, the road was still long before, from the summit of Monte del Gozo, the pilgrim caught a glimpse of Santiago de Compostela. First of all, he had to purify himself in the waters of the Lavamentula, then get rid of his rags, in other words, become presentable to be able to finally pray, during an entire night, kneeling in front of the apostle's sepulchre.

Alfonso VI

A SINGLE ROAD...

Little information is available about the routes followed by pilgrims once they had crossed the Pyrenees before the 11th century. Nobody knows which road was taken by Godescalc, Bishop of Le Puy, in 950 when he went to Santiago, except that he stopped over at the monastery of Albelda. However, one piece of information was given in the *Chronicle of Silos*, written in 1110. It is said that the king of Navarre, Sancho III the Great (1000-1035), "from the Pyrenees to the castle of Nájera, having eliminated the pagan presence in the lands separating them, made the road to Santiago go straight, whereas before pilgrims made a detour by the Alava". The notion of this territory being occupied by Moors is unlikely, since it is known that Christians had reconquered it long before. But it is certain that, in his policy of westward expansion, Sancho needed an established, busy and important axis of communication between Nájera and Burgos to move his troops. For this reason he encouraged the passage of ever growing crowds of pilgrims along this route. Before Sancho, pilgrims went from Roncesvalles to Pamplona, then passed through Salvatierrra, Vitoria, crossed the Ebro River near Miranda, reaching Briviesca and then Burgos. After Sancho, from Pamplona they followed an itinerary going through Puente la Reina, Estella, Logroño, Nájera, and Burgos. This stable, safe and nearly unique route, leading from Puente la Reina to Santiago de Compostela, was rapidly called *Iter francorum* or *Camino francés*, because many of its pilgrims came from north of the Pyrenees, but also because many *Francos* – clerics, monks, artisans or merchants – came to settle along the route. After Sancho, two contemporary kings played an important role in the development, consolidation and security of this route: Alfonso VI (1072-1109), King of Castile, and Sancho 1st Ramirez (1063-1094), King of Aragon. Alfonso VI eliminated the tolls that interfered with pilgrims' travel. He encouraged the foundation of hospitals in Cebreiro, Burgos and Foncebadón. He supported the efforts of Santo Domingo de la Calzada to build bridges and roads. He encouraged the arrival of *Francos* in Sahagún, Logroño, and Villafranca del Bierzo. The bridge at Ponferrada was built and San Zoilo Monastery in Carrión was founded during his reign. As for Sancho 1st Ramirez, he also abolished tolls, founded Estella, helped create the hospitals in Jaca and Pamplona, ceded lands and churches to great abbeys like Saint Foy of Conques and Sauve-Majeure near Bordeaux. By the beginning of the 12th century, the infrastructure of the *Camino francés* had been created. In the course of time and events, after the 13th century integration of Alava and Guipúzcoa into the kingdom of Castile, some pilgrims crossed the Bidassoa River at Irún and rejoined Burgos via Tolosa, San Adrian and Vitoria. Others followed the coast road that was badly equipped and blocked by natural obstacles. But during all this time, the *Camino francés* remained the great route of faith and hope for tens of millions of pilgrims. It was named a Unesco World Heritage Site in 1993.

Stages	Kms
Puente la Reina	703
Estella □	684
Los Arcos	663
Torres del Río	656
Logroño	635
Navarrete	625
Nájera □	607
Santo Domingo de la Calzada *	588
San Juan de Ortega	540
Burgos □	522
Castrojeriz	476
Frómista □	450
Villalcázar de Sirga	438
Carrión de los Condes	430
Sahagún □ *	390
Mansilla de las Mulas	340
Leon □ *	323
Hospital de Órbigo	292
Astorga	277
Rabanal del Camino □	254
Foncebadón	250
Ponferrada	221
Villafranca del Bierzo □	200
Cebreiro	171
Triacastela □	142
Samos	132
Portomarín	96
Palas de Rei □	70
Santiago de Compostela *	0

References to Aimery Picaud's Guide:
□: stages
*: presence of "holy bodies"

Bridge over Arga River in Puente la Reina

Doorway of San Román Church in Cirauqui

Saint Peter's Church, Puente la Reina

PUENTE LA REINA

In the 11th century, at the initiative of Doña Mayor, the wife of the king of Navarre, Sancho III the Great (1000-1035), or perhaps that of Doña Estefanía, wife of Don García "el de Nájera" (1035-1054), a six-arched bridge was built over the Arga River to facilitate the passage of ever more numerous pilgrims. The Arga, a tributary of the Ebro, was at this point the meeting place of the roads from Somport and Roncesvalles, and since 1964, a bronze statue of a pilgrim has been standing here. The bridge was mentioned in the *Chronicle of Pseudo-Turpin*, according to which Charlemagne had come *usque ad pontem Arge*. In 1190, at the request of the abbot of Irache Monastery, *Francos* built mills on the river and in 1121, Alfonso 1st the Warrior (1104-1134) entrusted a certain Monetario with the responsibility of founding a new town here. To encourage those willing to come and settle here, he ceded lands between the Arga and Obanos meadow. The town's regular, rectangular layout, organized around a central axis formed by the *Calle Mayor*, is reminiscent of some of the bastides in Aquitaine and Languedoc, that were founded later. Templars were invited to come and settle in the town in 1142 and received the right to sell bread and wine from King García Ramírez. At the entrance to the town, they built the church of Santa María de la Huertas, today called the Church of the Crucifix because it contains a magnificent Rhenish Christ, perhaps brought by a German pilgrim during the 14th century. After the dissolution of the Templar Order by the king of France, Philippe le Bel, in 1312, its possessions were taken over by the Hospitallers of Saint John of Jerusalem. In 1442, Jean de Beaumont, the Great Prior of the Hospitallers, founded a large hospital for pilgrims near the Church of the Crucifix. Entrance into the town, where ever since the early 13th century a first hospital welcomed Santiago pilgrims, is made between two towers, vestiges of one of the gates that opened in the 13th century walls, of which practically nothing remains. The *calle Major* crosses the town. Before reaching the bridge, it passes in front of Saint James's Church, mentioned already in 1142, but whose Romanesque doorway with five voussoirs, including a polyfoiled one of Mozarab inspiration, was made at the end of the 12th century. This church contains a wooden polychrome statue of Saint James dating from the 14th century called *Beltza*, black in Basque. Before reaching the bridge, a small street on the left leads to Saint Peter's Church, with a fine Romanesque chevet containing a statue of Our Lady of Le Puy or of *Txori*, the bird, that until the 19th century was sheltered by a little chapel on the bridge's roadway. The pilgrims' bridge with its six arches has retained its original appearance except for the fortified gate, built later, where pilgrims had to pay a toll, and the chapel of Our Lady, no longer in existence. Once over the bridge, the road runs towards Estella, passing through Cirauqui, whose name in Basque means vipers' nest. The 13th century San Román Church has a doorway with a polyfoiled voussoir, similar to that at Saint James's Church in Puente la Reina.

A BIRD OF GOOD OMEN

Legend has it that a bird of unknown species used to come, from time to time, to dip its wings in the waters of the Arga to wash the face on the statue of Our Lady of Le Puy that stood in a little chapel on the bridge. Before crowds of onlookers, the bird repeated its actions until the face was completely clean, then it disappeared. Its unforeseeable return was always a good omen.

Church of San Pedro de la Rúa in Estella

ESTELLA

In 1090, King Sancho Ramirez 1st (1063-1094) founded Estella at the foot of Lizarra castle, on the right bank of the Ega, a tributary of the Ebro River. Franks, attracted by privileges granted to them by the Navarrese king allowing them to trade with pilgrims, came to settle here, rapidly joined by a large Jewish community, whose synagogue was transformed into a parish church in 1145, Santa María Jus del Castillo. In the course of this same 12th century, the church of San Pedro de la Rúa was built, in the heart of the original urban centre. A century later, new quarters like that of San Juan, founded in 1187 by Sancho VI the Wise (1150-1194), or that of San Miguel developed on the other side of the river, around their respective churches. The northern doorway of San Miguel Church, from the late 12th century, is richly sculpted with scenes from the Bible with, in particular, the border with its haut-reliefs showing the holy women in front of Christ's tomb and Saint Michael slaying the dragon. At that time the city contained many hostelries, brotherhoods and hospitals to receive the Santiago pilgrims. Outside the town, Saint Lazarus hospital took care of lepers. In Estella, "where bread is good, the wine excellent, meat and fish are abundant, and which is full of delicacies", as reported by Aimery Picaud, the size of the Frankish population was such that in the 14th century, Provencal was still being spoken there. Pilgrims who had found shelter in a hospital depending on San Juan de la Peña, a few kilometres away, before the foundation of the town, crossed the Ega over the Prison Bridge, restored in 1971, to enter the Frankish town. They walked along the calle de la Rúa, lined with stalls and at the far eastern end of which stood the church of the Holy Sepulchre. The calle de la Rúa led to Saint Martin's square and the palace of the kings of Navarre, a secular building in Romanesque style dating from the 12th century. One of the pillars of its façade is topped with a his-

The holy women, San Miguel Church

ESTELLA BELLA

Legend says that in 1085 shepherds, alerted by a miraculous shower of stars, discovered the statue called Our Lady of Le Puy. And ever since, the original town, mentioned in the Roman period under the name of Gebalda, was called Estella, a name close to the Castilian term *estrella*, star. In any case, for pilgrims the town was Estella Bella, Estella the beautiful, and the basilica of the Virgin of Le Puy watches over the town.

Roland confronting Ferragut, capital in Palace of the Kings of Navarre

Palace of the Kings of Navarre

Doorway of San Pedro de la Rúa

toriated capital showing the combat between the valiant Roland and the Moorish giant Ferragut. Opposite the palace is the beginning of the stairs climbing to San Pedro de la Rúa Church, built on the slope of the hill where the castle stood. Its doorway is similar to those of Saint James's Church in Puente la Reina and San Román in Cirauqui. Inside, pilgrims prayed at the foot of Saint James's altar. Those who died were buried in the cloister of which only two galleries remain; the others were destroyed when a lieutenant of King Ferdinand of Aragon blew up the castle in 1512, during the conquest of Navarre. Pilgrims left Estella through the Castile Gate, the last vestige visible today of its ramparts, passed by the hermitage of Our Lady of Rocamadour and took the direction of the Benedictine monastery in Irache, mentioned in the 10th century, but perhaps founded during Visigothic times. Thanks to a donation from Don García "el de Nájera", the monastery was provided with a hospital for pilgrims in 1050.

INCOGNITO

Towards 1270, the bishop of Patras undertook a pilgrimage to Santiago. Alone, anonymous in the crowd of pilgrims, he carried with him a relic of Saint Andrew, who was martyred in the city in the north of the Peloponnesus. He travelled alone, on foot, with his precious asset in a wooden box. In Estella, he fell ill and died. He was buried in the cloister of San Pedro de la Rúa. The next night, the sexton saw lights above his tomb and the same thing happened on the following nights. The body was exhumed along with the box containing the precious relic, a shoulder blade but also a cross of enamelled copper and two cruets made of the same metal. In 1374, the relic was placed in a gold and enamel reliquary, made by Charles II the Bad. Today it is kept in the chapel adjoining San Pedro de la Rúa.

Irache Monastery

A Navarrese Section

Between Irache and Logroño, the route passes at the foot of Villamayor de Monjardin, where the outline of the Baroque steeple of San Andrés Church stands out. A historiated capital at the southern doorway of this church shows the combat between Roland and Ferragut. Monjardin Hill is crowned with the ruins of San Esteban Castle, a former Muslim fortress. In the *Chronicle of Pseudo-Turpin*, Monjardin was the scene of a battle between Charlemagne and Navarrese troops. The road then arrives in Arcos where pilgrims changed their Navarrese *coronados* for Castilian *maravedis*. In 1075, Sancho the Wise granted the town a statute by which Franks and Navarrese had the same rights. Santa María Church, in front of which the pilgrims passed, is a blend of Romanesque, Gothic, Plateresque and Baroque architecture. In Torres del Río, Holy Sepulchre Church, built towards 1200 with an octagonal layout, was perhaps a funerary chapel. Mudejar influence is visible in the architecture of its cupola. In 1219, Sancho VII the Strong founded the fortified town of Viana at the border between his kingdom and Castile, and in 1423, Charles III created the Principality of Viana, the prerogative of elder sons of the kings of Navarre. In the town that contained four pilgrims' hospitals during the 15th century, Santa María Church is a Gothic building dating from the 13th and 14th centuries.

Santa María Church in Los Arcos

Church in Torres del Río

Steeple of Viana Church

Villamayor de Monjardin

Santa María la Redonda Cathedral in Logroño

Logroño

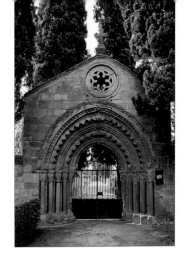

Gate to Navarrete cemetery

Having crossed the Ebro River by the stone bridge, pilgrims entered into Logroño. The present bridge dates from the end of the 19th century and replaces the one built, or reinforced, by Alfonso VI (1072-1109) at the end of the 11th century. Ever since 1076, the date of the annexation of la Rioja to Castile by the same Alfonso VI, Logroño occupied a strategic position at the frontier between the two kingdoms of Navarre and Castile. Santo Domingo de la Calzado and his disciple San Juan de Ortega participated in the work on the bridge, which consisted of twelve arches and three defensive towers. The medieval city spread along two streets, the *Rua Vieja*, taken by the pilgrims, and the *Rua Mayor*. There were two churches: Santa María del Palacio and Santiago el Real, near which the pilgrims' fountain and several hospitals were located. Tradition tells that Saint Francis, on his way to Santiago de Compostela, healed the son of Medrano, the lord of Agoncillo. In thanksgiving, the latter had a convent built on the right bank of the Ebro, downriver from the bridge. Construction had already progressed when the *Poverello* came through Logroño again on his way back. Pilgrims left Logroño through the *Porta del Camino* or *del Revellin* and took the road to Nájera. After a distance of nine kilometres, just before Navarrete, they reached the hospital of Saint John of Acre, whose doorway has been set at the entrance to the cemetery located at the town's western exit.

Clavijo

South of Logroño, the ruins of Clavijo Castle stand on a rocky peak. According to legend, in 844 Saint James Matamoros appeared here to the Asturian King Ramiro 1st, on the evening before his battle against Abd al-Rahmân II.

Clavijo

Knights' Cloister in monastery of Santa María la Real in Nájera

NÁJERA

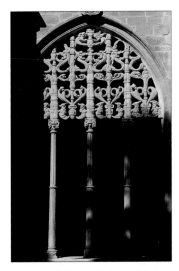

Detail of cloister in Santa María

THE GIANT'S NAVEL

According to popular tradition, Ferragut, the Moorish lord of Nájera, kept Christian knights as prisoners. Roland defied the giant from the top of the hill ever since called the Poyo de Roldán, and killed him by hitting him in the head with a stone. In the *Chronicle of Pseudo-Turpin*, Roland confronted Ferragut with Charlemagne's permission. After several attacks, the giant proposed a truce that his adversary accepted. The giant fell asleep and, when he awoke, before the next round of combat, the two men engaged in a theological debate, agreeing that the winner of the duel would be the holder of the truth. During the struggle, Roland stuck his dagger into Ferragut's navel, his only weak point. Charlemagne and his army could enter Nájera and deliver the captives.

On the way from Navarrete to Nájera, on its left the road leaves behind the Alto de San Antón, topped by the ruins of an Antonine establishment that ensured the pilgrims' safety, then on the right, the Poyo de Roldán, the site of the legendary confrontation between Roland and Ferragut. Nájera, whose name of Arabic origin means "place between the rocks", was occupied by the Moors in 714, and reconquered in 923 by Ordono II of Leon (914-924). At the beginning of the 11th century, Sancho III the Great (1000-1035) made it the capital of Navarre. This king, who struck the first money of the *Reconquista*, worked to have the route to Santiago de Compostela pass through his capital, which then became an important stage. At his death, his kingdom was divided among his sons and Don García "el de Nájera" (1035-1054) succeeded him at the head of the kingdom of Nájera-Pamplona. According to legend, in 1044 during a hunting party, the king's falcon pursuing a partridge entered a cave at the foot of the red cliff to the west of the city. Don García followed it and discovered a statue of the Virgin at the end of the cave. After recapturing Calahorra from the Moors in 1045, he and his wife, Doña Estefanía, founded the monastery of Santa María la Real on this legendary site, and endowed it with a hospital for pilgrims. In 1076, Alfonso VI (1072-1109) annexed la Rioja to Castile and in 1079 entrusted the monastery to Cluny. A community of monks, coming from north of the Pyrenees, replaced the indigenous community, creating tension with the bishop of Nájera, who transferred the seat of his bishopric to Calahorra. Pilgrims arrived in Nájera through the San Fernando quarter and crossed the Najerilla, a tributary of the Ebro River, over a bridge whose construction was attributed to San Juan de Ortega. Between Navarre and Castile, Nájera was the scene of a battle known as Navarrete, in 1367. Pedro 1st the Cruel (1350-1369), supported by the Black Prince, defeated Henri de Trastamare, backed by Du Guesclin. The monastery was then pillaged. Between 1422 and

Detail of tomb of Don García "el de Nájera", Santa María la Real

Tomb of Blanche of Navarre

1453, the Gothic church was built. In 1493, the stalls and the abbot's seat, topped by the statue of the founding king, were placed in the chancel. In the meantime, in 1486, the abbey had been separated from Cluny. The Knights' Cloister, a marriage of Gothic, Plateresque and Renaissance styles, was executed from 1517 to 1528, during which time Ignatius of Loyola was living in Nájera, from 1517 to 1521. On either side of the entrance to the cave, at the end of which the Romanesque Virgin had been found, tombs with recumbent effigies of the royal pantheon, dating from the 16th century, are lined up. Statues of Don García and Doña Estefanía, kneeling and praying, stand over their tombs. In front of the row of tombs in the Infants pantheon, the sarcophagus of Blanche de Navarre, daughter of Don García, sculpted in the 12th century, presents scenes of episodes from the Gospels as well as some from the life of the deceased. Leaving Nájera, some pilgrims did not go directly to Santo Domingo de la Calzada but instead detoured through Berceo, via San Millán de la Cogolla.

THESE NATURAL THINGS…

G onzalo de Berceo, a native of this village in la Rioja, north of the monastery of San Millán de la Cogolla, was born at the end of the 12th century. In about 1250, this monk from Cogolla wrote in Castilian the *Milagros de Nuestra Señora*, the Miracles of Our Lady, a few years before Alfonso X the Wise wrote his *Cantigas* in Galician. In the introduction to his work, Gonzalo presents himself as the pilgrim of Our Lady and, among the miracles that were to be read to the neighbouring monastic communities as well as to the many pilgrims wandering around the region, one story adds vigour and dramatic meaning to the framework of one of the twenty-two miracles attributed to Saint James and recounted in the *Liber sancti Jacobi* under number XVII. The young pilgrim who, before leaving on pilgrimage "frolicked with his friend", was convinced by the Devil, passing himself off as Saint James, to castrate himself and commit suicide. The Devil and the apostle gave themselves to the Queen of Heaven for judgement. The young pilgrim came back to life and as Gonzalo wrote, "He was cured, healed all over, to evacuate his waters there remained a little hole" since "these natural things he got rid of did not grow back".

Monasteries of Suso and Yuso, San Millán de la Cogolla

SAN MILLÁN DE LA COGOLLA

Millán was born in 473 in Berceo, on the shores of the Cardenas River whose source is found on the northern slopes of the Sierra de la Demanda, in the part of La Rioja in contact with Castile. At the time, the Visigothic kingdom was forming in the Iberian peninsula, under the authority of King Leogivild. His biography was written at the beginning of the 7th century by san Braulio, whose brother Frominiano had retired to Cogolla and had listened to the old monks talking about the saint's life. In a dream God appeared to Millán, the child of a modest family. He left his sheep behind and went to join san Felices de Bilibio, whose disciple he became. After years of priesthood, he retired to a cave in Suso. There, he healed the sick and gave food and drink to the poor and to pilgrims who began to arrive in large numbers. He died in 574, at the age of 101. His reputation for holiness was such that in 634, between two Councils in Toledo, Millán was added to the saints' calendar of the Spanish liturgy. He was the first saint originating in the Iberian peninsula to be included. He played an important role in the formation of the Castilian nation, miraculously intervening, like Saint James in Clavijo, during the battle of Hacinas to encourage the Castilian troops against the Moors. During the Muslim occupation, halfway through the 8th century until 923, the year of the reconquest of the region by Ordono II and Sancho 1st of Navarre, monastic life was uninterrupted at Suso. This is attested by the continuity of activity at the *scriptorium*: a copy of *Commentaries on the Apocalypse* by Beatus of Liebana is dated from the 8th century, the chronicle of San Millán and the writings of Leogivild of

Cordoba, from the 9th century. In 959, the primitive basilica in Suso was completed by Mozarab builders. At the end of the 10th century, al-Mansûr set fire to this basilica, which was restored and enlarged by Sancho III the Great (1000-1035), who imposed the Benedictine rule on the monastery and had san Millán's relics placed in a silver reliquary. Suso's spiritual influence was enormous. Pilgrims arrived from all over Castile and la Rioja, and many pilgrims going to Santiago made the detour to come to Cogolla. Many tombs have been discovered near Suso, the belief being that the closer one's burial site was to that of the saint, the greater were one's chances of salvation. Suso's spiritual influence was equalled by its cultural influence because it is also considered the birthplace of the Castilian language. It was indeed in this remote place that annotations in a Romance language, dated from 1040, were written in the margin of a paragraph of a codex of the *Glosas Emilianenses*. Two centuries later, another monk from Cogolla, Gonzalo de Berceo, wrote the *Milagros de Nuestra Señora*, establishing the language. In 1040, the prior of Suso, Domingo de Cañas, the future Domingo de Silos, opposed Don García "el de Nájera" who was perhaps too influenced by Cluniac ideas, and gave up his charge. In 1054, Don García wanted to move the

Death of San Millán

relics of san Millán to Nájera to endow the monastery of Santa María la Real that he had just founded. A hundred and sixty years later, the monk Fernando told the story in his *Translatio Sancti Aaemiliani*. The reliquary left Suso in a procession. In the valley where Yuso monastery was located, the reliquary stood straight up like an immobile stone. Then the king's men had to confront armed resistance by the population. In another version according to the *Chronicle of Nájera*, the reliquary was placed in a cart pulled by oxen who refused to move forward once they were in the valley. Don García, giving in to divine will, had the monastery of Yuso built in this valley. Entering Suso, the gallery contains the sarcophagi of the seven children of Lara and that of their tutor, as well as those of three queens of Navarre who could not find space for a burial site closer to that of Millán. The basilica's nave, from the 10th century, opens onto the chapel of Saint Oria. The 11th century extension of the nave opens onto the oratory of san Millán, where the saint's recumbent figure, a 12th century work, is kept, and onto the 6th century troglodytic cells, transformed into a necropolis. Yuso Monastery, in Renaissance and Baroque styles, was rebuilt between the 16th and 17th centuries because the Romanesque monastery had been sacked by the Black Prince after the battle of Navarrete in 1367. The reliquaries of san Millán and san Felices are kept in a sacristy. These reliquaries were restored in 1944 by Granda but the sculpted ivory plaques are the 11th century originals, made in the monastery's ivory workshop . Suso and Yuso were named Unesco World Heritage Sites in 1997.

Church façade of Santo Domingo de la Calzada

BURGOS

Burgos was founded in 884 by Count Diego Rodríguez at the request of King Alfonso III the Great (886-910), the king of Leon. The inhabitants gathered around a primitive castle standing on top of a hill on the right bank of the Arlanzón River. In 1035 the city became the capital of the kingdom of Castile and remained the capital until 1492, the year of the fall of the kingdom of Granada and the discovery of America by Christopher Columbus, when it ceded the role to Valladolid. Burgos was also a bishopric and an important stage on the route to Santiago de Compostela, so it developed rapidly in the 11th century on the spit of land formed by the confluence of the Vena and Arlanzón rivers, then in the 12th century it spread to the left bank of the Arlanzón. In 1221, Ferdinand III (1217-1252) laid the first stone of the cathedral that was built in two great stages, one during the 13th century, the other during the 15th, with the cloister dating from the 14th century.

When the German monk Hermann Künig von Vach passed through Burgos in 1495, the city contained no less than thirty-two pilgrim hospitals, including the hospital of San Juan Evangelista and the Hospital del Rey. The first, mentioned in 1085, was located on the left bank of the Vena River, facing the church today called San Lesmes, from the 14th century, built on the site of the former San Juan Evangelista Chapel. It was founded by Alfonso VI (1072-

Door Detail, Hospital del Rey Church

THE CASA DEL CORDÓN

T he Casa del Cordón is a mansion from the 15th century with a large Franciscan rope sculpted on its façade. The Catholic monarchs received Christopher Columbus there upon his return from his second voyage to America.

Drum vault of Burgos Cathedral

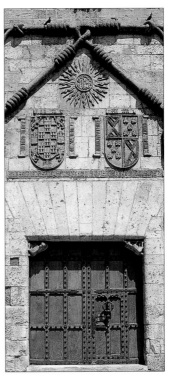

The Casa del Cordón

Sarcophagus of Alfonso VIII and Eleanor Plantagenet, Las Huelgas Reales Monastery

A CHARITABLE SOUL

Amaro, or Alleaume, a French pilgrim from the 15th century, appreciated the quality of the charitable reception reserved for pilgrims at the Hospital del Rey. He went to Santiago and, on his way back, stayed at the hospital to take care of pilgrims whom he served at the table and whose feet he washed. He used to go to meet them and carried the weakest on his back. When he died, the hospital seemed to be burning in a huge fire. The inhabitants of Burgos came running to put it out, but there were no flames and everyone understood that a miracle was happening. The bells began to ring all by themselves. The saint was buried, with other pilgrims who were dying at the hospital, in an adjoining field where a small chapel was built.

1109) who invited a monk from La Chaise-Dieu in France, Saint Lesmes, to come and establish a Benedictine community. Today only the cloister and the chapter-house remain from the monastery, both in Renaissance style. Pilgrims arrived at the Hospital del Rey after going out of the city through Saint Martin's Gate and crossing the Arlanzón River over the Malatos bridge. This hospital had been created in 1195 by Alfonso VIII (1158-1214), one of the victors of the Battle of Las Navas de Tolosa in 1212, along with Pedro II of Aragon (1196-1213). It depended on the abbey at Las Huelgas Reales, located a few hundred metres away and founded in 1187 by the same monarch. The hospital could receive any pilgrim arriving at its door, at any moment. All that remains of this establishment dates from the 16th century and has been the seat of the Burgos Faculty of Law since 1991. In the 16th century, the hospital was still extremely important since it was possible to go to confession in many languages. The Romero door and the church doorway are Plateresque in style. The wooden panels of the church door were carved by Juan de Valmaseda and show three generations of the same family on their way to Santiago. Among the characters is a woman breast feeding her child. In the pilgrims cemetery, San Amaro Chapel is dedicated to this French holy man who dedicated his life to pilgrims during the 15th century.

Starting in 1221, pilgrims crossing Burgos went past the cathedral under construction. In the 15th century, as they approached the city, they could spot from afar its two spires standing out against

CASTROJERIZ

On their way out of Burgos, the pilgrims passed close to the Hospital del Rey and then, just before crossing the Arlanzón, discovered another hospital, that of San Juan del Puente, depending on the bishopric. Between Burgos and Castrojeriz, Hornillos del Camino was the seat of a Benedictine monastery depending on Rocamadour, and Hontanas possessed a pilgrims hospital. Before reaching Castrojeriz, the road passes under Gothic arches from the 14th century, that linked the hospital, of which nothing remains, and the church, whose few walls and a doorway subsist. These are the vestiges of an Antonine monastery founded in 1146 by Alfonso VII (1126-1157). The castle of Castojeriz overlooks the plain from the summit of a hill, at the foot of which the village spreads. In 760, the Visigoth Sigeric built the *castrum* Sigerici there. In 882, it fell into Moorish hands. It was taken back by Christian troops and reinforced. In 1118, the bishop of Santiago de Compostela, Gelmírez, wanting to make Santiago into the seat of the archibishopric, sent clerics to Rome to plead his case. They were disguised as pilgrims, but carried a hundred and twenty ounces of gold. In Castrojeriz they were robbed by men of Alfonso 1st of Aragon (1104-1134), who held the castle. In 1131, Alfonso VII became its master and he definitely expelled the Aragonese garrison. Santa María de Manzano Collegiate Church precedes the village along the road. Founded in the 11th century, it was rebuilt in Romanesque style by Doña Berenguela, the wife of Alfonso IX (1188-1230), then restored and enlarged in the 18th century. It contains the statue of the Virgin of Manzano, *Santa María d'Almançan*, from the 13th century, praised by Alfonso X the Wise in his *Cantigas*. During the 19th century, Castrojeriz had up to seven hospitals and, besides the collegiate church, four churches of which Santo Domingo and San Juan are perfectly preserved. Between Castrojeriz and Frómista, a bridge with eleven arches, built by Alfonso VI (1072-1109), spans the Pisuerga River. This *puente Fitero* or *Ponteroso* is mentioned by Aimery Picaud in his *Guide*. Before the bridge, Saint Nicholas Chapel is the only vestige of a pilgrims hospital. The *Tierra de Campos* extends from the Pisuerga to Cea, a vast plain fought over by Leon and Castile. In 1068, at Lantadilla in the north, on the right bank of the Pisuerga, Sancho II (1065-1072), the king of Castile, and Alfonso his brother, submitted to the judgement of God in a duel to solve the conflict opposing them over provisions in the will and testament of their father Ferdinand 1st (1035-1065), who had attributed Castile to Sancho and Leon to Alfonso. The two men came to an agreement by stripping a third brother, García, of his Galician inheritance, before their own confrontation at the beginning of 1072 in the pitched battle at Golpejera. The death of Sancho II a short time later allowed Alfonso VI (1072-1109) to succeed him on the Castilian throne. A little way before Frómista, at Boadilla del Camino, a Plateresque *rollo de justicia*, dating from the 15th century, stands behind the chevet of Santa María Church. It symbolized judicial power; the accused were chained to it before their sentences were carried out.

Rollo de justicia

THE ANTONINE ORDER

A priory destined to contain the relics of Saint Anthony, brought from Constantinople by a knight, was founded in 1095 at La Motte-au-Bois, near Vienne, south of Lyons, by Benedictine monks from the Provencal abbey of Montmajour. Pilgrims arrived to obtain a cure for an illness common during the 10th and 11th centuries, Saint Anthony's Fire, or erysipelas, caused by rye, that provoked gangrene, hallucinations and convulsions. Guérin de Valloire, who suffered from this disease, went to the priory vowing that if he were cured, he would dedicate his life to victims of this fiery disease. His wish was fulfilled. He and his father, Gaston, created a first hospital and founded the Antonine Order, that adopted the rule of Saint Augustine. Urban II approved their statutes. But relations between Benedictines and Antonines worsened and, in 1297, Pope Boniface VIII took the side of the latter, and the former had to return to Montmajour. The order possessed over three hundred and seventy hospitals. On their black robes, the monks sewed a blue Greek tau, the emblem of the order organized into commanderies that, in 1776, was joined to the Knights of Malta.

San Martín in Frómista

FRÓMISTA

At the death of her husband Sancho the Great (1000-1035), the king of Navarre, Doña Mayor, from the dynasty of the counts of Castile, returned to the family fief. Near a town whose establishment she had encouraged, she founded the monastery of San Martín in Frómista. The church, entirely, perhaps too much, restored by the architect Manuel Aníbal Álvarez, from 1896 to 1904, is the only vestige of the monastery. In Doña Major's will, written in 1066, it is indicated that the monastery was under construction. In 1118, Doña Urraca, the daughter of Alfonso VI, placed the establishment under the supervision of San Zoilo in Carrión de los Condes. San Martín in Frómista thus entered the Cluniac sphere of influence. A hospital was dependent on the monastery. There were two other hospitals in the town that was a major stage on the *Camino francés*: Santiago and Palmeros. San Martín Church in Frómista is Romanesque. It was built while Romanesque art was being introduced to Spain with the support of Sancho the Great and his close relations. In 1035, the king of Navarre himself became associated with the construction of the Romanesque crypt of San Antolín in Palencia. In 1054, work began on San Isidoro of Leon, under the aegis of his son, Ferdinand 1st the Great. And after the bishopric of Jaca had been created in 1075, Don Ramiro of Aragon, one of his natural sons, launched the construction of Jaca cathedral, contemporary with San Martín in Frómista.

From the outside, the well bonded structure gives off a remarkably well-balanced impression. Its western façade is framed by two cylindrical towers and an octagonal lantern-tower tops the interior cupola, rising from the tiered roofs that translate the differences in height of the various naves and bays. In the east, the chevet is composed of a central apse adjoined by two apsidal chapels. The whole is lightened by the presence of cornices, fanlights and billet-moulding. Over three hundred modillions carved with geometrical figures, animal subjects or human models ornament the eaves. The inside is laid out like a basilica with a wider central nave, prolonged by the central apse, higher than the two lateral naves which are closed by apsidal chapels. On the five bays that separate these naves, the most eastward, onto which the apsidal chapels open, is widest, making a beginning of a transept. The crossing of this bay and the central nave form a perfect square topped by the cupola. Images from the tetramorph are carved on the squinches supporting this cupola. Capitals top the columns, some of them decorated with vegetal motifs, others showing animals, the latter being historiated. It is likely that they are the work of two artists. The first, more inspired, was the sculptor of the apse's capitals; the second of the capitals in the naves. In the central apse, a 12th century statue of Saint Martin and a 16th century statue of Saint James the Greater bring a bit of colour into this magnificent stone vessel.

Capital in San Martín in Frómista

SAINT TELMES

Near the church of San Pedro in Frómista stands the statue of Pedro González Telmo, a native of the village. Baptized in 1185 in San Martín Church, he studied in Palencia where his uncle was the bishop. A canon at first, he next entered the Dominican convent in Palencia. As a preaching friar, he criss-crossed Andalusia and Galicia. He died in Tuy in 1240. Although he had never been on a ship, sailors made this saint their patron because he had the reputation of dominating nature. They called Saint Telmes' fire the lights that form at the tops of ships' masts on stormy days, perhaps in an allusion to an episode in Pedro's life when he threw himself into some flames so that he would not be seduced by a woman.

Saint Telmes

Portico of Santa María la Blanca Church in Vallacázar de Sirga

VILLALCÁZAR DE SIRGA

During the 11th century, the route passed north of Villacázar, through Arconada where there was a monastery and a pilgrim hospital, attached in 1047 to San Zoilo in Carrión de los Condes. The establishment of a Templar commandery at Villacázar, an important element of security for pilgrims, was very likely the reason for the road passing through this village. The fortified Templar church, Santa María la Blanca, whose fine, carved southern doorway opens under a porch, was built during the 12th and 13th centuries. A hospital possessed by the Count of Osorno used to stand beside it. It was ceded in 1702 to the Order of Santiago. The church contains the two Gothic tombs with recumbent effigies of Philip, brother of Alfonso X the Wise (1252-1284), assassinated by the latter in 1271, and his wife Doña Leonor Ruiz de Castro, as well as a statue of the *Virgen blanca*, white Virgin, twelve of whose miracles are recounted in the *Cantigas* of Alfonso X the Wise. The Virgin of Villacázar had a reputation for miracle-working and, in particular, for healing pilgrims returning from Santiago de Compostela who had not been cured by the apostle. A French count, a great sinner, was not able to enter the church. The men accompanying him tried to force him inside but in vain, until the moment when the poor man, bleeding from the nose and mouth, sincerely repented for his sins.

Detail of Philip's tomb

THE MIRACLE OF THE STAFF

A Cathar *parfait* who had retracted his faith had to undertake a pilgrimage to Santiago de Compostela in penance. The staff he carried, weighing twenty-four pounds, was to be placed before the apostle's altar. Passing through Villalcázar de Sirga, he entered the church to pray to the White Virgin. While he was asking forgiveness for his sins, the staff broke in two and it was impossible to pick it up. His sins had been forgiven and he could continue his pilgrimage to Santiago with a lighter soul… and body.

The Virgen Blanca in Villalcázar

THE SOUL OF A POET

Although Alfonso X saw his dream of occupying the throne of the Holy Roman Empire disappear in 1257, he was a particularly cultured monarch. A lover of arts and literature, interested in science and law but also a chess player and interested in history, he wrote on all subjects, helped by numerous scribes, translators and scholars. In particular, he undertook the writing of the *Cronica general*, a history of Spain, the first to be written in Castilian. He wrote his poetry in Galician. The four hundred and thirty *Cantigas* were even intended to be sung. Under the title of *Cantigas de Santa María*, Hymns and praises of Holy Mary, he related the Virgin's miracles, mostly drawn from the *Speculum historiale* by Beauvais and the *Miracles of the Virgin* by Coincy, to which he added his talents of versifying. He used the stylistic device of the zejel, a poetic composition of Mozarab origin, based on octosyllabic lines. Among the miracles, that of the porter nun is one of the best known. This nun fell in love with a man, and before going off to live away from her monastery, she entrusted its keys to the Virgin. She had children, but filled with remorse, returned to her monastery where she realized that none of her fellow nuns had noticed her error nor her absence. The Virgin had taken over in the meantime. She found the keys where she had left them, put her habit back on and took up her post as though nothing had happened.

Christ Pantocrator on frieze of doorway, Santiago Church in Carrión de los Condes

Voussoir detail, Santiago de Carrión Church

Gallery in cloister of San Zoilo Monastery

CARRIÓN DE LOS CONDES

The road in Carrión de los Condes

MARTYRDOM OF SAN ZOILO

....

Diocletian (284-305) wanted to re-establish the religious unity of the Roman Empire, and death was the punishment for those who did not celebrate the cult of the pagan divinities of the Roman pantheon. Some Christians renounced their faith, but others, like Zoilo, refused and were martyred. This young man from Cordoba, the son of a wealthy family, was delivered to his executioners along with about twenty companions whose throats were cut. As for Zoilo, his kidneys were removed, then, since he was still breathing, he was beheaded. The mutilated bodies were buried in a place that was rapidly forgotten. At the beginning of the 7th century, Zoilo appeared in a dream to the bishop of Cordoba, san Agapio, and revealed his burial site. The remains of the holy martyr were brought to the church of Saint Felix of Cordoba.

In the heart of the *Tierra de Campos*, Carrión de los Condes, formerly Santa María de los Condes, was the town of the Counts of Carrión. In the *Poema del mio Cid*, two of them married and mistreated the daughters of the Castilian hero who, as the code of honour required, hurried to avenge the offence. The *Chronicle of Pseudo-Turpin* had Charlemagne passing through Carrión, and Aimery Picaud wrote that "it is rich in bread, wine and all kinds of products". At the entrance to the town, pilgrims arriving from Villalcázar de Sirga discovered the convent of Santa Clara from the 13th century where, according to tradition, Saint Francis had stopped on his way to Santiago de Compostela in 1213. The Romanesque church of Santa María del Camino was built during the first half of the 12th century. Under the porch on the southern side, the doorway framed by blocks sculpted with bulls' heads was probably a reminder of the legend of the hundred virgins: the animals, by charging the Moors, allowed the town not to pay the tribute of a hundred virgins that it owed every year. Near the *plaza Mayor*, the church of Saint James, or Santiago, from the second half of the 12th century, was burnt in 1809, during the War of Independence, but its doorway and carved frieze above it survived. On the doorway's central voussoir, a line of characters doing various manual or intellectual, peaceful or warlike activities can be seen. In the centre of the frieze, Christ Pantocrator is framed by the tetramorph where, on either side, the twelve apostles turn towards Him. Going out of the town, on the right bank of the Carrión, San Zoilo Monastery was founded in the 11th century by Count Gómez Díaz and his wife, Teresa, and was initially dedicated to Saint John the Baptist. During the second half of the 12th century, one of the founder's sons, Fernando, brought back the relics of San Zoilo, a martyr from Roman times, that were at Saint Felix of Cordoba church and gave them to the monastery, which then took the name of San Zoilo. In 1076, when her husband had been dead about twenty years, the Countess donated the monastery to Cluny. A hospital was created by the Cluniacs, but the establishment was never as important as the one at la Herrada, opposite Santa María Church. As its name indicates (a *herrada* is a tub), the hospital always had a tub of water standing in front of its door, for thirsty pilgrims after their long walk under the Castilian sun. In the 15th century, San Zoilo left the Cluniac Order to join that of the Benedictines of Valladolid. Of the primitive monastery, few vestiges remain other than a Romanesque doorway inside the church, with historiated tympana, and a window whose outline and the lines of the billets remind one of Frómista. The Plateresque cloister was built starting in 1537 according to plans by Juan de Badajoz, its vaults, keystones, and corbels are decorated with two hundred and thirty busts of characters from the ancestry of Christ or the Benedictines. The church contains several sarcophagi, including those of the Carrión Counts' families from the 11th and 12th centuries. And nearby, the stony path in the shade of poplar trees is an invitation to continue the journey.

San Tirso Church in Sahagún

SAHAGÚN

Facundo and Primitivo were, like Zoilo, victims of the persecution of Christians encouraged by Diocletian. Their mortal remains were thrown into the Cea River and collected by other Christians, who buried them on the shore. Several centuries later, a Visigothic shrine was built in this same place but it was destroyed by Moorish troops in 883. In 904, the Asturian king Alfonso III (866-910) founded a monastery here, that was devastated by al-Mansûr in 981, but was restored thanks to the many gifts and privileges granted by the monarchs of Leon and then Castile. Among its benefactors, Ferdinand 1st (1035-1065) liked to stay at the abbey and share the monks' food. During an interview in Burgos, Alfonso VI (1072-1109), whose tomb is located in the abbey church of Santa Cruz, asked the abbot Hugues de Cluny to send some of his monks. And so Robert and Marcelin arrived from Burgundy and the monastery became the main Cluniac establishment in the kingdom of Castile, with over fifty affiliated abbeys, possessions extending from the Cantabrian coast to the sierra of Guadarrama and a famous *scriptorium*. But practically no vestiges remain. In 1080, the abbot was Bernard de Sedirac who, after the recapture of Toledo by Alfonso VI in 1085, became its first archbishop. Also in 1085, the same king founded around the monastery the town that was to be called Sahagún

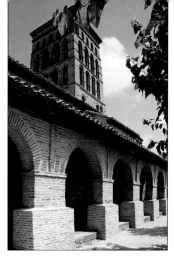

San Lorenzo Church in Sahagún

LA PEREGRINA

The church of La Peregrina in Sahagún belonged to a convent of Franciscan monks. Built towards the middle of the 13th century, it owed its name to the statue of the Virgin, dressed as a pilgrim, that it contained starting from the end of the 17th century.

La Peregrina Church in Sahagún

Sahagún, Field of Lances

THE FIELD OF LANCES

A ccording to the *Chronicle of Pseudo-Turpin*, Charlemagne founded the monastery of Sahagún and the town around it. It was the way the Frankish emperor celebrated his victory over the Saracens led by Agolant, on the shores of the Cea River. The author claimed that, the evening before the battle, the Christian soldiers planted their lances in front of their camp and the next morning – a miracle, they were covered with leafy bark and foliage. They cut them at ground level and from the roots, great ash trees grew, since the valiant knights' lances had been made from ash. Forty thousand lost their lives in the terrible battle that followed, in which Roland lost his father, Milon, and Charlemagne lost his horse.

Blind arcade, San Tirso Church

from the contraction of san Facundo, and had the Canto bridge built over the Cea River, on whose right bank the Field of Lances lay. In this new town, famous for its troubadours, where nine nationalities mingled, conflict rapidly arose between the inhabitants and the abbot who had extremely wide powers, such as that obtained by managing the communal oven, or the monopoly of selling wine. Although the communal oven was abolished in 1096, the situation did not improve and in 1110, peasants and citizens, supported by part of the secular clergy, rebelled. Alfonso VII (1126-1157) considerably reduced the abbey's power, and re-established lasting calm, even though in 1227 the inhabitants once again contested the power of the abbot Guillermo. Sahagún, with its influx of pilgrims, developed and became wealthy. Encircled by ramparts, it soon contained four hospitals, mentioned by Künig in the 15th century, among which that of the abbey offered seventy beds, a Franciscan convent, whose church was La Pelegrina, from the 13th century, and nine other churches. Four of these churches survive today: San Tirso, San Lorenzo, Santiago and La Trinidad. San Tirso, mentioned for the first time in 1123, and San Lorenzo, from the first half of the 13th century, are in Romanico-Mudejar style. After Sahagún, the road crossed an extremely desolate zone, passing through a few rare villages like El Burgo Raneró, placed under the control of the Cluniac abbey of Sahagún, before reaching Mansilla de las Mulas.

MUDEJAR ART

If the term Mozarab refers to Christian populations living on lands occupied by the Muslims, that of Mudejar is applied to Muslims remaining on territories recaptured by Christians during the *Reconquista*. The presence of these Mudejars, an economic necessity, was well accepted for a long time, even though in Castile, texts dated 1412 legalizing their situation imposed certain constraints while respecting their personal and religious freedoms. On the lands freed from the Muslim yoke by the *Reconquista*, many Mudejar colonies remained, especially in Aragon and in the area of Valencia. From the 11th to the 15th centuries, their artists and artisans continued to practice their arts and crafts for Christian masters. There was courtly Mudejar art, according to Elie Lambert's expression, that of the synagogue of Toledo, with its fine *artesonado* ceiling made of cedar wood, or the Alcazar of Sevilla – great creations for which Pedro the Cruel (1350-1369) used artists who came from Granada. There was also popular Mudejar art, practiced by local artisans, in the stucco ceilings of the San Fernando cloister at the Abbey of Las Huelgas Reales in Burgos, in the towers of Teruel, in the *artesonado* ceiling of the cathedral in Teruel, and also in the churches of San Tirso and San Lorenzo in Sahagún, with their walls decorated with blind arcades.

Ramparts, Mansilla de las Mulas

IN THE ESLA RIVER VALLEY

The town of Mansilla de las Mulas, on the left bank of the Esla River, a tributary of the Duero, was granted a charter by Ferdinand II (1157-1188), King of Leon, within the framework of the defensive organization of his kingdom. Mansilla was to be a solid stronghold, as can be seen by the vestiges of its walls behind which seven churches, two monasteries, and three hospitals welcomed pilgrims, some of whom also went to the abbey of Sandoval, several kilometres away, on the right bank of the Esla. This Cistercian abbey was founded by Don Ponce, majordomo of Alfonso VII (1126-1157), and his wife Doña Estefanía. Don Ponce, a prisoner of the Moors, escaped and took the road to Santiago. He stopped at the monastery of Carrizo, on the Orbigo River, created by his wife during his absence to receive pilgrims. Doña Estefanía herself provided them with care and comfort. When she began to wash the feet of Don Ponce, a ritual practice greatly appreciated in pilgrim hospitals, the husband and wife recognized each other. In thanksgiving, they founded the abbey of Sandoval, from *Saltus Novalis*, on lands granted to them in 1142 by Alfonso VII and his wife Doña Berenguela. Further upriver, on the right bank of the Esla, beyond the Mozarab church of San Miguel de la Escalada, stands another Cistercian abbey for the nuns of Santa María in Gradefes.

Santa María in Gradefes

Doorway of Sandoval Abbey

Martial the cupbearer, fresco in royal pantheon of San Isidoro, Leon

LEON

It was on the strip of land formed by the confluence of the Bernesga and Torio Rivers that the VIIth Legion Gemina established its camp at the end of the first century. Although few physical vestiges remain from this period, the toponymy of the city of Leon has a definite relationship with this *legio*, created by the emperor Galba in 68. When, in 846, Abd el-Rahmân II's own son captured Leon with his war machines, the city was already encircled by ramparts that the Arab chief vainly tried to destroy. At the end of the 10th century, al-Mansûr in turn invested the city that had been the capital of the kingdom of Leon since 913. He succeeded in dismantling the ramparts that had been restored by Alfonso V (999-1028). A well-preserved section of these walls is still visible behind San Isidoro Basilica. Until the conquest of Toledo in 1085, Leon was the most important city in Christian Spain, a pre-eminence that it gradually lost with the shifting of the geopolitical centre of gravity implied by that important step in the *Reconquista*. But it retained a patrimony of monasteries, churches, and hospitals that remained very active, because of the passage of numerous pilgrims. Doña Sancha, the heiress to the kingdom of Leon, married Ferdinand 1st (1035-1065), the king of Castile, and convinced him to be buried in Leon, in the wood and stone church of Saint John the Baptist, built by Doña Sancha's father, Alfonso V to contain his own tomb. Ferdinand 1st had the shrine with its royal pantheon rebuilt out of stone, to the plans of the Asturian church of San Salvador de Valdedios. In 1063, the relics of Saint Isidore were transferred there from Sevilla. On December 21, Santo Domingo de Silos attended the consecration of the new church, that took the name of the holy doctor of the Visigothic church. Doña Urraca (1109-1126) had the church rebuilt. Work continued during the reign of Alfonso VII (1126-1157) and the new church was consecrated in 1149. In 1148,

Capital in Santa Marta de Tera

SANTA MARTA DE TERA

The bishops of Leon and Astorga brought the relics of San Isidoro from Sevilla in 1063. To thank them, Ferdinand 1st granted to Ordoño, the bishop of Astorga, the monastery of Santa Marta de Tera, to the west of Benavente, that had been founded in the 10th century by Mozarab monks. The church, rebuilt at the end of the 11th century, shows some similarities with that of San Isidoro in Leon. Its southern doorway is framed by statues of two apostles: on the left, Saint James the Greater, and on the right, that of John or Peter. Alfonso VII was one of the benefactors of this monastery, a pilgrimage site, that perhaps possessed the relics of Saint Martha, the martyr of Astorga in the last days of Roman presence. During the spring and autumn equinoxes, a ray of sunshine enters the church through an oculus in the chevet and lights up a capital set to the right of the altar. A naked, asexual body, representing Saint Martha's soul, is carried towards the heavens by angels on a kind of tray forming a mandorla. It seems that the light of the rising sun, a divine symbol, is carrying the martyr's soul towards the heavens.

Royal pantheon in San Isidoro, Leon

"IGNORANCE IS THE MOTHER OF ALL ERRORS..."

In 552, *Carthago Nova* (Carthagena), occupied by Justinian's troops, was recaptured and destroyed by Atanagild, king of the Visigoths. Severianus fled with his wife and two children, Leander and Florentine, to settle in Sevilla, where the Hispano-Roman couple later had two more children, Fulgence and Isidore, born in 560. Leander became the abbot of the monastery of Sevilla, where one of his pupils was his young brother Isidore, whose tutor he became when their father died while Isidore was still a young child. Leander became archbishop of the city in 576. After rejecting Arianism, he instructed Recared and presided with him over the Council of Toledo in 589, during which the conversion of the Visigothic king to Christianity became official. He died in 599, and in turn Isidore occupied the archbishopric of Baetica. During his ministry, his constant worry was the formation and education of his clerics. He started episcopal schools in Sevilla. Drawing on the very rich

Material lining the reliquary chest, San Isidoro

library in Sevilla and relying on a large group of copyists, he compiled a huge amount of knowledge intended to endow the new Catholic church with solid intellectual foundations. This immense work touched on all fields of knowledge. Hence, in the *Differences*, he attempted to specify the meaning of certain words. As far as religion was concerned, he wrote *On Heresies*, established the list of *Dates of Birth and Death of the Fathers*, and wrote a *Rule of the Monks*. But the

major work of the end of his life was constituted by the twenty volumes of *Etymologies on the Origins of Certain Things*. Going back to the sources of language, the author touched on all the fields of knowledge: the seven liberal arts – grammar, rhetoric, dialectics, arithmetic, geometry, music and astronomy, natural and physical sciences, passing through techniques, architecture, and geography. He dedicated another work to law, the *Hispana vetus*. Although Isidore imposed Hispano-Roman culture on the Germanic minority who held political power in the young Visigothic kingdom, he also provided it with its basic charter with his *History of the Goths*. And at the Council of Toledo in 633, with his formula of *Rex, Gens, Patria* (one King, one People, one Fatherland) he gathered together Hispano-Romans and Goths into a single nation. Isidore died in Sevilla on April 4, 636. In 653, the Council of Toledo named him *doctor egregius*. And in 1063, on a mandate from Ferdinand 1st, the bishops of Leon and Astorga, Alvito and Ordoño, came to get the relics of the holy doctor from Sevilla and transferred them to San Juan de Leon Church, from then on called San Isidoro.

Banner of Baeza, treasure of San Isidoro

Alfonso VII had invited a community of Augustinian canons to establish themselves there. At that time, pilgrims did not pass through San Isisdoro, but Ferdinand II (1157-1188) published a decree in 1168 placing the monastery on the route of the road that then joined San Marcos bridge.

Only the royal pantheon, one of the first Romanesque works in Spain, remains from the 11th century church. Forty-six capitals, historiated or with floral décor, top as many columns. The paintings covering the walls and vaults and that have earned the shrine the name of "the Sistine chapel of Romanesque art", were done between 1160 and 1170 by an unknown artist. They show scenes from the New Testament but also a calendar of work on the land. Twenty-three kings, twelve infantes, and nine counts of Leon rest in this pantheon. The doorways of the Lamb and the Pardon are Romanesque and date from the reconstruction undertaken by Doña Urraca, contrasting with some of the Renaissance or Baroque details on the façade. The door of Pardon, framed by haut relief sculptures of Saint Peter and Saint Paul, was the door generally used by pilgrims. Several fine pieces make up the treasure of San Isidoro: Doña Urraca's chalice from the 11th century, the ivory shrine, the reliquary urn of Saint John the Baptist and Saint Pelayo from 1059, the chest of relics of San Isidoro, a Mozarab bible from 960, as well as the banner of Baeza, embroidered by the ladies of Leon on the battlefield where Alfonso VII conquered, thanks to the miraculous intervention of Saint Isidore, shown on the cloth like Saint James Matamoros at the Battle of Clavijo or Saint Millán at Hacina, with a sword in one hand, a cross in the other, riding a white steed.

Santa María de la Regla was one of the other churches in Leon, built on the site of the second century Roman baths. Damaged during the attack by al-Mansûr, it was restored at the end of the 11th century, during the episcopacy of Don Pelayo. During the reign of Alfonso IX (1188-1230), it was destroyed and work began on the cathedral, *pulchra leonina*, a masterpiece of Spanish Gothic

Pardon Doorway, San Isidoro

Chalice of Doña Urraca

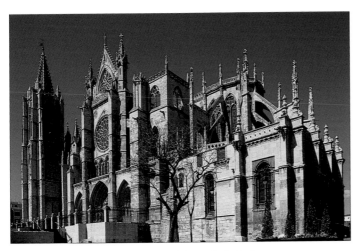

South façade of Leon Cathedral

Window in Leon Cathedral

Detail of façade of San Marcos

architecture. At the beginning of the 12th century, work stopped and did not begin again until 1250, to end in the 15th century after a new interruption during the 14th century. Three doorways open on the western façade, framed by two towers. On the pier of the central doorway, stands the statue of Santa María la Blanca; on the left side of this doorway, a statue of Saint James the Greater stands among other apostles. The interior is lit by an exceptional set of stained glass windows, comparable in their beauty to Chartres, representing a total surface of twelve hundred square metres. Juan de Badajoz drew the plans of the transcoro and behind the high altar, the reredos was painted in the 15th century by Nicolás Francés, who also did the wall paintings in the cloister. This reredos was composed of eighteen large paintings and over four hundred small ones, that were taken apart in 1721 and scattered. Only five large paintings by this master have been returned to the reredos visible nowadays, including the one at the top showing the translation of the apostle James. It was completed by other paintings taken from reredos in churches in the area.

Many hospitals – seventeen were mentioned – welcomed pilgrims, those who left directly for Santiago de Compostela, as well as those who made a pilgrimage within a pilgrimage to go and worship the Holy Saviour in Oviedo. The hospital of San Marcos was founded in the second half of the 12th century but the monumental whole, in Plateresque style, and which is today partially occupied by a *parador de turismo*, was built by the Order of Santiago at the beginning of the 14th century, at the initiative of King Ferdinand the Catholic, at the time the Order's Grand Master. The church was consecrated in 1541 and the upper section of its façade is dotted with carved scallop shells. The lower section of the enormous façade, above the base, is crossed by a series of carved medallions, an immense portrait gallery in which, among others, El Cid encounters Alfonso II and the Catholic kings. Work on the cloister, of which Juan de Badajoz made two galleries, ended at the beginning of the 18th century.

LA VIRGEN DEL CAMINO

A fter crossing the Bernesga River by the San Marcos bridge, pilgrims took the direction of Astorga. About six kilometres from Leon, on July 2, 1505, the Virgin appeared to a shepherd and, so that he could prove it, threw a stone that grew bigger to the place where she wished to be worshipped. By 1515, pilgrims stopped at the original hermitage built on the designated site, that was replaced in 1961 by the shrine of the Virgen del Camino, conceived by the Dominican architect Fray Francisco Coello.

The Virgen del Camino

Bridge and former San Marcos hospital

"HE WHO WENT TO SAINT JAMES AND NOT TO THE HOLY SAVIOUR…"

Towards 761, Frómista and his nephew founded a hermitage on a hill called Oveto. "In this abandoned and uninhabited place", King Froila and his wife, Queen Munia, were buried. Alfonso the Chaste (792-842) transferred the capital of his kingdom from Pravia to Oviedo and, on the same hill, had various shrines built, including a church dedicated to the Holy Saviour, Saint Mary's Church that was to become the royal pantheon, and San Tirso Church. To the south of Holy Saviour Church, extended the buildings of the royal palace, prolonged in the east by the palatine chapel. In this chapel, called Saint Michael's, a reliquary containing very many relics was placed. This reliquary had been brought from Toledo after the fall of the Visigothic king-

lid of this reliquary are covered by carved sheets of silver. It is still visible in the *Cámara Santa*, the name given since then to Saint Michael's chapel, integrated into Oviedo's Gothic cathedral, between the *capilla mayor* and the cloister, and where, on the shafts of the columns, pairs of apostles were sculpted in the 12th century. A document established in 1075 indicates that the original reliquary contained eighty-three relics, including those of many characters from the Old and New Testaments, and those of martyrs victims of Roman persecution, like Facundo and Primitivo. Among other relics that were not kept in the reliquary were one of the carafes of the wedding at Cana. Alfonso VI's interest in the Holy Reliquary and the stir created by the relics' inventory was at the origin

Statue of the Holy Saviour of Oviedo

of Pajares. Pilgrims' songs evoked the difficulty of this journey. "When we were at Mount Etuve/ that is so cold and so harsh/ and makes many hearts mournful/ It makes several wives widows/ Orphans little children…". Going down towards Oviedo, pilgrims passed at the church of Santa Cristina de Lena. In Oviedo Cathedral, Saint James is indeed present, a reminder that a route, less crowded than the *Camino francés*, follows the coast from Irún. On the splaying of the Gothic portal of the chapel of Alfonso the Chaste, Saint James appears as a pilgrim, and a painting in the reredos of Saint Peter's chapel, from the 18th century, evokes one of the apostle's miracles when he intervened in the Battle of Coimbra. And on one of the pillars of the *capilla mayor*, topped with a capital decorated with pilgrims' shells, stands the statue of the Holy Saviour. A saying quoted in the New Guide printed in Paris in 1583 reminds us that, " He who went to Saint James/ and not to the Holy Saviour/ Has visited the servant/ and left behind the Lord.".

Holy reliquary in Oviedo

dom by Christians wanting to store it in a safe place in the Asturian mountains. This Holy Reliquary soon became the object of a local pilgrimage. In 1075, King Alfonso VI (1072-1109) went to Oviedo, attended the opening of the original reliquary, carried out an inventory and had the Holy Reliquary made. The sides and

of the development of the pilgrimage to Oviedo. Many pilgrims starting from Leon went to the Asturias before continuing on the road to Santiago de Compostela. They had to cross the Cantabrian range, then called Mont d'Estures, where they found a hospital, mentioned by 1103, at Arbas, just before crossing the pass

Bridge over the Orbigo in Hospital de Orbigo

Ramparts of Astorga, with the cathedral chevet and Gaudí's episcopal palace

ASTORGA

Between *Legio* (Leon) and *Asturica* (Astorga), the route that follows the old Roman road passes through Villadangos del Páramo, to the north of this region with its well-deserved name whose translation is *barren area*. At Hospital de Orbigo, Suevi and Visigoths confronted each other in 456. Cordoban troops and those of Alfonso III the Great (866-910) did so in the year 900. A two hundred and four-metre long bridge with twenty-four arches spans the Orbigo River. In 1434, any worthy knight had to take up the challenge thrown down by Don Suero de Quiñones to be allowed to cross it.

Asturica was founded in 14-15 BC by Augustus, who surrounded it with thick walls to protect it from Asturian and Cantabrian tribes. The town was located at the crossroads of two of the three great routes that, with the *via Augusta*, covered the Iberian peninsula: the *via de la Plata*, coming from the south, and the road that linked *Tarraco* (Tarragona), *Caesar Augusta* (Zaragoza), *Legio* (Leon) and *Asturica* (Astorga). Astorga, a bishopric starting in the 3rd century, was by the 4th century a centre of the Priscillianist heresy. After Theodoric's victory over the Suevi on the Orbigo, Astorga, a Suevi town, was destroyed. In 714, the Moorish chief Tariq captured it, but it was recaptured in 744 by Alfonso 1st (739-757). At the end of the 10th century, the town was attacked by al-Mansûr, and its walls were slightly damaged. They were restored in 1230 by Bishop Don Nuno.

KNIGHTLY SPIRIT

The year 1434 was a Jubilee year. A knight from Leon, Suero de Quiñones, thought of celebrating it by organizing a tournament, the *Paso Honroso*, near the bridge over the Orbigo River. In order to free himself from the dependence caused by his love for a lady, in whose honour every Thursday he wore a gilded silver necklace, he challenged, along with nine other supporters, any knight who dared to cross the bridge, swearing to break up to three hundred lances against any who would take up his challenge. The tournament lasted thirty days, from July 10 to August 9, with a rest on Saint James's Day, July 25. A palisade was put up on an esplanade close to the bridge. Jousts were determined by a twenty-two chapter-long set of rules, presented along with an account of events, in the *Book of the Honourable Step*, probably dictated by Don Suero to his equerry Pedro Rodríguez de Lena. The first combat opposed Don Suero and a German knight, in the presence of the king. Sixty-seven other knights appeared, one of whom died after receiving a lance in the eye. At the end of the tournament, the knights from both teams left for Santiago de Compostela, where Don Suero presented his necklace to the apostle. It is around the neck of the reliquary bust of Saint James Alphaeus in the San Fernando chapel of the cathedral. In 1458, twenty-four years later, Don Suero died in an ambush set by Guttiere de Quejada, a knight he had beaten at the *Paso Honroso*.

Priscillian, the Heretic

During the second half of the 4th century, Christian communities of men and women advocating strict Encratism, in the line of Eastern Gnostic and Manichaean doctrines, appeared in the Iberian peninsula and in southern Gaul. Refusing all meat and practicing fasting, their members considered marriage and the sexual act that produced bodies as diabolical creations and lived in abstinence, hence their name of *Continent*. It was within one of these groups that Priscillian, an educated Spanish layman from a wealthy Christian family of senatorial rank, began to preach towards 370-375. Condemning the licentious lives of the clergy, he proposed harsh asceticism, fed by a negative conception of the material world. Partly based on the reading of apocryphal documents and understanding astrological influences, his preaching was extremely successful in Gallecia, in the Asturias, in Lusitania and as far as Baetica, but soon encountered the hostility of the Spanish Church. The bishops Hydatius of Merida and Ithacius

of Ossonuba were the first to oppose Priscillianism, and had it condemned at the Council of Zaragoza in 380. However, Priscillian had also found supporters within the clergy, and even won over two bishops, Instancius and Salvian. Far from accepting the decisions of the council, these two clergymen tried to increase the preacher's authority and consecrated him bishop of Avila, in Lusitania. Salvian died a short time later. At the same time, Ithacius and Hydatius obtained from Emperor Gratian the ratification of a decree against Manichaeism, with the purpose of hampering the progress of Priscillianism, which had by then spread to southern Gaul, where it found many supporters, including the noblewoman Euchrotia. Faced with this threat, Priscillian went to Italy to obtain the support of the powerful bishop of Milan, Ambroise, and the no less influent Damasus, Bishop of Rome. The Bishop of Avila was refused any support but he nonetheless managed to have Gratian's decree annulled. However,

taking advantage of the rise to power of the usurper Maximus (383), Ithacius went to Trier, where he easily obtained the condemnation of Priscillian and a meeting of a council in Bordeaux. In 384, the council declared Priscillianism a heresy, and deposed Instancius. Refusing to appear before the council, Priscillian went to Trier to plead his cause directly with the emperor. In vain. The new council convoked in the imperial city, attended by the highest religious authorities, among them Ambroise of Milan and Martin of Tours, confirmed the Bordeaux condemnation. However, Hydatius and Ithacius were not fully satisfied and at their request, Priscillian and his friends were called to appear before the prefect of the court for breach of morals and magic practices. At a time when evil spells were harshly punished by Christian emperors, the sentence was bound to be fatal and atrocious. After being put to the question (flagellation, torture on the rack and with hot irons) Priscillian, Euchrotia, the bishop Instancius, the Aquitanian poet Latronianus, as well as two new supporters, the clerics Armenius and Felicissimus, were beheaded in Trier in 385. Brought back to Spain probably by river and then by sea, the tortured bodies were buried with great pomp in a still unknown place, and were raised to the rank of martyrs. Despite the condemnations pronounced by the councils called in Toledo in 396 and 400, Priscillianism remained very active in the north of the Iberian peninsula, particularly in western Gallecia, today's Galicia. Present until the end of the 6th century, it left a deep mark there.

Trier Cathedral

Pilgrims crossed the town by the calle de las Tiendas where Jewish and Frankish shopkeepers sold their wares. There was a Franciscan convent near the *Puerta del Sol* through which pilgrims entered the town. The most important hospital was that of San Juan, beside Santa María Cathedral. Construction of this Gothic style church began in 1471, but work was not completed until 1693, hence explaining details in Renaissance, Baroque and Plateresque styles on the façade and the towers. The doorway's tympanum is sculpted with episodes from the life of Christ: the resurrection of Lazarus, the merchants in the temple, the Resurrection. At the summit of the apse's pinnacle stands the statue of Pero Mato, an inhabitant of Astorga who participated in the Battle of Clavijo. A small street that skirts the group of buildings comprising San Juan hospital, Santa Marta Church, and the chapel of San Esteban, leads from the cathedral to the episcopal palace, built between 1889 and 1913 to plans by Gaudí, and the seat of the Museum of Los Caminos. The window of the cell of the Immured opens onto this street: loose women, to whom the pilgrims gave food through thick bars, were locked up here. On the *plaza de España*, the baroque Town Hall is topped with a clock whose two automatons, representing maragatos, bang out the hours. The *maragatos*, skilful muleteers, perhaps originally a cross between Moors and Visigoths, are the inhabitants of the Maragatería, the harsh and isolated region to the west of Astorga, which is its capital, that the pilgrims reached after leaving the town through the *Puerta del Obispo*.

St James, Museum of the Roads

THE MUSEUMS OF ASTORGA

Within the walls of the Astorga episcopal palace, the Museo de Los Caminos (Museum of Roads), dedicated to local history, devotes one of its rooms to the Santiago pilgrimage, showing statues of the apostle, and various pilgrims' objects and documents. The Cathedral Museum occupies part of the monastic buildings. The painting of the Roman matron Luparia is among its collections of religious art. According to Compostela legend, this pagan noblewoman converted to the faith of James the Greater's disciples, after making them undergo trials and tribulations. The disciples had arrived by sea from Jerusalem, site of his martyrdom, to bury his body on Spanish soil. Luparia wanted James to be buried on the site of an old temple she owned. Her name Luparia – from *lupa*, she-wolf, is the subject of a long digression in the translation of Saint James, written by an abbot of Fleury in the 11th century. "[Luparia's] name was savage, grasping and proud [...]. But [...] first of all insane because of her pride and, in conformity with the name she bore, terrifying the servants of Christ, [...] she got rid of her aggressive ferocity and [...] was associated with the college of the lambs of Christ."

The Legend of Queen Luparia, Cathedral Museum

RUTA DE LA PLATA

Originally, the *via de la Plata* linked *Emerita* (Merida) to *Asturica* (Astorga). It was described in Antoninus's itinerary, the repertory of roads in the entire Roman empire, established during the 2nd century, giving for each road its various stages and the distances between them. In this booklet, the *Iter ab Emerita Asturicam* was number XXIV. It extended to the south towards *Italica* (Santiponce) and *Hispalis* (Sevilla) and, to the north, towards *Lucus Asturum* (Oviedo) and *Gigia* (Gijón) through Legio (Leon). After the *via Augusta* that linked *Summum Pyreneum* (le Perthus) to *Carthago Nova* (Carthagena) through *Barcino* (Barcelona), the *via de la Plata* was the most important Roman road in the Iberian peninsula. A first roadway had been drawn starting in 139 BC by the praetor Servilio Scipion, after he had ordered the assassination of the Lusitanian chief Viriato. But it was Emperor Augustus (27 BC – 14 AD) who started the construction of this great strategic route, that was continued under Tiberius. The work followed the usual structure of Roman roads. On a foundation of large blocks of stone, a gravel bed, the *rudus*, was laid out, then a layer of sand, the *nucleus*,

Sevilla

on which rested the top layer that could be driven on. This was the *summum dorsum* or *summa cresta*, made of stone slabs. The width of the road, limited by the side ditches, varied between six and twelve metres. Every *mille passuum*, there was a milliary column; a thousand steps represented a distance of one kilometre, four hundred and eighty metres, since the Roman step measured one metre forty-eight. Many works of art were built, like the bridge crossing the Guadiana River at Merida. Every twenty to twenty-five (Roman) miles, staging posts, *mansiones*, lodged and fed travellers, and staging posts called *mutationes*, provided fresh horses for wagons and chariots. Of this work called cyclopean by the traveller Richard Ford, only a few bridges and stretches of road remain. Their stones were used for building churches, abbeys, castles or houses. The etymology of the name of this Roman road, that finally became the *ruta de la Plata*, has often raised questions. The only point of convergence of all the opinions expressed on the question is that in no case did it have anything to do with silver, *plata* in Castilian. Some have found a Latin (*lata*) or Greek (*plateia*) origin, both of these terms meaning "wide". Others

Roman bridge in Merida

propose an Arab origin – *balath* translated by "lined with stones". This latter hypothesis could be validated by the fact that Moorish troops, especially those of al-Mansûr, at the end of the 10th century, used this magnificent road to penetrate the northern Christian territories during their raids. Before and after them, others used this road like the Romans, who built it and travelled it north and south; the Goths followed it from north to south, as did the armies of the *Reconquista*. Under Alfonso X

Façade of Astorga Cathedral

the Wise (1252-1284), the *ruta de la Plata* was one of the nine *cañadas reales*, or royal roads, of his kingdom. It was one of the routes to Santiago de Compostela, and as such, called the Mozarab road to Saint James, or else the southern route. Coming from the south of the Iberian peninsula, sometimes from Mediterranean or Atlantic ports where they had landed, pilgrims taking it rejoined the *Camino francés* at Astorga, a town they entered by the Postigo, a postern opened in the southern line

of city walls, from which they rapidly reached the *calle de las Tiendas*. Along this more than two thousand year-old road, over the centuries an excep-

The Casa de las Conchas in Salamanca

tional patrimony of towns, sites and monuments has accumulated: Sevilla, Santiponce, Almendralejo, Merida, Caceres, Plasencia, Bejar, Salamanca,

University doorway in Salamanca

Zamora, Benavente, La Bañeza, Astorga, and beyond, to the north, Valencia de Don Juan, Leon, Mieres, Oviedo, Avilès and Gijón. This incomplete list is enough to prove the immense role played by the *ruta de la Plata* in the history of Spain, for which it has been a veritable stratigraph for over two thousand years.

Castle in Valencia de Don Juan

Iron cross at Foncebadón Pass

The Maragatería

Pilgrims who did not wish to climb Monte Irago skirted it in the north by the puerto de Manzanal. After crossing the pass, they found a hospital of the Knights of Saint John of Jerusalem, whose presence in itself proves that this path was often used by the walkers for God, like Hermann Künig von Vach in the 15th century. The others confronted the isolation of the Maragatería. The route avoided Castrillo de los Polvazares, a typical Maragato village, crossed Santa Catalina de Somoza and El Ganso, and arrived at Rabanal del Camino, at the foot of Monte Irago. The 12th century church of Santa María in this village was Templar. These Templars, who depended on Ponferrada, ensured pilgrims' safety in these hostile lands. Close to the summit of Monte Irago, Foncebadón, today an abandoned village, was an important stage on the way to Santiago, already mentioned in the 10th century. In 1103, Alfonso VI (1172-1109) granted the privilege of immunity to the pilgrim shelter in Foncebadón and to the church of San Salvador of Monte Irago, both placed under the authority of the hermit Gaucelme. At Foncebadón Pass, at an altitude of 1,504 metres, the *Cruz de Ferro*, or Iron Cross, stands on top of its wooden mast, on a mound made of stones thrown by Galician harvesters, who hired themselves out in Castile, and by pilgrims.

Rabanal del Camino

MOUNT OF MERCURY

The hermit Gaucelme, in the early 9th century, before the pilgrimage, raised the mast of the Cruz de Ferro (iron cross) on this stony hill. The Romans called these mounds, mounts of Mercury. Mercury and his children, the Lares, were the gods of crossroads.

Castrillo de los Polvazares

Ponferrada Castle

THE BIERZO

Molinaseca, Pilgrims Bridge

LAS MÉDULAS

....

O n the north-western slopes
of the Aquilian mountains,
south-west of Ponferrada, for
three centuries slaves sieved three
hundred million tonnes of soil dug
out of the ground by pipes and
pressure pipelines, to enrich Rome
by a million kilograms of gold.

Once past the Foncebadón Pass, the route runs down the western
slopes of Monte Irago to reach Manjarín, the first village in the
Bierzo, then Acebo. At Molinaseca, it crosses the Meruelo River
over the Pilgrims bridge. The Boeza is a tributary of the Sil. The
Romans had installed a fort on the spit of land formed by their
confluence, a strategic location near the gold-mining centre of Las
Médulas. Theodoric captured the position in 456 and a few centuries later, the Muslims occupied it. Also between the two rivers,
the church of Santo Tomas de las Ollas, well named "de las
Entrambasaguas", between two waters, has a Mozarab apse.
Pilgrims crossed the Boeza in small boats until the Mascaron
bridge was built. In 1082, Bishop Osmundo had the *Pons ferratus* set
over the Sil River, mentioned by Aimery Picaud. Ponferrada developed under the impetus of Ferdinand II (1157-1188). In 1178, this
monarch invited the Templar Order to settle there in order to control the region of passage that the Bierzo constituted and hence
ensure pilgrims' safety. Between 1218 and 1282, on the left bank of
the Sil, the Templars built a fortress that spread over more than
eight thousand square metres, and occupied it until the dissolution
of their order in 1312. In 1498, Isabelle the Catholic endowed the
town with a pilgrims hospital. This hospital, called the Queen's is
located on Hospital Street.

Las Médulas

MOZARAB CHURCHES

The term "Mozarab" is used for Christian populations living on lands conquered by Muslim troops. Paradoxically, the most typical Mozarab churches are found on lands the most quickly liberated from the Moorish hold. After the repression to which Christians had been subjected under Mohammed 1st (852-886), they had no choice other than converting or fleeing towards the north of the Iberian peninsula, at the limit between the territory controlled by al-Andalus and that bitterly defended by the Asturian kings. Hence, four of these Mozarab churches greatly influenced by Cordoban achievements are San Miguel de la Escalada, between

San Miguel de la Escalada

Sahagún and Leon, Santo Tomas de las Ollas, in Ponferrada, Santiago de Peñalba, in the south of the town, and San Miguel de Celanova, south of Orense. The first three are very close to the route to Santiago de Compostela, and this is probably not accidental. To the north-east of Mansilla de las Mulas, the monastery of San Miguel de la Escalada was founded at the end of the 9th cen-

tury, during the reign of Alfonso III (866-910) by monks having fled Cordoba, with the abbot Alfonso at their head. The church was built on the ruins of a Visigothic church. A new church was consecrated on November 20, 913, since the original shrine had become too small given the increase in the number of monks at the monastery. In 1050, new transformations were made in the church. It had a plan like a basilica with three naves and six bays. The bay beside the chevet is the largest and is used as a transept, with three apses opening in it. The floor plan of these three apses makes a very closed horseshoe, a stylistic effect typical of Mozarab art, that is also found in the horseshoe arches of the church and the portico and the window of the external gallery. The bell-tower, from the 11th century, is Romanesque. The monastery of Santiago de Peñalba was founded at the beginning of the 10th century by a monk, Gennade, "in memory of Saint James", in a mountainous cirque bristling with limestone rocks whose colour was at the origin of the name

Santiago de Peñalba

Peñalba (white mountain). Gennade became the bishop of Astorga before retiring to his foundation. Under its flat-stone roof, the building plan is basilical and the Mozarab character of the arches and domes is obvious. The south lateral porch, with its twinned arches of horseshoe shape and framed by an alfiz, is without a doubt an accomplished example of an art imported from the south of the Iberian peninsula.

San Miguel de la Escalada

After Ponferrada, pilgrims crossed the village of Cacabelos, set north of the Cistercian abbey Santa María la Real de Carracedo. They then entered Villafranca del Bierzo, after passing in front of the Romanesque church of Saint James. In a privilege granted by Pope Calixtus III (1455-1458), during Jubilee years, pilgrims who found it impossible to continue their journey could cross the threshold at the Pardon doorway of this church and receive the same indulgences as they would have obtained by going to Santiago de Compostela. The town that the pilgrims crossed by following the calle del Agua, is set on the left bank of the Burbia, at the place where the river meets up with its tributary, the Valcarce. Alfonso VI (1072-1109) invited Franks and Cluniac monks to settle there. It was on the site of their monastery, Santa María de Cluniaco, that in 1544 the collegiate church of Santa María de Cruñego was built.

Capital in Villafranca del Bierzo

Chevet of Saint James Church in Villafranca del Bierzo

MONASTICISM IN THE BIERZO

During the 7th century, Saint Fructuoso de Braga, with the help of his disciple Valerian, had provided the impetus by founding several monasteries in the Bierzo, including Compludo, near Acebo, and that of San Pedro do Montes, several kilometres north of Santiago de Peñalba. He provided his foundations with an extremely strict rule with respect to discipline and abstinence. His example was to be widely followed since in the 10th century, the Bierzo already had over twenty monasteries. Most of the orders had one or several establishments: Cluniacs, Cistercians, Premonstrants, Canons of Saint Augustine, Franciscans, but also Templars and Hospitallers. Located at greater or lesser distances from the road to Santiago, all had the role of receiving, protecting or edifying pilgrims who approached their destination.

Santa María Church in the Cebreiro

THE ROAD FROM PORTUGAL

Saint James Church in Coimbra

P ilgrims also came from Portugal. From Lisbon, they reached Tomar, the seat of the Order of Christ starting in 1319, then arrived in Coimbra, where there was a Saint James Church. They crossed Porto on the right bank of the Douro River, near its mouth, before reaching Braga. To the west of Braga, in the little town of Barcelos on the right bank of the Cávado River, a miracle, whose conclusion was similar to that of the *hanged-unhanged*, occurred. In the 14th century, a Santiago pilgrim accused of robbery was condemned to be hanged. He vainly tried to convince the judge and begged the apostle James to intercede. He announced that, to prove his innocence, the rooster that was then roasting and the judge was preparing to eat, would come back to life and crow. The miracle happened and the pilgrim, freed, had a monument raised to the glory of Saint James. It is visible today in the archaeological museum in the former Palace of the Counts-Dukes of Barcelos. And in the town, large numbers of little roosters, carved out of wood and marvellously decorated commemorate the event. North of Braga, pilgrims crossed the Miño River, then after Padrón where they never hesitated to pause, they arrived in Santiago de Compostela, the city of the apostle, that they entered through the Fajeira Gate.

Porto

The rooster of Barcelos

303

The Obradoiro, façade of Santiago de Compostela Cathedral

Santiago de Compostela

Tree of Jesse, Portico of Glory

After the discovery of the apostle's tomb on the right bank of the Sar River, a tributary of the Ulla, Alfonso II the Chaste (792-842) had a modest oratory built to shelter it, "a little work of stone and clay", that was rapidly surrounded, in the north, by the San Juan baptistery and, in the east, by a Benedictine abbey, later called of Antealtares because of its location in front of the apostle's altar, as well as two other churches. The bishop of Iria, Theodomir, protected these holy places with a circle of ramparts that also enclosed the original urban centre of Santiago de Compostela surrounding them. During the reign of Alfonso III the Great (866-910), Bishop Sisnando had a new, larger church built, nonetheless conserving in its original condition the oratory in which the apostle's tomb had been placed. In 971, Norsemen approached Galicia's coasts and the caliphate of Cordoba intended to take advantage of the situation and to catch the kingdom of Leon in a pincer movement and hence, to deal it a fatal blow. But Saint Rosendo organized defences, galvanized the Leon fighters and pushed back both attacks. On August 10, 997, al-Mansûr who had just reorganized the army of the Omeyyad caliphate, entered the city that had been abandoned by its inhabitants, sacked it, destroyed the apostle's church but, probably through superstition, respected his tomb and spared its guardian. The Muslim chief took with him to Cordoba the church's bells and the doors of the city gates. The church rose from its ruins and was consecrated in 1009 by Bishop Pierre de Mesontio, who was also the composer of *Salve Regina*. It was demolished only in 1112, when work on the Romanesque cathedral had sufficiently advanced. During the 11th century, worried by the still latent Norman threat, Bishop Cresconius reinforced and developed the city's defences. At the mouth of the Ulla River, the castle of Honesto was to confront danger coming from the sea. With the constant increase in the flow of pilgrims, the church rapidly became too small. In 1078, Bishop Diego Peláez undertook the construction of a new church. Work slowed considerably when, in 1088, the prelate was accused of supporting Galician separatism and thrown into prison by Alfonso VI (1072-1109). In 1095, the episcopal seat was transferred from Iria to Santiago de Compostela and, in 1100, Diego Gelmírez (1100-1140), by succeeding Diego Peláez, put a term to the period of vacancy that the bishopric had suffered from after the imprisonment of Diego Peláez. He restarted construction work and, in 1105, consecrated most of the altars. But in 1117, along with Queen Doña Urraca (1109-1126), he had to confront an uprising by the town's inhabitants, who set fire to the building. The fire was so strong that, according to *Historia Compostelana*, the bronze of the church bells was brought to melting point. Despite these events, at his death, the *capilla mayor* and the chancel were completed, the door of Las Platerías had been inaugurated and the cloister was under construction. Aimery Picaud, who came to Santiago in about 1130, described a nearly completed cathedral in his *Guide*. However, he was not able to

HISTORIA COMPOSTELANA

It was under the abbacy of Diego Gelmirez that, from 1109 to 1140, the *Historia Compostelana* was written in Latin by three canons at the cathedral of Santiago de Compostela: Munio, Hugo, and Girardus. This document provided very interesting information about the pilgrimage to Santiago during the first half of the 12th century. It thus included the testimony of Emir Ali ben Yusuf (1106-1142) who had come to Compostela to meet the queen Doña Urraca. This gives an idea of the importance of the flow of pilgrims coming to worship at the apostle's tomb. Impressed by the size of the crowd, the emir asked the guide accompanying him, "Who is this character so great and famous that Christians come to pray to him from the Pyrenees and even further away? The multitude of those coming and going is so great that hardly any space is left open on the road in the direction of the west."

St Luke, Portico of Glory

THE MASTER'S SIGNATURE

....

The lintels of the Portico of
Glory carry the following
carved text: "The year of the
incarnation of the Lord 1188, of
the era 1226, the days of the calends
of April, were set in place the lintels
of the principal doorways of the
church of the blessed Saint James,
by master Mateo, who directed the
work of these doorways, from their
foundations…".

admire the Portico of Glory to which Maestro Mateo put the finishing touches in 1188. Aimery Picaud described in great detail the original doorway of the Transfiguration, later replaced by the Portico of Glory. In 1211, the cathedral of Santiago de Compostela was solemnly consecrated in the presence of Alfonso IX (1188-1230). Between 1738 and 1750, the Galician architect Fernando de Casas y Novoa added a Baroque façade – the Obradoiro – onto the western façade of the cathedral. This "golden work" is, in any case, an authentic masterpiece in which the wealth of sculpted details, emphasized by the patina of time and highlighted by the natural elements of sun and rain, takes nothing away from the spirit and lightness of the whole. At the summit of the building's central section, James the Greater, to whom the two large lateral seventy-metre high towers, perfectly symmetrical and slightly recessed, seem to provide an honour guard, dominates the whole with all his grandeur as an apostle and all his simplicity as a pilgrim. At his feet, to the right and left, Athanasius and Theodore are also dressed as pilgrims. From the parvis of the Obradoiro, a stairway, whose two flights frame the door of the 12th century Romanesque crypt, leads to the cathedral parvis. Once through the doorway, the space between the rear of the Obradoiro and what used to be the façade of the cathedral forms a narrow narthex. The Portico of Glory, before providing an invitation to enter the cathedral, captures the visitor's interest by the wealth and beauty of its sculpted works that retain fine traces of their original polychrome finish.

The "Saint of the Bumps"

Peter, Paul, James and John, Portico of Glory, Santiago Cathedral

THE PORTICO OF GLORY

Like many masters of medieval workshops, Master Mateo is known only from his work and, in particular, by his masterpiece, the Portico of Glory. Was he French, Italian, Galician? Tradition suggested that the *saint of the bumps*, kneeling and openly repenting behind the pier of the doorway, inside the cathedral, was the sculpted image of the master. Pilgrims used to bump their heads three times with the statue, which was supposed to instil in them some of the artist's genius. Master Mateo was certainly an architect, since he built the bridge of Cesures, over the Ulla. Was he a sculptor? Probably, but he was most likely helped in his work by other artists. At the request of Ferdinand II (1157-1188), Master Mateo began to work on the Portico of Glory in 1168, and completed it in 1188. The work, whose style was already a preview of the Gothic, has come down to us intact except for its polychrome colouring that has either changed or been altered. It is undeniably true that, in this portico, pilgrims found a metaphysical echo of their aspirations when they decided to set out on the road to Santiago de Compostela, a justification of their efforts and hardships endured along the way and, also, a confirmation by an image of the reality of the world of the sacred and their faith. Their fervour has left an indelible imprint in the pier's marble, dug and polished by the five fingers of millions of hands. The height of the prints provides us with the ever repeated scene of kneeling pilgrims, their heads bowed, in contemplation. And it is nearly possible to hear, repeated endlessly although never really pronounced, all those

breathless thanks. The portico is comprised of three doorways corresponding to the interior outline of the cathedral. The lateral doorways open onto the side aisles and the central one, onto the central nave. For the canon Lopez Ferreiro, each doorway corresponds to a church: that on the left, to the Jewish church, the central one to the Catholic church, and that on the right, to the church of the Devil. In any case, the portico took its inspiration from both the Old and

Saint James

the New Testaments and constitutes a veritable genesis of Christianity, whose continuity is ensured by the pilgrim contemplating it. The column of the pier of the central doorway is carved with the tree of Jesse, or Jesus Christ's human genealogy. It is topped with the capital of the Trinity, a reference to his divine genealogy. Above, a statue of the apostle James seems to welcome pilgrims. On the tympanum, showing his wounds, Christ resuscitated is framed by the four evangelists, each holding his symbolic animal of the tetramorph. On either side, on the lower register, angels present the instruments of the Passion: the Cross, the crown of thorns, the nails, the jar of vinegar, the spear and the sponge. On the upper register, in the background, in a fine effect of perspective, the Just appear. On the archivolt, the twenty-four old men of the Apocalypse hold vials of perfume and musical instruments. On the left and right of the doorway, at the same height as the statue of James the Greater on the pier, and also standing on columns, on the left statues of the prophets Jeremiah, Daniel, Isaiah, and Moses; on the right, the apostles Peter, Paul, James and John. Similar statues representing prophets and apostles frame the lateral doorways: on the right of the right door, Bartholomew and Thomas; on the voussoir of the left hand door, Christ in limbo appears between Adam and Eve. Jesus Christ and the Archangel Michael occupy the keystones of the archivolt and the voussoir of the right hand doorway with, on one side, the Just and on the other, the procession of the Damned.

Entrance of former royal hospital

MASTER BUILDERS

A imery Picaud's *Pilgrim's Guide* provides precise information about the master builders who worked on the Romanesque cathedral of Santiago de Compostela during the 12th century. "The masters of stone who undertook the construction of the basilica of the blessed Saint James were called Bernard the Old – he was an inspired master – and Robert, with the help of other stone masons about fifty in number under the direction of Don Segeredo, vicar and master of the chapter, and of Abbot Gundesindo, during the reign of Alfonso, King of Spain and Diego 1st, a courageous knight and generous man."

Saint James Alphaeus

The square of the Obradoiro is framed in the north by the former royal hospital, founded by the Catholic kings and whose construction began in 1501. Today it is a *Parador de turismo*. To the west stands the palace of Rajoy, that has become the City Hall, topped by a statue of Saint James Matamoros, and to the south, the college of San Jeronimo. The cathedral and its annexes, the cloister and the episcopal palace, are encircled by a series of small streets and squares, a veritable exterior ambulatory, going around which allows the discovery of the whole, but also of the monuments on its periphery. At the south-eastern corner of the square, Fonseca Street leads to the plaza of Las Platerías, where the doorway of the same name provides access to the southern arm of the cathedral's transept. To the right of the doorway stands the Clock Tower, a former fortified tower from the 14th century, that in the 17th century was topped with a Baroque steeple, a work of Domingo de Andrade. Several steps lead down towards the Plaza of the Quintana, marked off by the façade of San Payo convent, the Chapter house and the chevet of the cathedral where, since 1611, the Door of Pardon stands open during Jubilee years. On either side of this door, also called the Holy Door, twenty-four statues from the chancel were re-used. They had been sculpted in granite by Master Mateo after he had finished the Portico of Glory, but had been destroyed in 1604 by Bishop Juan de Sanclemente. The Door of Pardon is surmounted by a statue of Saint James as a pilgrim, framed by Athanasius and Theodore. Another doorway, Baroque in style, opens onto the same plaza – the royal door of Quintana, made in 1667. And in the angle formed by the northern side of the cathedral and the episcopal palace, the Plaza de l'Inmaculada is closed in the north by San Martín Pinario Monastery. This is where pilgrims coming along the *Camino francés* used to arrive. Through the northern door, or French door, demolished in the 18th century and replaced by the Door of Azabachería, they entered the cathedral through the transept.

The layout of Saint James's Cathedral is characteristic of pilgrimage churches such as Saint Sernin in Toulouse or Saint Foy in Conques. A large number of worshippers had to be able to enter, pray and move around easily. Two lateral naves surmounted with galleries, frame the central nave. The two transept arms also have aisles. An ambulatory, onto which six radial chapels open, encircles the *capilla mayor*. The axial chapel is dedicated to the Holy Saviour; in 1102, Bishop Gelmirez placed the relics of Saint Fructuoso there. It is also known as the chapel of the king of France, because the French king Charles V the Wise (1364-1380) made a donation of three thousand florins so that a mass would be celebrated in that chapel every day. Here too, after confession which could be done in many different languages, and after taking communion, pilgrims received the *Compostela*. Other chapels open onto the lateral naves – beside the chapel of Relics, San Fernando Chapel containing the Treasure and the reliquary bust of Saint James Alphaeus, or the Less, with around its neck, the necklace supposedly brought in 1434 by Don Suero Quiñones. In the

THE LAS PLATERÍAS DOORWAY

The southern façade of Santiago de Compostela cathedral, the only one with Romanesque details near the Baroque balustrade surmounting it, is called Las Platerías because in front of it silver jewellery used to be sold, just as the northern façade is called la Azabachería, because jet jewellery was sold there. The Las Platerías façade opens with a gemeled doorway, surmounted by a composite whole of sculpted elements forming a kind of frieze put together like a puzzle. Above this frieze, a cornice is supported by sixteen modillions. Taking into account the various chronological signs, including an inscription referring to Alfonso VI, the year the Las Platerías doorway was completed can be situated between 1112 and 1117. The two tympana are formed of carved blocks joined together, done by several artists. The disorderly aspect of the construction could be due to the fact that the fire of 1117 seriously damaged the doorway, and it was partly restored with elements brought from elsewhere. The tympanum of the left-hand doorway presents the Temptation of Christ, in four scenes done by the master of the Temptation. Other elements were made by the chisel of the master of Las Platerías, who was the master in charge of carrying out the doorway. The most amazing of these elements, and the artist's masterpiece, is the one on the right, that had to be re-carved so that it would enter into the space on the tympanum: a half-undressed woman holds a skull on her lap. And Aimery Picaud commented, "And we should not forget to mention the woman who is beside the Temptation: she holds, between her hands, the horrible head of her seducer that was cut off by her own husband and that,

twice a day, on his orders, she has to kiss. O horrible and admirable punishment of the adulterous woman that has to be told to all." Another interpretation of this sculpture has been suggested: this woman could be Eve, mother of the dead man. The tympanum of the right-hand doorway shows scenes from the Passion of Christ, but also the miracle of the blind man. Some of the sculptures of the doorway's buttress and the uprights of the doors came from the northern doorway after it had been redone in the 18th century. Among them, on the left buttress, we see King David, the creation of Adam and a Christ in majesty,

and on the right upright of the right-hand door, a woman with a lion cub. Other elements of the northern doorway have been re-used above the doorway, like on the left, Adam and Eve driven out of Paradise. They were joined there by other sculptures removed from the western doorway beside the Portico of Glory, such as Saint James turning towards Christ placed in the centre of the work. On the left and right of the latter, two separate groups of apostles must have belonged to a complete and united group of the twelve apostles, that probably constituted the principal sculpted item of the original frieze.

The Las Paterías Doorway

Cathedral cloister

The Translatio, Goodyear Reredos

Gothic dome in the cathedral

transept's southern arm, beside the doorway of Las Platerías, is the Clavijo tympanum, probably brought from the 13th century Gothic cloister. Just next to it, a passage leads to the 16th century cloister through the western gallery from which there is access to the library, where the *botafumeiros* are presented. It is prolonged by the chapter house and the museum that, besides rich collections of tapestries, contains an alabaster reredos from the 15th century, offered by John Goodyear, that in five panels shows episodes in the life of Saint James the Greater. In the northern arm of the transept, a passage leads to the Corticela chapel, the result of a 13th century restoration of the shrine built by Bishop Sisnando in the 9th century.

In the centre of the *capilla mayor*, under an enormous Baroque baldaquin, a polychrome stone statue of Saint James, made in 1211, is placed in a precious *camarín* on the high altar. Pilgrims could, and can still, accede to the *camarín* by a staircase passing behind the apostle's statue in order to kiss it. At one time, Saint James wore a crown and it was traditional for pilgrims to place this crown on their own heads and put their hat onto the apostle. The statue wears a silver cape offered at the end of the 17th century by Bishop Monroy, whose tomb is located in the neighbouring Pilar chapel. In his left hand, James holds a staff, and in the right, a strip of material on which the text, "*Hic est Iacobi Apostoli et Hispaniarum Patroni*" is written. His index finger, pointing downwards, adds the gesture to the word, inviting pilgrims to take the staircase leading down to the crypt located under the high altar, at the very place where the tomb of the apostle and his disciples was discovered at the beginning of the 9th century. This crypt, rearranged in the holy year 1885, holds the silver chest containing the relics of Saint James and Saints Theodore and Athanasius.

The transept crossing is covered with a Gothic dome. Two metallic arches that, at their meeting point, support the jointed pulley onto which the great rope of the *botafumeiro* is wound, rest on brackets placed at the bottom of the four squinches. During great occasions, this gigantic censer swings above the heads of the faithful and rises up to the vaults of the central nave. Its weight is such that eight men, the *tiraboleiros*, those who pull the rope, have to bend right back to move it. The existence of the *botafumeiro* is mentioned in 1322, but the present system was not put in place until the 16th century. A few stairs separate the transept crossing from the *capilla mayor*. On either side of these steps rise two of the four pillars supporting the dome; a polychrome statue stands against each one of them. The statue of Saint James Alphaeus dates from the 14th century, and that of Saint Mary Salome, the mother of *Boanerges*, James the Greater and John, from the 16th century.

From Santiago de Compostela, pilgrims went to Padrón, the old Iria Flavia, because, "*Quen va Santiago e non va a Padrón/ O faz remeria o non*". Here, on the shores of the Sar River, a carved stone represents two pilgrims praying in front of a small boat. As for the stone to which the boat was attached, it is allegedly the one placed under the high altar of the town's collegiate church.

A SEPULCHRE FOR ETERNITY

The original tomb of the apostle James and of his disciples Athanasius and Theodore was shaped like a small oratory measuring about six metres by four, built over a funerary chamber that contained the sarcophagi of the three martyrs. This mausoleum, in which other bodies had been buried, had been built in the 1st or 2nd century. A Greek inscription on one of the sarcophagi had been deciphered: *Athanasios martyr*. As soon as the mausoleum was built, the burial place certainly became an object of local devotion by Christians, and continued to be so during the following centuries, with the constitution of a necropolis around the mausoleum. A legendary substratum was elaborated during this period and was largely exploited after the discovery of the apostle's tomb in the 11th century. The cult became obsolete, probably when Muslim troops invaded the Iberian peninsula. The constructions of

Alfonso IX in the 9th century and Alfonso X in the 10th century, then of Pierre de Mesontio in the 11th, always respected the original mausoleum. In 1112, it was Bishop Diego Gelmírez who had it demolished in the framework of construction of the Romanesque cathedral. The room containing the sepulchre became nearly inaccessible, and the high altar was placed above it. Beforehand, the bishop had had a survey of the relics carried out, and he removed a right mastoid apophysis to present to Atto, the bishop of Pistoia. Several centuries later, in 1589, Francis Drake attacked La Coruña and fears for the relics of Saint James of Compostela caused them to be removed and hidden. Once the danger was past, they remained where they had been placed, perhaps to discourage attempts by Spanish kings who would have like to put them at the Escorial. And their hiding place was forgotten. In 1878, the archbishop of Santiago,

Cardinal Payá y Rico, began to look for them. Of course, they were not in the sepulchre that had been closed by Gelmírez. Guided by a popular belief, excavations were undertaken under the high altar and, in the night of January 28-29, 1879, an urn containing nearly complete skeletons of three individuals was discovered. After a long enquiry, on March 12, 1883, a decree by the Archdiocese declared that the remains were indeed those of the apostle and his two disciples. Pope Leon XII ordered a complementary enquiry. Within its framework, the Pistoia relic was examined and analyzed and was found to correspond to one of the Santiago skeletons. On November 1, 1884, the Pope in his bull *Deus omnipotens*, confirmed the 1883 decree and invited the faithful to go to Santiago de Compostela on pilgrimage "according to the custom of our forefathers". In 1891, the new crypt was inaugurated.

The tomb of Saint James

REFERENCE POINTS

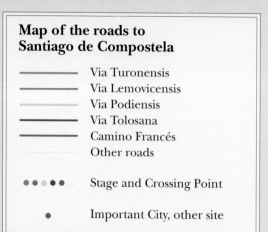

Map of the roads to
Santiago de Compostela

——————	Via Turonensis
——————	Via Lemovicensis
——————	Via Podiensis
——————	Via Tolosana
——————	Camino Francés
——————	Other roads
••••••	Stage and Crossing Point
•	Important City, other site

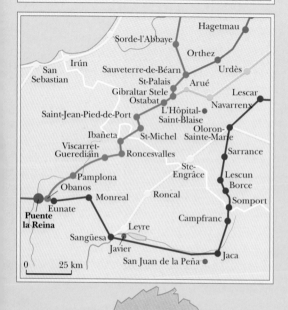

Hagetmau
Sorde-l'Abbaye
Orthez
Irún
San   Sauveterre-de-Béarn   Urdès
Sebastian   St-Palais   Arué
Gibraltar Stele   Lescar
Ostabat   Navarrenx
Saint-Jean-Pied-de-Port   L'Hôpital-
                          Saint-Blaise
Ibañeta   St-Michel   Oloron-
Viscarret-   Sainte-Marie
Guerediáin   Roncesvalles   Sarrance
Pamplona   Ste-
Obanos   Engrâce   Lescun
Monreal   Borce
Puente   Roncal   Somport
la Reina Eunate
             Leyre   Campfranc
Sangüesa
         Javier   Jaca
      San Juan de la Peña

0   25 km

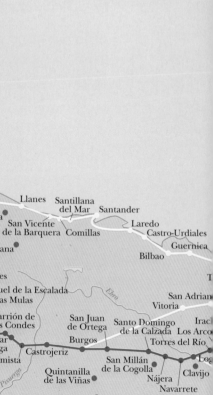

La Coruña   Ribadeo
         Mondoñedo   Luarca
SANTIAGO Villalba
DE COMPOSTELA   Canero   La Espina   Gijón
Cape   Sobrado de   Cornellana
Finisterra   Labacolla los Monjes
         Leboreiro Lugo   Oviedo
Padrón   Palas de Rei Vilar de Donas   Llanes   Santillana
         Portomarín Sarria   del Mar   Santander
              Triacastela   Santa Cristina   Covadonga San Vicente   Laredo
         Samos Cebreiro   de Lena   de la Barquera Comillas Castro-Urdiales
              Villafranca Hospital Virgen del   Liébana   Guernica
              del Bierzo de Orbigo Camino   Bilbao
              Ponferrada   León   Gradefes
         Santiago de Peñalba   Sandoval San Miguel de la Escalada   San Adrian
              Foncebadón   Mansilla de las Mulas   Vitoria
              Astorga   San Juan   Iraci
Barcelos   La Bañeza   Sahagún   Carrión de   de Ortega Santo Domingo Los Arco
Braga   los Condes   de la Calzada Torres del Río
                          Benavente   Villalcázar   Burgos   Log
PORTUGAL   de Sirga Castrojeriz   San Millán
                                     Frómista   de la Cogolla Clavijo
Porto   Quintanilla   Nájera
                             de las Viñas   Navarrete
                   Zamora
                                     Santo Domingo
                                     de Silos   SPA

Salamanca

ATLANTIC
OCEAN

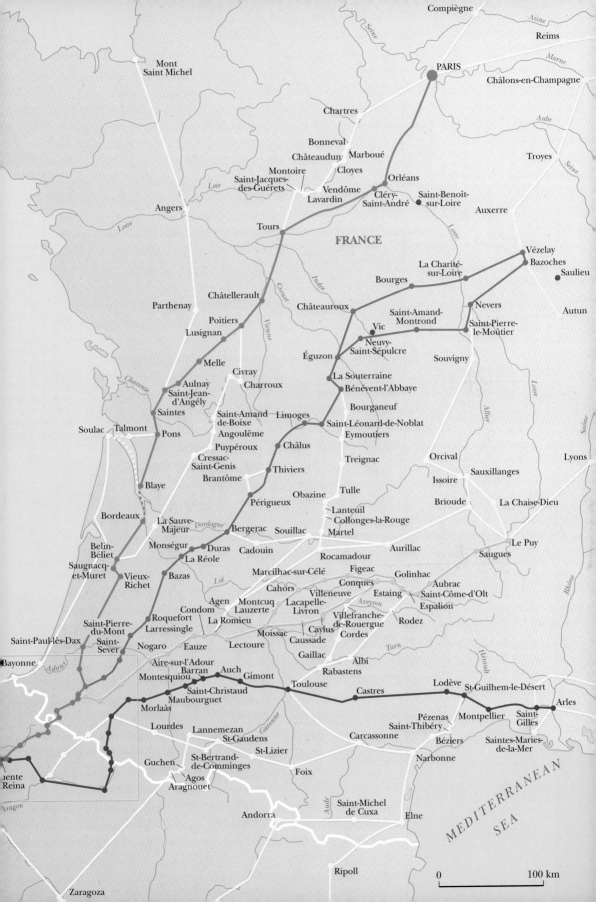

INDEX

A

Aachen , 11, 30, 41, 56, 57, 109, 110, 111, 125, 152, 225
Abd al-Rahmân I, 23, 26-27, 28, 59, 130, 239
Abd al-Rahmân II, 31, 59, 253, 281
Abd al-Rahmân III, 27, 60, 63
Acquapendente, 112, 193
Agen, 56, 171, 173, 201, 212
Aimery Picaud, 43, 77, 78, 133, 160, 305
Aire-sur-l'Adour, 189, 214
Alarcos, 59, 68
Alaric II, 14, 20
Alava, 20, 60, 245
Albelda, 59, 70, 71, 245
Alcuin, 30, 31, 125
Alexander III, 66, 67, 108
Algeciras, 25, 59, 64, 68
Alfonso 1st the Warrior, 29, 36, 64, 151, 237, 240, 247, 263, 287
Alfonso II the Chaste, 23, 29, 31, 41, 51, 59, 66, 87, 284, 285, 305, 311
Alfonso III the Great, 51, 59, 60, 67, 68, 263, 277, 287, 296, 305, 311
Alfonso V of Leon, 64, 281
Alfonso VI, 59, 64, 65, 72, 75, 78, 244, 245, 253, 255, 256, 263, 267, 269, 271, 277, 285, 293, 299, 305, 309
Alfonso VII, 59, 65, 78, 155, 207, 261, 269, 278, 279, 281, 283
Alfonso VIII, 59, 65, 66, 67, 68, 153, 207, 264, 265
Alfonso IX of Leon, 60, 66, 68, 78, 269, 283, 306
Alfonso X the Wise, 68, 79, 256, 265, 269, 273, 291
Al-Mansûr, 59, 63, 64, 65, 72, 73, 75, 257, 277, 281, 283, 287, 291, 305
Amaya, 18, 25, 59
Ambroise of Milan, 39, 98,
126, 133
Amiens, 109, 110, 122, 126, 164
Ampurias, 12, 29
Angoulême, 131, 143
Aniane, 31, 223, 225
Antioch, 38, 39, 181
Aphat-Ospital, 147
Aragnouet, 266
Arius, 15, 16
Arles, 23, 26, 39, 57, 77, 110, 114, 216-219, 220
Arras, 108, 109, 110
Arthous, 144, 145, 147
Arué, 147, 215
Asquins, 160
Astorga, 14, 25, 29, 59, 147, 149, 151, 207, 245, 281, 284, 286-291
Atanagild, 16, 282,
Athanasius, 15, 35, 46, 47, 102, 306, 308, 310, 311
Aubrac, 86, 87, 189, 192, 193, 195
Auch, 214, 217, 232, 233
Aulnay, 119, 134, 135, 136
Aurillac, 171, 202, 207, 299
Autun, 26, 39, 161, 168
Auxerre, 110, 161
Avignon, 23, 26, 98, 110, 114, 115, 157, 184

B

Baeza, 18, 153, 282, 283
Barbarossa, 111, 217
Barcelona, 25, 29, 63, 110, 223, 290
Barran, 217, 232
Bassoues, 232, 233
Bazas, 175, 184, 185
Bazoches, 157, 166
Beatus of Liebana, 30, 31, 36, 37, 73, 186, 257
Becket, Thomas à, 176, 207
Belin-Béliet, 119
Belmonte, 67
Benedict of Aniane, 55, 75, 125, 223, 224, 225
Benedict of Nursia, 125, 143, 213, 223, 265
Bénévent-l'Abbaye, 157, 172, 175, 207
Bergerac, 180, 183, 377
Bernard de Clairvaux, 158, 207, 231
Bessuéjouls, 196
Béziers, 55, 126, 128, 224
Bilbao, 141, 301
Blaye, 57, 119, 140, 152
Bologna, 88, 98, 112, 114, 184, 212
Borce, 217, 236
Bordeaux, 26, 57, 77, 110, 119, 130, 140-144, 147, 149, 151, 153, 225, 288
Bourges, 35, 157, 160, 162, 163, 164, 168
Braga, 14, 21, 29, 30, 31, 74, 92, 297, 303
Brantôme, 179
Briançon, 98, 114
Brioude, 171, 207, 223
Bruges, 110
Burgos, 59, 60, 87, 89, 90, 141, 207, 245, 259, 262-267, 277, 278

C

Cáceres, 66, 67
Cadix, 16, 25, 68
Cadouin, 180, 181
Cahors, 173, 189, 205
Calahorra, 255, 259
Calatrava, 59, 65, 66, 67, 68, 153
Calixtus II, 43, 74, 91, 260
Calmont-d'Olt, 194, 195
Campfranc, 217, 237
Cape Finisterra, 46, 71
Carcassonne, 26, 224, 226
Carrión de los Condes, 245, 271, 273, 274-275
Carthagena, 16, 219, 282, 290
Castañeda, 89, 300, 302
Castres, 217, 224
Castrillo de los Polvazares, 293
Castrojeriz, 245, 268-269
Cebreiro, 51, 89, 90, 171, 245, 298, 299, 300, 302
Celles-sur-Belle, 132, 133
Césaire (Saint), 130, 217
Châlons-en-Champagne,
51, 110, 161
Châlus, 157, 176, 177, 179
Charlemagne, 23-31, 41, 43, 51, 54-57, 101, 111, 122, 124, 127, 131, 140, 142, 144, 149, 151, 152, 153, 155, 179, 191, 209, 220, 229, 230, 247, 251, 255, 275, 278
Charles Martel, 23, 26, 55, 130, 151, 223
Charles the Bald, 29, 55, 122, 157
Charles III the Noble, 155, 251
Charles V, 66, 95, 111, 267
Charroux, 131, 143, 173
Chartres, 9, 33, 57, 110, 119, 121, 122-123, 127, 164, 241, 284
Châteauroux, 157, 160, 165
Châtellerault, 119, 127
Chindaswind, 20
Cirauqui, 246, 247, 250
Cîteaux, 151, 169, 239, 265
Civray, 131
Cize (Pass), 44, 57, 77, 119, 149, 151
Clavijo, 59, 60, 69, 197, 253, 257, 283, 289, 310
Cléry-Saint-André, 119, 120
Clovis, 13, 14, 125, 130, 175, 209
Clunia, 60, 63
Cluny, 72, 74, 75, 119, 136, 171
Coimbra, 25, 45, 59, 60, 63, 64, 65, 285, 303
Collonges-la-Rouge, 273
Columbus, Christopher, 60, 79, 263
Condom, 173, 182, 212, 213
Conques, 77, 155, 159, 180, 181, 192, 195, 196, 197, 198-201, 202, 205, 210, 245, 308
Constantine, 15, 39, 53, 116, 133
Cordoba, 16, 18, 19, 23, 25, 27, 28, 30, 31, 36, 56,

INDEX

BIBLIOGRAPHY

BARRET (P.) ET GURGAND (J.-N.): *Priez pour nous à Compostelle*, Hachette, 1978
BEATUS DE LIEBANA: *L'Apocalypse de Jean*, Catleya Éditions, 1998
BENNASSAR (B.): *Saint Jacques de Compostelle*, Julliard, 1970
BERARDINO (A. DI) (under the direction of): *Dictionnaire Encyclopédique du Christianisme Ancien*, Cerf, 1990
BERNHEIM (P.-A.): *Jacques, frère de Jésus*, Noêsis, 1996
BOTTINEAU (Y.): *Les chemins de Saint-Jacques*, Arthaud, 1983
BRANTHOMME (H.) ET CHÉLINI (J.) : *Les chemins de Dieu, Histoire des pèlerinages chrétiens des origines à nos jours*, Hachette, 1982
BRAVO LOZANO (M.): *Chemin de Saint-Jacques-de-Compostelle*, MSM, 1992/ *Guide Pratique du Pèlerin*, Everest, 1998
CHOCHEYRAS (J.): *Saint Jacques à Compostelle*, Ouest-France, 1997
DUHOURCAU (B.): *Vers Compostelle, la voie du piémont Pyrénéen*, J & D, Biarritz, 1993
DURLIAT (M.): *La sculpture romane de la route de Saint-Jacques, de Conques à Compostelle*, CEHAG, 1990
GEARY (P.-J.): *Le vol des reliques au Moyen Âge*, Aubier, 1993
GERARD (A.-M.): *Dictionnaire de la Bible*, Robert Laffont, 1989
GERBET (M.-C.): *L'Espagne au Moyen Âge*, Armand Colin, 1992
GODIN (J. ET N.): *Rocamadour, sous la légende, l'histoire*, in Notre Histoire n° 25
HASENOHR (G.) ET ZINK (M.) (under the direction of): *Dictionnaire des Lettres Françaises, Le Moyen Âge*, Fayard, 1964
HEERS (J.): *Précis d'histoire au Moyen Âge*, PUF, 1968
La Bible, Cerf, 1996
JACOMET (H.): *Pèlerinage et culte de saint Jacques en France: bilan et perspectives* in *Pèlerinage et Croisades*, CTHS, 1995/ *Un miracle de saint Jacques, Le pendu-dépendu* in Archéologia, n° 278/ *Le bourdon, la besace et la coquille* in Archéologia, n° 258/ *La confrérie des pèlerins de Saint-Jacques à Paris* in Archéologia, n° 289/ *Pèlerin du Moyen Âge et pèlerins d'aujourd'hui, Raison et déraison du pèlerinage* in *Le Pèlerinage*, Communio, n° 132/ *Compostelle au XII*e *et au XX*e *siècles, du mythe*

à l'utopie ? in *Europe Romane*, Revue d'Auvergne, Aurillac, 1993/ *À l'appel du Jubilé* in *Compostelle*, Cahiers d'Études, de Recherche et d'Histoire Compostellanes, n° 2, 1993/ *L'apôtre au manteau constellé de coquilles, Iconographie de saint Jacques à la cathédrale de Chartres*, Actes du colloque du VIIIe centenaire de la cathédrale, Picard, 1994
JUGNOT (G.): *Deux fondations augustiniennes en faveur des pèlerins: Aubrac et Roncevaux* in Cahiers de Fanjeaux n° 13, Privat, 1978/ *La via Podiensis* in Chemins de Compostelle n° 1 et 2, 1997-1998
LACAU SAINT GUILY (A.) ET HUREAU (J.): *Le Mont-Saint-Michel au péril du temps* in Notre Histoire n° 68
LA COSTE-MESSELIÈRE (R. DE): *Sur les Chemins de Saint-Jacques*, Perrin, 1993
LACOSTE (J.) (under the direction of): *La sculpture romane en Saintonge*, Christian Pirot éditeur, Tours, 1998
Le Pèlerinage, Cahier de Fanjeaux, n° 15, Privat, 1980
LENOIR (F.) ET MASQUELIER (Y.-T.) (under the direction of): *Encyclopédie des religions*, Bayard, 1997
MANTRAN (R.): *L'Expansion Musulmane*, PUF, 1969
MARTIN-BAGNAUDEZ (J.): *Martin de Tours, évêque et routard* in Notre Histoire n° 142
OURSEL (R.): *Pèlerins du Moyen Âge*, Fayard, 1978
PÉRICAD-MÉA (D.) (rédacteur en chef): *Les chemins de Saint-Jacques et la culture européenne*, Campus Stellae n° 1, Klincksieck, 1991
RUCQUOI (A.): *Histoire médiévale de la Péninsule ibérique*, Le Seuil, 1993
Saint-Jacques-de-Compostelle, (collectif) Brepols, 1995
SIGAL (P.-A.) (under the direction of): *L'image du pèlerin au Moyen Âge et sous l'Ancien Régime*, Association des amis de Rocamadour, 1994
STIERLIN (H.): *L'art du Haut Moyen Âge en Espagne*, PUF, Que sais-je ? n° 2907, 1994
URRUTIBÉHÉTY (C.): *Pèlerins de Saint-Jacques, La traversée du Pays Basque*, J & D, Biarritz, 1993
VAUCHEZ (A.) (under the direction of): *Dictionnaire encyclopédique du Moyen Âge*, Cerf, 1997
VÁZQUEZ DE PARGA (L.), LACARRA (J.-M.) URÍA RIU (J.):

Las peregrinaciones a Santiago de Compostela, 3 vol., Madrid, 1948-1949
VIELLIARD (J.): *Le Guide de Saint-Jacques de Compostelle*, J. Vrin, Paris, 1990
VORAGINE (J. DE): *La légende dorée*, GF-Flammarion, 1967
ZODIAQUE, La nuit des temps

ILLUSTRATIONS

This list gives additional information about some illustrations and their origin where space in their caption was insufficient.

Front cover: Blazon of the Founders, Las Huelgas Reales, Burgos; Reliquary foot, Treasury of Oignies, Namur; Pilgrim's attributes, Compostela Cathedral; Work of the Months, San Isidoro, Leon; St James, Issoudun Chapel; Eunate Chapel; Translatio of relics of St James, Pistoia Cathedral; Silos cloister; Santiago pilgrim, Holy Saviour Church, Villeneuve-d'Aveyron
Back cover: St James pilgrim, Leon Cathedral; Deer, Saint-Gilles Church façade; St James, Museum of the Ways of Astorga; Sun, Church façade in Quintanilla de las Viñas; St James Alphaeus, Compostela Cathedral; Gourd, Museum of the Ways of Astorga
Pages 4-5: Compostela
Page 6: Saint James, Batalha
Page 7: Cordoba
Page 9 top: Chartres
Page 10: Aachen
Page 15: Yilanli Kilise, Göreme
Page 21: Treasure of Guarrazar, Archaeological Museum, Madrid
Page 22: Attack..., *Las Cantigas de Santa María*, Escorial
Page 23: *Charles Martel*, Saint Denis Basilica
Page 32: The Golden Legend, B.M. of Rennes
Page 34: Saint-Jean-des-Vignes Abbey, Soissons
Page 35: The Virgin of Pilar, Compostela Cathedral
Page 37: *The Apocalypse*, Escorial
Page 40: Theodomir..., Archives of Compostela Cathedral
Page 43: *Codex Calixtinus*
Page 44: Fresco, Santa Maria Novella, Florencee
Page 45: The Miracle of the Gallows, Unterlinden

Museum, Colmar; Pons de Saint-Gilles..., *Miroir Historial* by Vincent de Beauvais, Condé Museum, Chantilly; The Matamoros, Burgos Cathedral
Page 48: Hotel de Cluny, Paris
Page 49: Las Navas de Tolosa, Museum of the History of France, Versailles
Page 54: The dream..., La Grande *Chronique de Saint Denis*, B.M. of Toulouse
Page 55: *Codex Calixtinus*
Page 56: Chartres Cathedral
Page 58: The Reconquest, *Las Cantigas de Santa María*, Escorial
Page 60: The banner ... Las Huelgas Reales, Burgos
Page 70: The monk Gómez... MS parm 1650c. 102v°, Palatine Library of Parma
Page 72: Arms of Cluny, Ochier Museum, Cluny
Page 78: Saint Francis, Assisi
Page 80: *Codex Calixtinus*
Page 81: Pilgrims, Paul-Dupuy Museum, Toulouse
Page 82: Benediction... *Pontifical*, Ms 565, f° 175bis, B.M. of Lyon
Page 84: Pilgrims... Condé Museum, Chantilly
Page 89: Triacastela...*Heures dites de la duchesse de Bourgogne*, Condé Museum, Chantilly ; *Dante*, Santa Maria Novella, Florence
Page 90: Compostela (1644), National Museum of Art and History, Luxembourg
Page 99: *Louis XV...*, French School, (18th c.) Château de Versailles et de Trianon
Page 101: *Virgin with Child* by Botticelli, Petit-Palais, Avignon
Pages 104-105: *Monte del Gozo*
Page 106: Saint-Pierre, Aulnay
Page 107: Le Puy
Page 126: Saint Martin..., Bourges Cathedral
Page 136: Reims Cathedral
Page 159: Chartres
Page 163: Saint James, Chartres
Page 168: Reliquary of Saint Bernadette, Nevers
Page 183: Canterbury
Page 193: Cloister Museum, Tulle
Page 219: Saint James, Arles
Page 242: Christ pilgrim, Silos
Page 243: Leboreiro Bridge
Page 256: Tomb... Nájera
Page 257: Detail of reliquary chest of San Millán, Yuso
Page 259: David, Santo Domingo de la Calzada
Page 312: Clavijo
Page 313: Landscape near Terradillos de los Templarios